Movements that Heal

Rhythmic Movement Training and
Primitive Reflex Integration

Harald Blomberg M.D.
With
Moira Dempsey

Illustrations by Phua San San and Moira Dempsey

Movements that Heal

Authors: Harald Blomberg M.D. with Moira Dempsey

Edition: 1st

ISBN: 9781791985127 (pbk.)

Published by BookPal
www.bookpal.com.au
PO Box 3422
Sunnybank Hills LPO
QLD 4109
Australia

Originally published in Sweden in 2008 as *Rörelser som helar* by Harald Blomberg. Published by Cupiditas Discendi AB

'Frank and Ernest' in Chapter 9 reprinted courtesy of the Thaves family

Illustrations © Phua San San and Moira Dempsey, permission to use and reproduce in any format must be obtained from, copyright holders.

Contents

Preface

For many years I have been a psychiatrist in Sweden and worked with clients using a movement method I call Rhythmic Movement Training (RMT) which is a movement and primitive infant reflex integration programme for people with learning, emotional and behavioural challenges. While my practice is in Stockholm I have also had the opportunity to develop and expand the training by teaching workshops in Europe, Asia, Australia and America. In these courses, I have addressed teachers, physiotherapists, occupational therapists, behavioural optometrists, masseurs, kinesiologists and other professionals as well as parents of children with different challenges.

I originally learned the basis of the movements from Kerstin Linde, an experienced and accomplished photographer. Her close scrutiny of infants, children and adults inspired the method which came from her observations of rhythmic developmental movements spontaneously made by infants. For several years, during the second half of the 1980s, I followed her work and wrote about my experiences and observations of our work together in my 1998 book *Helande Liv*.

The rhythmic elements of the movements are characteristic of her method. Other approaches that help children with motor and learning challenges inspired by baby movements, lack the rhythmical elements that I have found so useful. One of many effects of Kerstin Linde's method was the integration of primitive infant reflexes. She emphasized that the rhythmic exercises integrate primitive reflexes if they are done in a correct or exact way. This may be true for small children but for older children and adults the rhythmic movements need to be supplemented with other methods. One effective supplementary method is an isometric pressure technique I originally learned from Russian psychologist Svetlana Masgutova.

My intention in writing this book is to provide a plausible scientific explanation for the remarkable effectiveness of RMT - which has been my experience that is now shared by others - when working with the diverse learning needs of children and adults. This book therefore contains some elaborate sections about the structure and function of the brain and the nervous system and their connections to the primitive reflexes.

I want to thank sociologist Sophia Lövgren, Ph.D. who has generously contributed her great expert knowledge to the afterword of this book. I am also very thankful for the support and assistance I have received from Dr Mårten Kalling who supplied many valuable insights and also shared many scientific articles that have helped me explain the mode of action of RMT.

I especially want to thank Moira Dempsey who has not only done a tremendous job editing my manuscript and correcting linguistic and grammatical errors, but also given me much helpful assistance and advice as to the final version of the book, and provided some illustrations.

I would also like to thank Phua San San in Singapore for her illustrations of movements and reflexes, and Sandra Almenberg who have provided the illustrations in the original Swedish version of this book.

To the many people throughout the world who have been models, given feedback and helped refine the work, attended classes and to all the instructors who have all been instrumental in growing RMT around the world, I owe and give my sincere gratitude.

Harald Blomberg, Stockholm, Sweden

I have been a teacher for many years, working in Australia, Sarawak-Malaysia and Singapore. In 1991 I came across Educational Kinesiology/Brain Gym®, Touch for Health, and other forms of kinesiology and I became quite fascinated by them, as they were extremely beneficial in helping me to overcome many emotional and learning challenges. Eventually I trained as a consultant and instructor in these fields.

In 1997 I met Claire Hocking, an Educational Kinesiologist from Australia and first heard about retained primitive reflexes and the effect that they have on development, learning, emotions and behaviour. It certainly opened up a new way of looking at learning difficulties and I started to use this information with my kinesiology clients in Singapore.

I first met Dr. Blomberg at a camp for children with special needs in Poland in 2003. He was using these seemingly simple movements with children that were having a wonderful effect. Over three nights of the camp Dr. Blomberg talked about the Rhythmic Movements and why he thought they worked. I was so surprised that when I attempted to do the movements I just couldn't organise my body to work out how to do them unless I was given help. Dr. Blomberg agreed to come to Singapore to teach this work.

Since then I have worked at gaining a greater understanding of these remarkable movements. I have been fortunate in being able to work with Dr. Blomberg at developing this programme and taking it out to the world.

Moving back to Australia in 2005 gave me the opportunity to help with writing the manuals and materials for the classes.

My thanks go to all the people around the world who have given feedback, suggestions, been models and listening ears. Most especially I would like to thank Javant Biarujia, Claire Gien Snelgar, Bren Peters, Evonne Bennell and Tan Li-Anne, who read and made suggestions; Pam Whitman, who gave me a quiet space to finish; the late Judy Grant, who organised my first classes in North America; all the instructors, providers and would be instructors who so enthusiastically take this remarkable work out to the world; San San who kept on drawing, all the children, parents and clients who have allowed me to play and practise; all my teachers of kinesiology and reflexes, who taught me so much; and lastly, and most importantly, to Harald.

Moira Dempsey, Melbourne, Australia

Introduction

Why is it that there seems to be such an increase in the number of people with ADD/ADHD, autism, dyslexia, speech and language difficulties, depression, etc? To answer this question I think we need to look at the very foundations of what is essential for development - movement and a good environment - to even begin to understand why these foundations are not being well laid for many children.

Movement is essential for babies. They have to follow their inborn primitive reflex pattern programmes from when they first start developing in utero through to their complete integration into the whole body movement system. When steps are missed along the way whether because of pre-natal trauma, birth injury, environmental conditions or just too long a time spent in inappropriate baby equipment with very little time spent exploring on the floor, then the foundations of brain organization and postural abilities are not well established. If we combine this with environmental stresses such as pollution, electro-magnetic field (EMF) irradiation, heavy metal toxicity and poor diet then many children struggle to develop, function and have challenges with good health.

Rhythmic Movement Training (RMT) is about resetting these foundations. This book describes how simple healing exercises originally developed by Kerstin Linde stimulate the ability of the brain and the nervous system to renew and create new nerve connections and how these exercises help a person to develop, mature and heal physically, emotionally and mentally. These movements exist as inborn motor primitive reflex patterns which need to be activated and integrated in order for a child to develop normally. I have combined these movements, together with other techniques, e.g. isometric pressure, to create the programme.

Children are being Affected by our Harmful Environment?

The environment we live in today can be harmful to our physical and psychological health. Environmental pollution, mercury and other heavy metals, vaccines, unhealthy food sugars, sweeteners, MSG and other food additives and irradiation from mobile phones, mobile masts, cordless phones and other wireless technology are only some of the ongoing threats to our health.

Foetuses, children and youths are especially sensitive to this environmental exposure. Their immune and central nervous systems are immature and therefore more sensitive than in adults. This has led to an ever increasing number of children being born with deformities, allergies, depression, attention deficit disorders, and the attendant disorders that fall along the Pervasive Development Disorder syndromes.

Swedish statistics indicate in increase in deformities of 15% and an increase of 16% in chromosomal aberrations during the period of 1999 and 2004.

The young of today's Sweden are the first generation whose sense of well-being has deteriorated in comparison to those of previous generations. Since 1980 there has been:

- A fourfold increase of suicide attempts in young people
- A threefold increase in young people who feel apprehension and anxiety
- An almost threefold increase in young people who suffer from insomnia and more young people feeling constantly tired[1]

Mercury, aspartame, food colouring and additives, electromagnetic radiation and electric smog all play a part in the deteriorating health of our children, and is discussed in depth throughout this book.

The Freiburg Appeal

An increasing number of doctors have noticed an alarming upsurge in severe disease and disorders during the last decade. In 2002, a group of German doctors published the Freiburg Appeal which was signed by more than 1,000 German doctors. The doctors "noticed a dramatic increase of severe and chronic diseases" during the previous few years, including the following:

- Learning and concentration problems and behavioural disorders in children, e.g. hyperactivity
- Cancer, leukaemia and brain tumours

The appeal continued: "In addition we more often observe different disorders, which are incorrectly perceived as psycho-somatic, e.g.: headache, migraine, chronic fatigue syndrome, insomnia, tinnitus, nerve pain and pain of soft tissue."

The appeal also called attention to the fact that an accumulation of such cases can be observed in areas and places with strong irradiation and that the symptoms often improve or disappear when the irradiation is decreased.

How does the Swedish Medical Profession Respond?

When children have been affected by our harmful environment and show various symptoms most Swedish doctors do not respond like the German doctors who signed the Freiburg appeal. Instead they respond by giving these children psychiatric diagnoses and medication. A prominent Swedish psychiatrist argues that psychiatric illness is far more common among children than has previously been recognized. According to this expert, epidemiological studies have shown that the rate of psychiatric illness among children runs currently at 20-25%. Of these, 6% are considered to suffer from depression and 7% from Attention Deficit Hyperactivity Disorder (ADHD). According to other experts, 1 child out of 10 suffers from ADHD.[2]

Diagnoses are social constructs, as Sophia Lövgren explains in the afterword of this book. The medical profession defines them by combining various symptoms and declaring these combinations to constitute diseases and disorders. Children who suffer from attention deficit, impulsivity and hyperactivity are considered to suffer from ADHD. Although there is no consensus within the medical profession about the cause(s) of ADHD, the recommended treatment of ADHD with central nervous system (CNS) stimulants (drugs that speed up physical and mental processes) such as Concerta and Ritalin is not questioned.

Children and adolescents who are irritable, passive and sad, who have a lack of energy, fatigue and insomnia are diagnosed as depressed and treated with antidepressants.

How do the Media and Politicians Respond?

In the Swedish media there is seldom any serious discussion about the causes of the deteriorating health in children and young people. The media usually emphasizes the increased stress in society as a main cause. Scientific studies that demonstrate how children are harmed by irradiation, vaccinations, medication or food additives remain in the shadows while studies that show 'no harmful effects', are uncritically over reported. Reports about effective and safe methods to help children with problems are conspicuous by their absence.

In Sweden the government addresses these problems by increasing funds to child psychiatry thereby increasing the number of children who can be seen, diagnosed and treated with medication.

I think that the health of children is decreasing is as big a threat to our future as global warming. That there is no serious discussion about this in the media and the fact that no responsible authorities are prepared to treat these problems seriously is bizarre. It's as strange as it would be if the media did not discuss the causes of global warming and politicians just ignored the issue.

Who Needs Diagnoses?

In Sweden there are now many people who work in the area of diagnosing children with behavioural disorders. A growing body of experts, including doctors, psychologists and social workers have been trained to diagnose and work with these children.

There are many people who may benefit in different ways in upholding the social construct of diagnosing children who have reactions to their environment and development. These benefits cover a range of economic, political and professional areas:

- Pharmaceutical companies are able to sell their drugs
- Scientists working in the area can apply for grants for research
- Doctors, psychologists and social workers can get jobs and forge careers
- Politicians can say they are doing something about a growing societal problem
- Parents and teachers get support and resources and may escape feeling like failures

Children on the other hand do not need diagnoses. Children who have problems with attention and hyperactivity do not need to be treated as suffering from disorders that, according to experts, "seriously affect their health and development undermining their basis for satisfactory lives as adults". They do not need to hear that they run the risk of "academic and professional failure and often having serious social and psychiatric problems in adulthood."[3]

Children with challenges need help. They need real help to feel and function well. They do not need to be stigmatized by diagnoses and poisoned by drugs that subdue their symptoms and are harmful to their systems.

A Biologically and Ecologically Sustainable Environment

First and foremost, children need a biologically and ecologically sustainable and healthy environment. It should be the responsibility of society to provide for this, but it is not always being done. And when politicians, health authorities and the medical profession let children down by sacrificing their health, the only way out is knowledge and individual initiative from parents, teachers and all people around children to improve the environment for the benefit of their long-term health.

Some Suggested Beginnings

- Clean up the environment for foetuses, infants and small children from unnecessary electromagnetic irradiations, like cordless and wireless technology
- Do not use cordless Digital Enhanced Cordless Telecommunications (DECT) telephones around children and mobile telephones no closer than 2 metres from them.
  - Pregnant mothers shouldn't use mobile phones
  - Restrict the use of mobile phones and cordless and wireless technology by children and young people and don't allow them to use cordless DECT telephones
- Restrict the amount of television watched
- Eliminate sugar, sweeteners, MSG, colourings and other food additives from children's diets

- o Make sure their nutritional needs are met with sufficient minerals and vitamins
  - o Give them a supplement of vitamins, minerals and omega-3 if this is indicated
- Search for alternatives to the central stimulants and antidepressants that doctors prescribe
- Study the risks of vaccinations and think about if and when you want your child to be vaccinated
- Restrict the use of baby equipment such as baby walkers
  - o Infants need time on the floor to move, develop neural connections, integrate primitive reflexes and in so doing facilitate sensory processing

Healing Movements

I have written this book for all those looking for simple, safe and effective ways to help people develop, function and feel well, without the use of medications.

The movements and other techniques may appear to have a magical effect within a short period of time; however this does not mean that they are magic. I have done my best to explain scientifically how such simple exercises can have such powerful effects and I sincerely hope that the reader will not feel weighed down by my explanations.

Throughout this book there are case studies that illustrate the effectiveness of the movements. In the appendix there is my own story as well as stories written by people whom have had direct experience, either for themselves or their children, using the movements and reflex integration activities. I believe that these will add to your understanding of the effectiveness and ease of using these movements for you, your children and your clients.

Chapter 1
How Doctors Traditionally Treat ADHD

Central Stimulants and ADHD

Children who are hyperactive, inattentive, easily distracted, easily bored with what they are doing, have difficulty organizing their activities and controlling their impulses are diagnosed with Attention Deficit Hyperactivity Disorder (ADHD).

Hyperactivity in the US has traditionally been treated with central stimulants, namely Ritalin and Concerta. The 1990s saw a ten-fold increase in Ritalin prescriptions. It is estimated that 7-10% of American children, mostly boys, are treated with Ritalin or other central stimulants. In addition, intake by adults of central stimulants has increased. From 2000 to 2004 the sale of central stimulants increased from $759 million to $3.1billion.[1]

Promoters of this development have been pharmaceutical companies and the American National Institute for Mental Health (NIMH). NIMH is a government institution led by psychiatrists who are outspoken promoters of treating hyperactive children with central stimulants.

One of the duties of NIMH is to distribute money for research. According to an article in *U.S. News & World Report* NIMH has "focused its studies almost exclusively on brain research and on genetic underpinnings of emotional illness... The decision to reorder the federal research portfolio was both scientific and political".[2]

According to American psychiatrist Peter Breggin, who has criticized the increased prescription of stimulants to US children, NIMH has granted millions of dollars for research about central stimulants. Nearly all of the money has gone to ADHD/Ritalin advocates, and none to critics.

The Theory that ADHD is a Biological Disorder is Refuted

In 1998 NIMH organized a consensus conference with the apparent purpose of recognizing ADHD as a genetically-determined biological disorder. One of the papers presented at the conference was a review of the whole range of brain scan

1

reports that supposedly showed a biological basis for ADHD. These brain scan studies claimed to have found brain abnormalities in certain areas of the brains of children diagnosed with ADHD. However, in many of these studies, the children diagnosed with ADHD had been treated with stimulants. None of these studies could be proven to have been based exclusively on children with ADHD who had not been treated with central stimulants.[3] Accordingly, the differences between the brains of normal children and those diagnosed with ADHD were more likely the effect of the medication, In studies on monkeys, the same medication was known to cause brain damage in similar areas of the brain.

Several papers presented also highlighted the severe risks and side-effects of central stimulants. After having listened to a number of lectures and studied numerous papers by scientists researching ADHD, the panel cast reasonable doubt on the validity of the ADHD diagnosis. Most disappointing to the medication advocates of NIMH was the conclusion in the final consensus draft distributed to the press, which stated that there "were no data to indicate that ADHD is due to a brain mal-function".

In 2000 the American Academy of Pediatrics issued a similar statement saying that brain scans and similar studies "do not show reliable differences between children with ADHD and controls".[4]

The Multimodal Treatment of Children with ADHD (MTA) Study of 1999

Central stimulants have been prescribed to an increasing number of American children for more than 50 years. In spite of the fact that many children have taken these drugs for 5 years or more, until recently, none of NIMH's research grants have been aimed at discovering the dangers of long-time use of Ritalin and other stimulants.

In 1999 the Multimodal Treatment of Children with ADHD (MTA) study of 579 children who had been medicated with stimulants for one year was published. Before this, most studies followed up treated children for a few months at most.

One of the principal researchers of this first MTA study, Professor Peter Jensen, made the following statement: "We did the best study which ever has been done on planet Earth, which helped parents and teachers with these children – and what did it show? It showed that medication was still much more effective for these children."[5]

According to a well-known British child psychiatrist, Eric Taylor, the most important conclusion of the study was that carefully carried through medication was better than any other treatment. This would require medication to be available for all children with ADHD.

This first MTA study was a triumph for the pharmaceutical companies and the ADHD/Ritalin advocates among psychiatrists. At the same time, it would turn out to be a disgrace for the global child psychiatric community and a catastrophe for the increasing number of children who would be labelled with ADHD and treated with stimulants, as a consequence of the study.

The results of this study were widely publicized all over the world. In more than 10 countries that I have visited to teach RMT I have heard reports of this increasing number of children who are treated with central stimulants.

The Recent MTA Study, a Follow-Up Study after Three Years

In 2007 a follow-up of the MTA study, made by the same research team, was published. In this study 485 of the original group of medicated children were followed for 3 years.

The result of this study was very disappointing to the research team. One of the principal researchers, Professor William Pelham, made an appearance in the BBC programme "Panorama" stating that after 36 months of treatment there were no positive effects whatsoever, contrary to what the research team had expected. He said that nothing indicated that drugs are better than no treatment at all in a longer perspective and he stressed that this information should be made very clear to parents.[6]

According to Professor Pelham the report showed that the initial positive effects of the treatment in children with the most severe problems had completely disappeared when the children grew older.

The report also established that central stimulants obstruct the normal growth of children, which also affects their growing brain. The study also demonstrated that central stimulants are connected with more aggressive and antisocial behaviour and increased risks of future criminality and drug abuse. Children aged between 11 and 13 years, who participated in the study, used alcohol and illegal substances more often compared to those in control groups. The report concluded that this growing incidence of substance abuse at an early age requires clinical attention.

Professor Pelham stated on BBC Panorama in 2007, "I think we exaggerated the positive effects of medication in the first study."

Although the result of this new study was publicized in the US, UK and Australia, the Swedish media remained silent about it. To my knowledge, the findings have not caused widespread discussion among psychiatrists or in the media as we would expect. Medical professionals, like many of us, seldom admit to making mistakes and, in the case of central stimulants, Swedish psychiatrists seem to prefer to behave as if nothing has happened.

Studies in the 1970s Showed that Central Stimulants Reduce Growth

If the researchers responsible for the MTA study had done their homework, and analysed the many previous studies on the effect of central stimulants, they would not have been so surprised by the results.

The fact that central stimulants reduce overall growth has been demonstrated in dozens of studies. One obvious cause is that central stimulants suppress appetite; however another more insidious cause is that they disrupt growth hormone production. This was shown in 1976 by a Norwegian research group study.[7] In another study from 1986 of 24 young adults, who had been treated with central stimulants for hyperactivity in childhood, shrinkage of the brain was found in more than 50% of the cases.

Since the 1970s Several Studies have shown that Central Stimulants do not Improve Academic Success

In spite of what is often stated by ADHD/Ritalin advocates among psychiatrists, central stimulants do not improve school success in treated children. A 1976 double blind study could not show any improvement of scholastic achievement in a group of children treated with central stimulants, compared to a control group, even when the treated children's behaviour was rated as improved. On the contrary, the researchers found that central stimulants in fact suppressed "desirable behaviours that facilitate learning".[8]

In 1992 James Swanson, a prominent ADHD/Ritalin advocate, and his colleagues warned that "cognitive toxicity may occur at commonly prescribed clinical doses ... The children become withdrawn and over focused and may seem "zombie-like." According to Swanson cognitive toxicity is common and may occur in 40% of treated cases and the over-focusing of attention may impair rather than improve learning.[9]

Increased Risk of Drug Abuse

The increased risk of drug abuse aforementioned has been substantiated in earlier research. The US Drug Enforcement Administration (DEA) has repeatedly expressed great concern that treatment with Ritalin will lead to abuse of other drugs. In 1995 the DEA reported that, "a number of recent studies, drug abuse cases, and trends among adolescents from various sources, indicate that methylphenidate (Ritalin) use may be a risk factor for substance abuse."[10]

At the 1998 NIMH conference organized, Professor Nadine Lambert of the University of California, Berkeley, presented a unique longitudinal study comparing future drug abuse in two groups labelled ADHD. The study compared one group who had been prescribed stimulants as children with another group that had not been given medication.

Professor Lambert found a significant correlation between stimulant treatment in childhood and later drug abuse. She told the conference that the prescription of stimulants to children for a year or more was correlated with increased "lifetime use of cocaine and stimulants". She concluded that childhood use of stimulants "is significantly and pervasively implicated in the uptake of regular smoking, in daily smoking in adulthood, in cocaine dependence, and in lifetime use of cocaine and stimulants."[11]

For obvious reasons it would be difficult to demonstrate adverse effects of central stimulants, such as suppressed growth or increased risk of drug abuse by following children for a year or less. These effects would not become obvious until years later. Many children take central stimulants for 5 to 10 years or more. What will happen to these children in the future? For now we can only speculate. No follow-up research lasting for more than 3 years has yet been made and in my opinion it is doubtful if it ever will be made since the results of such studies are potentially more devastating to the pharmaceutical companies than the recently published MTA study.

Why do Initially Positive Effects of the Treatment in Children with the most Severe Problems Completely Disappear after 3 Years?

If the researchers responsible for the MTA study had investigated previous research on central stimulants conducted with monkeys, they would have been able to predict the outcome that the apparent positive effects of central stimulants disappear after a few years.

According to one hypothesis, ADHD is caused by an insufficient functioning of the neurotransmitter dopamine in two areas of the brain, the prefrontal cortex and the basal ganglia. The prefrontal cortex is responsible for executive functions: attention, judgement, and planning, impulse control and, in conjunction with the basal ganglia, our ability to sit still.

Central stimulants increase the amount of dopamine and other neurotransmitters released into the prefrontal cortex and the basal ganglia. However, it simultaneously reduces the rate of its removal from the synapses. As a result, central stimulants increase the amount of dopamine in these areas, which causes an immediate, short-term calming of the system. Therefore an over-active child who spends a lot of time jumping and running around and is a burden to all around him will, after medication, be able to sit still and focus. This makes an indelible impression on many teachers and parents. However, this effect is not only short-lived; it comes at a high price.

The increase of dopamine causes a compensatory die out of dopamine receptors in the brain far outlasting the acute drug effect and, consequentially, leads to the death of brain cells.[12] In a study conducted on monkeys in 1997 it could be shown that the administration of two relatively small acute doses of amphet-amine (2 mg/kg taken 4 hours apart) produced a persistent, marked decrease in dopamine synthesis and concentration for up to 3 months. One animal showed continued dysfunction after 8 months.

The stimulant dosage for children is often as high as those reported in several studies on animals and have caused brain damage in those animals.

According to the follow-up MTA study, central stimulants lose their positive effect when children are treated for between 1 to 3 years. This is logical considering that the long-term effect of central stimulants on the brain decreases the production of dopamine producing nerve cells. Consequently doses of central stimulants have to be continually increased so as to keep achieving the same effect.

Sweden – A Case-Study

The fallout of the 1999 MTA study was a world-wide increase in the diagnoses, labelling and treatment with central stimulants of ADHD children. Conversely the 2007 follow-up study appears to have had little or no impact on these practices. How is this possible?

Sweden, over the last few decades, has been ever-increasing its application and use of central stimulants in the treatment of ADHD. There has been an increase of 2,000 to 15,000 Swedish children diagnosed with and treated with central stimulants in the 8 years from 2000 to 2008. In addition 14,000 adults diagnosed with ADHD were treated in 2008. The drugs of choice were Ritalin and Concerta.

This helps to explain the surprising lack of response to the latest MTA study of many Swedish medical professionals, health authorities and media

Ritalin was Prohibited in Sweden for Many Years

It is remarkable that there has been an increase in the use of central stimulants in Sweden considering the fact that Ritalin was withdrawn from use in 1968 due to its widespread abuse. In addition, during the late 1960s and 70s it was only those who were licensed by the Swedish National Board of Health and Welfare (SNBHW), who were able to write out prescriptions. Consequently it was rare that they were given to people.

The first time I realized the effect stimulants could have on children was in 1972. I was working in a children's psychiatric clinic and one of the patients was an 11-year-old boy with elective mutism who would not talk to anyone but his mother. Many treatments had been unsuccessful including behaviour therapy and electro-shock treatment. As a last resort the chief psychiatrist decided to apply for a licence to treat the boy with central stimulants. I recall arriving at work one day to find the normally cheerful and lively boy looking sad and tired. Realizing that something was amiss I investigated and found that he had been given his first dose of Ritalin that morning. Needless to say Ritalin did not make the boy speak. Eventually he received the psychological help he needed to begin speaking once the chief psychiatrist resigned and took up an appointment as a professor of child psychiatry at a Swedish university hospital.

Central stimulants become Accepted in Sweden

During the 1980s and 90s more and more children were diagnosed with DAMP (Deficits in Attention, Motor Control and Perception), the formerly preferred diagnosis of Swedish child psychiatrists, now replaced by ADHD. Treatment of ADHD with central stimulants gradually became more accepted by child psychiatrists and the number of treated children grew.

In 2000 an expert group of Swedish child psychiatrists wrote a report where they promoted the view that ADHD is a biological disorder[13]. They based this view on the American brain-scan studies claiming to have shown brain abnormalities in the frontal lobes and basal ganglia in children diagnosed with ADHD. As we have seen, however, these conclusions had been refuted by the NIMH consensus conference in 1998 and later in a statement by the American Academy of Pediatrics. According to the Academy, brain-scans and similar studies "do not show reliable differences between children with ADHD and controls".[14]

The Swedish National Board of Health and Welfare Establishes the Cause of ADHD

In 2004, the SNBHW published a booklet titled "Briefly about ADHD in children and adults" in which it reiterated many of the opinions of the expert group.[15]

The Board emphasized heredity as the cause of ADHD and wrote: "Heredity is brought about by genes. Genes control the transmitter substances that convey information between the neurons of the brain. Shortage or insufficient effect of these substances in certain areas of the brain causes changes of psychological/cognitive function that may cause problems for the child to control his/her behaviour. This in its turn will result in the typical symptoms of ADHD like restlessness, attention problems and impulsivity".

This sensational statement about the cause of ADHD does not have any scientific foundation and is contrary to the research presented at the American Consensus Conference organized by NIMH in 1998 and the final consensus draft of that conference.

The SNBHW Recommends Central Stimulants as a Treatment

The Board recommended the use of central stimulants as a treatment for ADHD and emphasized how well-documented the use of these drugs are especially in large studies on children, how effective they are and how slight their side-effects.

According to the Board there are no other psychoactive drugs that have been so thoroughly studied as central stimulants and it makes the following statement:

"Due to the rapidly growing knowledge about ADHD in Sweden and the fact that we now have taken part in international experiences [sic] of medication the number of children treated with central stimulants has rapidly increased in the same way as in other countries."

However, the Board admits that it is not yet known how effective these drugs will be in the long run after many years' treatment. The SNBHW praised central stimulants for increasing the power of concentration and decreasing hyperactivity. Moreover "the drugs seem to improve cognitive abilities like problem solving."

Concerning the danger of addiction and future abuse the Board states there is no such risk and claims that treatment with central stimulants "instead seems to diminish the risk of future abuse".

The Board also writes that follow-up studies of children diagnosed with ADHD often painted a gloomy picture "with poor academic and professional success and often serious psychiatric problems in adult age". The Board considered that ADHD should be met as a public problem, "since it concerns many individuals and has a serious effect on their health, development and possibilities to live a fully adequate life as adults".

An Analysis of the Position of the Swedish National Board of Health and Welfare

The arguments of the Board deserve closer scrutiny. Even if it is true that no other psychoactive drugs have been as thoroughly studied as stimulants, the Board does not seem to know the results of this research. If it had studied the outcomes, it would have known that central stimulants do not "improve cognitive abilities like problem solving". It would not have made the completely ridiculous statement that central stimulants "seem to diminish the risk of future abuse". Such a statement gives rise to the question as to whether the Board will next recommend that parents treat their children with small amounts of other addictive substances, e.g. alcohol or nicotine, each day "to diminish the risk of future abuse".

If the Board had carefully studied the extensive research done on ADHD it would not have found any scientific basis for its opinion that ADHD is a genetically determined biological disorder. Neither would it have been taken in by the apparent "good" results of the previous MTA study, uncritically advertising central stimulants as an effective and safe treatment of ADHD.

If the Board had carefully examined the American research on ADHD it would have realized that the follow-up studies, which showed that children diagnosed with ADHD had a gloomy prognosis, were made mainly on children who had been treated with stimulants. In all probability their poor prospects were therefore caused by the medication.

Certainly, the Board made the reservation that it was still not known how effective central stimulants would be after many years of treatment. So what happened when it was shown that they had no positive affects whatsoever after 3 years' treatment?

The New MTA Study Refutes the Board's Standpoint

The recent MTA study shows that after 3 years' medication, stimulants have no positive effects whatsoever. They are simply no better than no treatment at all. Therefore it must have been a mistake to label stimulants as effective drugs for treating ADHD.

Far from diminishing the risk of future abuse as the SNBHW has claimed the MTA study has demonstrated that central stimulants are connected with more aggressive and antisocial behaviour that cause an increased risk of future drug abuse and criminality.

By reason of this finding the recent MTA study has also corroborated that it is not the diagnosis of ADHD but the medication with central stimulants that has "a serious effect on children's health, development and possibilities to live a fully adequate life as adults".

Now that the Board knows that stimulants are not at all effective after 3 years' use I would have expected it to come out and correct its previous statement that it is still not known how effective central stimulants are after many years' treatment. I would also have expected it to follow the advice of one of the principal researchers of the MTA study and make it very clear to parents that nothing indicates that drugs are better than no treatment at all in a longer perspective. However the Board has not done this. After more than 3 years of knowing about the effects, it has still not commented on the study at all. Nor does it seem likely that it ever will.

The Reasons for the Cover-Up of the Recent MTA Study

Swedish psychiatrists and child psychiatrists have been most successful in persuading politicians to give resources to psychiatrists to label children and adults with ADHD and treat them with central stimulants. In addition, psychologists and social workers have been employed and have received special training to be able to assist doctors in diagnosing people who are supposed to need treatment with stimulants. In the beginning, there was some resistance to drugging children with stimulants but with the united forces of the media and the SNBHW the drugging enterprise was soon riding high on the crest of a wave. When more children were diagnosed and treated, more doctors, psychologists and social workers were needed, causing more children to be diagnosed, etc. Now there are a host of professionals serving the ever increasing undertaking of diagnosing and treating ADHD.

And the result of this, as we know, is this sixfold increase, over an 8-year period of children diagnosed with ADHD and treated with stimulants.

This development has not been without its problems. According to reports in the Swedish press many children must wait too long for a neuropsychiatric examination. In 2007, in the Stockholm region alone, 450 children had to wait for more than 3 months to be seen.[16] And the pressure increases. In 2007, 40% more referrals were written than the previous year. And so another problem arises which is the shortage of employees with the competence to make neuropsychiatric investigations.

However, now politicians have intervened to improve this situation. The current politician responsible, Birgitta Rydberg, declared that "in those cases where medical treatment is required, for instance with small doses of amphetamine, this must be done immediately". She reassures that further training is under way to speed up the process and adds: "We vacuum the region for all available competence." Another step is to give economic incentives: "The more investigations a unit makes, the more payment it will receive."[17]

Considering these circumstances, it has become obvious that the SNBHW, doctors, psychologists, other health workers and politicians have no interest at all in revealing the true facts about central stimulants and ADHD.

The Swedish National Board of Health and Welfare and its psychiatric experts naturally do not want to lose their credibility by having their incompetence exposed.

Doctors and health workers obviously want to protect their jobs and livelihood. Politicians also do not want to be exposed as gullible fools wasting tax-payers' money on an improper non-scientifically documented scam that has exposed thousands to severe long-term repercussions.

So the Swedish tax-payer continues to pay. The non-effective drugging of children continues with no restrictions. The fact that these drugs cause damage, and will continue to cause damage, does not seem to be of any concern to the authorities or personnel involved in this merry-go-round.

Chapter 2

An Alternative Way of Regarding and Treating Attention Disorders

It is Normal for Small Children to have Attention Problems and be Hyperactive

By studying our youngest children it is possible to see alternative approaches to attention disorders and how children's challenges can be remedied, other than those advocated by the psychiatric establishment and pharmaceutical companies. Children with Attention Deficit Hyperactivity Disorder (ADHD) display similar behaviour to toddlers of around the age of one, especially those who have been allowed to move around freely and not forced to sit in baby-walkers or car seats for long periods of time.

Infants and toddlers move around, cling and climb and do not sit still. They are impulsive, easily distracted and quickly tire with what they are doing. They have difficulties listening, following instructions and organizing their activities. They do not have the ability to control their emotions and temper.

However, unlike older children who are labelled as having ADHD, most children as they grow older manage to learn attention and control of movement without too much trouble. So how is it that a child who has normal developmental behaviour is different from a child who develops ADHD? What secret knowledge is it he possesses that enables him to prevail over his attention challenges? Could it be that children with ADHD have a genetically caused shortage of transmitter substances in the brain, such as the Swedish National Board of Health and Welfare (SNBHW) claims, or can there be other more plausible and less far-fetched explanations?

The Plastic Brain

The British obstetrician and researcher Robert Winston, in his book *The Human Mind*, describes the ability of the brain to regenerate. This has been called the plastic brain.

In the 1940s, brain researchers found that communication between neurons goes in both directions. When a nerve cell of the brain (a neuron) receives a signal from another neuron it passes the signal on to other neurons and at the same time sends a feedback signal to the cell that originally sent the signal. When this first process is over, another process begins. The affected neurons multiply the connections with each other by growing new nerve synapses and increasing the supply of transmitter substances, thereby facilitating the firing of the nerve signals in the new pattern.

"This feedback and learning mechanism within the brain means that every synaptic connection is 'told' whether it has contributed to the final outcome of the communication. If it has, it is encouraged to react a little more strongly next time too, by growing new connection sites and by sending more neurotransmitters across the synaptic cleft. If it hasn't, it will inhibit its actions."[1]

The Infant's Brain is Undeveloped

The brain of the infant has not matured. In a newborn baby, only the brain stem has all its functions firmly established, while the other parts are still developing their uses. Before an individual is able to bring into play all of his brain, the nets between the nerve cells of the brain must develop through the growth of branches from the nerve cells, and the nerve fibres must develop

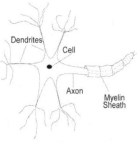

Motor neuron with axon and myelin sheath

an insulating sheath of myelin. This maturing of the brain will take place all throughout childhood; however it is the very first year after birth that is the most crucial period for laying the foundation for later development. It has been estimated that every minute in the life of a newborn baby, more than 4 million new nerve cell branches are created in the brain.

This process does not happen by itself. The brain needs stimulation from the senses for branching and myelination to occur. Stimulation from the vestibular, tactile and kinaesthetic senses is especially important for this. The baby gets this stimulation by being touched and rocked by his parents and by continually making rhythmic baby movements on his own. Such movements develop in a certain order according to an inborn programme which can have individual variations. Turning around, creeping on the stomach, rocking and crawling on hands and knees are some important milestones in this development. The stimulation the brain receives from such rhythmical baby movements during the first year of life is fundamental for the future development and maturing of the brain.

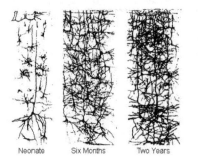

Neonate   Six Months   Two Years

Development of neural pathways in first two years through movement and sensory stimulation

When the nerve connections and synapses of the brain increase in number, additional parts of the brain start to perform their functions in new nerve patterns, which are stimulated by the infant's movements. This is a process that continues automatically even when the nerve cells do not get direct stimulation. At the same time there is a pruning of nerve connections corresponding to old behavioural patterns that the child no longer needs.

In children who have not had sufficient stimulation of this kind, the maturing of the brain is delayed or impaired. Such delayed development can appear as an attention disorder with or without hyperactivity.

According to the American scientist Paul MacLean, who studied the development of the brain in reptiles, mammals and humans, the human brain consists of three layers that cap the brain stem like the layers of an onion[2] and work as guiding operators for the neural chassis.

The first layer is the reptilian brain which corresponds to the brain of reptiles. In 'humans the reptilian brain is called the basal ganglia, one task of which is to control our postural reflexes.

The reptilian brain must also inhibit the primitive reflexes: which are inborn, stereotyped movement patterns controlled by the brain stem. The primitive reflexes constitute the movements of the foetus and the newborn infant. They must be transformed into the postural life-long reflex movement patterns in order for the child to be able to rise, walk and keep his balance. The basal ganglia also regulate the level of activity of the child and ensure that the child is not revved up most of the time.

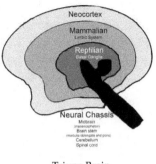

Triune Brain

The next layer is the mammalian brain, or the limbic system, that controls, among other things, our emotions, memory, learning and the ability to play.

The outer layer is the neocortex. Signals from the sense organs must reach the neocortex and be processed there in order for us to be aware of what happens around us and be able to act consciously. The very front part of the neocortex, the prefrontal cortex is of crucial importance for our judgement, attention, and power of initiative and control of impulses.

The Importance of the Rhythmic Baby Movements for the Linking up of the Brain

When we are born, all parts of the brain have been established however are not yet working well together. In order for all parts to function as a unit they must be developed and linked up to each other. This is achieved by the rhythmic infant movements that stimulate the growth and the branching off of the nerve cells and the myelination of the nerve fibres.

The infant needs to develop sufficient muscle tone in order to be able to move around and stimulate this linking together. To establish tone, the infant needs to be touched, hugged, and rocked, as well as being allowed to move around freely. Such stimulation sends signals from the sense organs of the tactile, balance and kinaesthetic senses to those centres of the brain stem that regulate muscle tone. If the baby gets insufficient stimulation from these senses the tone of the extensor muscles will be low.[3] This may make it difficult for the baby to lift his head and chest and move around, further reducing the stimulation from the balance, tactile and kinaesthetic senses, leading to a particularly vicious cycle of developmental delay.

When a baby is unable to move around freely, too little stimulation is conveyed to the neocortex via the Reticular Activation System (RAS) of the brain stem. The task of this system is to arouse the neocortex. When there is insufficient arousal, the child will become sluggish and inattentive to sensory signals. Moreover the nerve cells and the nerve nets of the neocortex will not develop properly.

The cerebellum is also important for the linking up of the brain and development of our ability to pay attention. One task of the cerebellum is to make our movements rhythmic, coordinated and smooth. From the cerebellum, there are important nerve connections up to the prefrontal cortex and the centres of speech in the frontal lobe of the left hemisphere.

At birth, the cerebellum is immature and it grows substantially after the age of 6 months. The rhythmic baby movements develop the nerve nets and nerve cells of the cerebellum and its connections to the frontal lobes. That is one reason why rhythmic baby movements are so important for the linking up of the frontal cortex and the development of the power of attention and speech.

Why Babies have Challenges Sitting Still and Being Attentive

Infants do not know how to maintain attention and concentrate on specific tasks. Nor do they yet have the neural connections into the frontal lobes to control their impulses. This is why infants do not behave like small adults.

Infants have not yet developed the ability to regulate their movements and activities. By the age of 10-12 months they are moving around continually and find it difficult to sit still. Most normal babies are hyperactive at this age because the basal ganglia, that regulate the level of activity, have not yet developed well and are not linked up adequately with other levels of the brain.

On the other hand, babies who are not able to move around enough due to low muscle tone or other circumstances get too little stimulation of their neocortex and frontal lobes and run the risk of becoming sluggish, hypoactive, inattentive and late to develop.

Similarities between Small Children and Children with ADHD

In both small children and those with ADHD there are many indicators that the basal ganglia are not yet functioning efficiently. They find it difficult to regulate activity, have active primitive reflexes and balance problems – all pointers to the immaturity of the basal ganglia.

It is also common that children with attention disorders have an inability to make simple movements in a rhythmical and smooth way, another indicator that the nerve nets of the cerebellum have not yet adequately developed. As the cerebellum is of crucial importance for the proper functioning of the frontal lobes this inability can be an important contributing factor behind attention problems and impulsivity.

Many children with ADHD have low muscle tone and hunched posture causing shallow breathing and insufficient arousal of the neocortex. These children may alternate between hyperactivity and passivity, the hyperactivity being their way of stimulating the neocortex.

Attention Disorder as Delayed Maturity of the Brain

As we have seen, many experts consider ADHD to be genetically caused. An alternative explanation is that the symptoms are caused by a delayed or thwarted maturity process of the brain. For some reason the brain of the child has not received sufficient stimulation for the neurons to branch off and create new synapses. This lack of stimulation may also hinder the formation of myelin around the nerve fibres. If there is insufficient myelination of the nerves it will affect the speed of propagation of the nerve signals. Taken together all this may delay the development and linking together of the different parts of the brain and prevent the brain functioning well as a whole.

Circumstances such as prematurity, brain injury inflicted during delivery, Caesarean delivery, vaccinations, hereditary factors, electromagnetic fields (EMF), and microwaves from mobile phones, toxicity or disease may cause the infant to omit crucial steps in motor development, which in turn impedes brain development.

A lack of stimulation from those closest to the infant, being left alone without tactile or vestibular stimulation or forced to spend his time in baby-walkers and car seats instead of moving around on the floor will also prevent the brain from maturing properly.

Rhythmic Movement Training

As has been shown, there are many similarities between infants and children with ADHD regarding both behaviour and immaturity of the brain.

We must therefore ask if children with ADHD or ADD can improve their attention abilities by imitating the rhythmic movements that infants spontaneously make. Such movement training has been used in Sweden for more than 25 years.

The movements in RMT were first developed by Kerstin Linde and are based on the natural rhythmic movements of the infant. To be effective these movements need to be done daily for 10-15 minutes. The movements are done in lying or sitting positions as well as on hands and knees.

The movements used in the training are active or passive rhythmic whole body movements. Passive movements are done by gently pushing the client's body rhythmically from the feet with the client in a supine position or from his hip in the direction of the head in a foetal position. With the client lying face down, the bottom can be rhythmically pushed from side to side. In a supine position the legs may be passively rolled so that the big toes meet in the middle.

These movements can also be made actively. In a supine position with his knees bent the client may push from the feet rhythmically or roll his legs to and fro from the sides to the middle so that the big toes meet and then move out again. In a prone position the client may roll his bottom from side to side. Other active movements include crawling and rocking on all fours.

Whether done actively or passively these movements are suitable for everyone however disabled they may be. These movements should ideally be made in a very exact way. In severely disabled people, this is of course impossible and one long-term goal is to successively teach them to be done more and more exactly.

It is easy to see that these movements strongly stimulate several senses. The movements of the head stimulate the balance sense. The rhythmical pushing along the spine from the feet or bottom stimulates proprioception in many joints as well as the organs of the belly. The rhythmic movements also stimulate the tactile sense receptors of the skin by causing friction between the back or front and the floor.

There is a description of some of the Rhythmic Movements in Chapter 19.

The Effects of Rhythmic Movement Training on Behaviour

The sensory stimulation caused by the rhythmic movements encourages the growth of the nerve nets of the brain stem, cerebellum, basal ganglia and neocortex to develop. This causes attention and concentration to improve and hyperactivity and impulsivity to decrease.

Effects of rhythmic movements made by people doing RMT

The rhythmic movements also increase the muscle tone of the extensor muscles that straighten the back and keep the head in an upright position. Body posture, breathing and endurance will improve and the neocortex will be aroused by stimulation via the brain stem, which improves attention and concentration.

The movements stimulate the cerebellum and its nerve pathways to the prefrontal cortex, which also improves attention and concentration and diminishes impulsivity. RMT also stimulates the basal ganglia to mature and integrate the primitive reflexes, which then facilitates the ability to regulate levels of activity and be still.

The Significance of the Rhythm in the Rhythmic Movements

It is the rhythm in the spontaneous movements of a baby that stimulates, organizes and develops his brain. According to the cell biologist James Oschman in his book *Energy Medicine – the scientific basis* the body is a living matrix in which all parts are in contact with each other from the skin to the cell nuclei. The information between the different parts is transmitted not only by nerve signals but by electromagnetic impulses of different frequencies.

The rhythm of the movements gives an alternating stimulation of the brain through nerve signals from sensory cells in the vestibular, tactile and proprioceptive senses. Nerve signals are transmitted to the brain via the transmitter substances such as dopamine, glutamate and gamma-Aminobutyric acid (GABA). An alternating stimulation is much more efficient than an uninterrupted one since the brain can't get used to alternating stimulation. The brain quickly gets used to a fast, constant stimulus and the arousing effect of this rapidly ceases.

Information throughout the living matrix of the body is also transmitted by different kinds of energy. Energy is fundamentally vibration in the form of light or electromagnetic energy, sound, chemical or mechanical elastic energy. Many of the most important molecules of the muscles and skeleton are formed as spirals. This makes them elastic and gives them good resonance properties. When the body is set in oscillation by the rhythmic movements weak electromagnetic fields are created which transmit information to all parts of the body, especially the nervous system and brain.

Ascertaining the Training Children Need

In order to know what exercises to use, we must get an idea about the difficulties of the child. It is important to conduct a thorough interview with the parents and child to have an understanding of the history and the problems that the child feels most affected by. The interview should be supplemented with an examination of the child's motor abilities. It is especially important to find out which primitive reflexes have not been integrated and if the child has problems doing simple rhythmic movements. A careful visual examination and an audiogram can also be valuable, especially where there are learning challenges. On the basis of the interview and the result of the examination it is possible to get a rough idea about which functions the child needs to improve.

Children with symptoms of ADHD and learning difficulties always have retained primitive reflexes. However, they may not seem to have obvious motor problems. Sometimes children with attention and learning difficulties may even have good motor abilities and be good at sports and gymnastics. I find that more often than not children with attention problems have low muscle tone, poor posture and difficulties doing simple rhythmic movements. In such cases the motor problems are usually more prominent.

The training programme of the child should be based on the interview and the result of the motor examination. In the beginning this programme should take no more than 10 minutes to do and needs to be done daily or no less than five times a week. As motor abilities improve and the reflexes are integrated the programme will change.

With the integration of the reflexes and the improvement of the rhythm in the simple rhythmic movements the symptoms of the child will improve. Attention, control of impulses and the ability to sit still are some of the challenges that will improve. In most cases it will take a year or more before the challenges are permanently gone. If the exercises are not done for enough time the new pathways in the brain may not have time to consolidate and some of the symptoms may reappear.

Many children and adults who have retained primitive reflexes have never had any attention or learning problems. They may instead have visual, motor or emotional problems or long-term pain in the muscles and joints.

The following case-study illustrates the effects of RMT in attention disorders. It shows how the rhythmic movements improve attention and diminish impulsivity and hyperactivity.

Case-Study: Anna

Anna was 10-years-old when she began RMT. Her motor development had been normal except for her fine motor development. She crawled on hands and knees as a baby and walked at one.

It was very difficult for her to concentrate and sit still at school. She was easily distracted and had very poor perseverance. She had no problems reading and writing but great problems with mathematics. She had her own assistant during mathematics classes and if the assistant was absent she would do nothing but run around disturbing the other students.

Anna acted on impulse and found it very difficult to pay attention and follow instructions, especially during PE classes which she really did not want to attend. Her ankles were weak and easily sprained. She found it hard to do tasks that require fine motor control, especially tying shoe laces and doing up buttons. Her handwriting was poor and messy.

Anna had emotional problems. She was afraid of the dark, anxious and apprehensive, especially at nights. She had severe difficulties with her peer relationships. The girls in her class used to tease her and then she would run away and hide.

During her first visit I tested her for primitive reflexes, many of which were active. The Spinal Galant Reflex was especially active which explained her inability to sit still and her great dislike of wearing tight clothes. Her Moro Reflex was also extremely active causing sensitivity to sounds and touch and many of her emotional problems. Her Palmar and Grasp Reflexes were also active, causing problems with fine motor ability.

Anna's Training

Anna visited me about once a month for a little more than a year. She did rhythmic movements at home for 10-15 minutes every day. At each visit I gave her new rhythmic movements to do. She continued to do some of the movements every day for the entire time I saw her. She had assistance at home in order to do them as exactly as possible. In addition she had isometric exercises for reflex integration that her mother helped her with.

After four months her mother noticed that Anna had become more defiant and ill-tempered. After five months these symptoms had decreased and she was more self-confident. She could concentrate better at school and her school-work, including mathematics, improved. A few weeks later she had caught up with her classmates in mathematics. She also started to like PE classes as she found the activities easier - especially long and high jumping.

After the summer vacation she moved to another school and her mother chose to say nothing about Anna's problems. It turned out that she could concentrate well and no longer needed an assistant. She had good relationships with her classmates and she was no longer teased. Her ankles had become much stronger and she started football training. Her fine motor ability also improved considerably.

After a little more than a year of movement training she was no longer afraid of the dark. Anna was also no longer hypersensitive to sound and touch and was not so easily disturbed by others. She had no problems sitting still or wearing tight clothes. Her fine motor ability had improved considerably although she still had some problems doing up buttons. She had practically no difficulties with concentration and her endurance and perseverance were good.

Chapter 3
Two Ways of Looking at Children with Challenges
Diseases and their Causes are Cultural Phenomena

Many scientific experts, whether they are doctors, psychologists or learning specialists, backed by politicians and bureaucratic organizations, have a tendency to label children with challenges as suffering from specific diseases or dysfunctions such as ADD, ADHD, autism, dyslexia, etc. As the sociologist Sophia Lövgren points out in the afterword of this book, such diagnoses are actually social constructs and cultural phenomena where different subjective symptoms are brought together and formed into a disease that is then discerned to be something to be treated.

In order to treat a diagnosed disease successfully it is advantageous to know what causes it. After medical experts have identified and characterized a disease, which seems to be the easy part, they start looking for the cause. In general, scientific medicine looks for a solitary cause of any disease or diagnosis. The discovery of bacteria and infectious diseases has especially promoted this approach.

However at other times different kinds of causes have been popular. After bacteria, viruses became popular as agents that cause diseases, and now it is genes that are the most popular causes of diseases.

Obviously not only diagnoses but also the recognized causes of diseases and disorders are cultural phenomena. This can be no better illustrated than by developments in the psychiatric field.

The Triumph of the Medical Model in Psychiatry in the 1980s and 1990s

When I trained as a doctor in the 1960s psychological and emotional factors were considered to be relevant as causes of diseases, especially of mental illnesses. Psychiatrists as upholders of the traditional medical paradigm that the mind is only an effect of physical processes were becoming marginalized. Psychologists, social workers, counsellors, family therapists and other non-psychiatrists were taking over the mental-health field. In the beginning of the 1980s the American Psychiatric Association decided to create a partnership with drug companies which would give psychiatry access to funds from the drug companies to promote the medical model, psychopharmacology and the authority and influence of psychiatry.[1] This turned out to be a very successful strategy, if not for patients, then at least for psychiatrists and pharmaceutical companies.

This process was not limited to the US but spread all over the world. In Sweden leading psychiatrists have been especially successful in promoting the medical model and pharmacological treatment particularly when it comes to behavioural symptoms in children. In a way, Swedish child psychiatrists seem to have taken the lead in the promotion of the medical model in their speciality. While there is still not a consensus among US paediatricians and child psychiatrists that ADHD is caused by a brain malfunction, the Swedish National Board of Health and Welfare (SNBHW) boldly states that the typical symptoms of ADHD such as restlessness, attention problems and impulsivity are due to a genetically determined lack of transmitter substances. In addition, Swedish psychiatrists have also managed to convert psychologists and social workers in Sweden to the medical model and make them their associates in the labelling and psycho-pharmacological treatment of children.

The Connection between Race Biology and Genetics in Sweden

The enthusiasm with which most Swedish psychiatrists have picked up the genetic model of explanation for ADHD may seem odd. However I believe there are historical and cultural reasons for the attraction of Swedish psychiatrists to the genetic model and the absence of any questioning of it. In the 1930s and the beginning of the 1940s race biology was a generally accepted ideology in Sweden as it was in other countries. Politicians funded an Institute of Race Biology in Uppsala which undertook the task of studying and documenting the different race groups in Sweden. By measuring the skulls and photographing the naked bodies of the Lapp and Finnish sections of the population in the north of Sweden the researchers were attempting to prove, scientifically, the racial inferiority of these groups compared to the dominant Aryan Swedish population. Many people in Lapland can still recall how as children they were forced to take part in these studies against their will. They are quite cognizant of the fact that if the Nazis had won the war that many of them would have ended up in extermination camps rather than just suffering humiliation and fright at the hands of those who carried out these despicable studies.

After the Second World War race biology became obsolete and the Institute of Race Biology in Uppsala was not allowed to continue its activities. It was quietly merged with the Department of Genetics in the Faculty of Medicine, which still harbours its research materials. When I studied genetics in Uppsala during my medical training the history of the department was discussed among the students but never openly with the teachers. In the following years there has been no ideological settling of accounts of race biology among doctors and geneticists nor has the topic been adequately studied by historians and sociologists. Unlike the Aborigines of Australia the Lapp and Finnish peoples in Sweden are still waiting for an official apology for the discriminatory and racist treatment inflicted on them by the state.

I believe that this absence of an official settling of accounts for the deplorable treatment of these peoples has had an influence on the attitudes and actions not only of the Swedish medical profession but of many other sectors of Swedish society. The total absence of questioning that ADHD is a genetically determined lack of transmitter substances in the brain is especially significant in this respect. So is the readiness of the medical profession to treat these children with addictive and seriously harmful drugs. The support of these practises by the media and the benevolent funding of it by politicians have also enabled these practises to continue and grow.

As has been demonstrated, the idea that ADHD is a genetically determined lack of transmitter substances in the brain, has no more scientific foundation than the idea that the Lapp and Finnish sections of the Swedish population were genetically inferior. And, furthermore, is contradicted by many facts.

Eight out of Ten Swedish Children Diagnosed with ADHD Come from Lower Socioeconomic Groups

Christoffer Gillberg, professor of child psychiatry in Gothenburg, Sweden, has studied children with ADHD. He is one of the experts who promote the view that ADHD is a genetically determined biological disorder. When sociologist Eva Kärfve analysed his research material she found, to her surprise, that 8 out of 10 children who had been labelled ADHD belonged to lower socioeconomic groups. There was no evident explanation for this fact[2]. To scientists who believe that ADHD is genetically determined, the obvious conclusion of this finding would be that lower socioeconomic groups are genetically predisposed to have a higher incidence of ADHD than higher socioeconomic groups. In other words they are genetically inferior. However such an idea is not politically correct in Sweden and is not embraced by the scientific community and can therefore not be expounded by the SNBHW. On the other hand, if the genetic predisposition of ADHD is the same in all socioeconomic groups (as is the accepted notion), 8 out of 10 children with ADHD cannot possibly belong to the lower socioeconomic groups. Such a result would refute the idea that ADHD is a genetically determined biological disorder. Within this context, Gillberg's results would actually point to social and environmental circumstances as causal factors of ADHD.

On the other hand, if it were a generally embraced concept among scientists that the lower social strata were genetically pre-disposed to develop ADHD, Gillberg's result would not only give scientific corroboration of their genetic inferiority but also of the notion that ADHD is a genetically determined condition.

Treating Children with Central Stimulants is a Violation

The efficiency and thoroughness with which Swedish politicians and the medical establishment organize the diagnosing and treatment of children with ADHD is on a par with the effectiveness with how the Institute of Race Biology organized the measuring of the skulls of the Lapp and Finnish peoples in Sweden in the 1930s and 1940s. This efficiency and thoroughness would even be admirable if the purpose and consequences were not so destructive.

Like the Lapp and Finnish children in the 1930s, children being diagnosed with ADHD have no say in the matter. They are prescribed central stimulants whether they want them or not. Even if initially they protest against taking the drug, eventually it will make them more compliant and willing to do as they are told.

Unlike the Lapp and Finnish children of the 1930s and 1940s, children with ADHD are not threatened with physical extinction – it is only their brain cells being endangered when they are treated with central stimulants. Many animal studies on monkeys have shown that relatively low doses of central stimulants cause destruction of brain cells and permanent brain damage especially in the frontal lobes and the basal ganglia. When the central stimulants cause the synapses to be over stimulated by dopamine they will perish causing impaired functioning of these parts of the brain. According to scientific reports children are being treated with equivalent mg/kg dose amphetamine levels as high as those reported to cause brain damage in animals.[3]

Stimulants Make Children Manageable at the Cost of their Spirit

The promoters of central stimulants emphasize how these drugs improve the functioning of children with ADHD and facilitate their interaction with other children. However what really happens to children treated with these drugs is something quite different. They become more compliant and willing and able to do as they are told, especially in regard to boring and repetitive tasks at school. In addition they become less spontaneous and curious and they often withdraw from inter-action and play with other children.

Numerous studies conducted on animals using central stimulants show striking similarities between the reaction of animals and those of children who are prescribed these drugs. Peter Breggin summed up the result of these studies in the following way at the NIMH conference:

"First, stimulants suppress normal spontaneous or self-regulated activity, including curiosity, socializing and play. Second, stimulants promote stereotyped, obsessive-compulsive, overly focused behaviours that are often repetitive and meaningless."[4]

Even if such reactions may result in fewer conflicts with others and in that way facilitate interaction then we must question if they really imply that the functioning of children has improved. Shouldn't we instead see such conduct as being a reason for concern requiring careful consideration?

In the US a consortium of attorneys is bringing a series of class-action suits against Novartis (the manufacturer of Ritalin) and the American Psychiatric Association. One of these attorneys writes in the foreword of Peter Breggin's book *Talking Back to Ritalin*: "I asked myself if the large sums of money earned by the pharmaceutical industry could corrupt their research in the same way as in the tobacco industry. Much as the tobacco industry promoted and marketed its products with children in mind, I began to wonder if our vulnerable children were again being targeted for corporate profit. Ultimately stimulants steal childhood. They make children more manageable at the cost of their spirit. "

Side-Effects of Central Stimulants

According to promoters of central stimulants, e.g. the SNBHW, these drugs have relatively few side-effects. However, the facts are quite different.

From Breggin's survey it is evident that the side-effects of stimulants, far from being insignificant, are both serious and extremely common. In several studies the frequency of side-effects is more than 50%. The most common side-effects are loss of appetite, drowsiness, withdrawal, loss of interest in others and depression. In one study of 41 children between 4 and 6 years of age 75% suffered from loss of appetite, 62% from drowsiness and 62% were uninterested in others. In another study of 83 older children 45% had side-effects that were mostly of withdrawal, sadness or crying.

Obsessive-compulsive symptoms are very common side-effects. They appear as a compulsive repetition of simple activities such as endlessly playing computer games. In one study of 45 children 51% developed compulsive symptoms that in certain cases were very serious. One child became so obsessed with doing a good job raking leaves he would wait for each one to fall from the tree. Another played Lego for 36 hours without breaking to eat or sleep.

In another study 42% of the children produced an obsessive over-focusing after a single dose of stimulants. The children were sometimes unable to stop performing a task that had been assigned to them.

Tics and movement disorder are also very common side-effects. In a study with 45 children, 58% developed tics and abnormal movements. In another study of 122 children, 9% developed tics and abnormal movements. One child did not recover and developed an irreversible syndrome with facial twitching, head turning, lip-smacking, forehead wiping, and vocalizations.

A Canadian study from 1999 demonstrated that at least 9% of the 98 children who had been treated with central stimulants developed psychotic symptoms.

It has long been known that central stimulants decrease blood circulation in the brain, damage blood vessels and cause haemorrhages. In a 1995 textbook of psychiatry Jaffe writes: "In monkeys the toxic effects of chronic amphetamine use include damage to the cerebral blood vessels, neuronal loss [brain cell death] and microhaemorrhages."[5]

It is only recently that attention has been paid to such side-effects in children and adults instigated by the many reports in the rise of blood pressure, stroke and sudden heart death in treated patients. In 2005 the central stimulant Adderal was with-drawn from the market after reports of 20 cases of sudden heart death and 12 cases of stroke.[6] In February 2006 Reuters reported that 51 patients who had been medicated with central stimulants had suddenly passed away, which caused the FDA to urge pre-scribers to pay attention to heart attacks and high blood pressure.

Another 30 deaths in patients treated with Ritalin had also been reported.

Strattera

Strattera is produced by the drug company Eli Lilly and was originally an antidepressant drug which turned out to have no effect on depression. Instead, in 2002, it was introduced as a remedy for ADHD. It is not addictive like other drugs used in ADHD. However, its effects are questionable and its side-effects are appalling. According to a Swedish study of 100 children medicated with Strattera they experienced no positive effects when taking the drug. However, about 40% complained of one or more side-effects including stomach pain, headache, tiredness, loss of appetite and nausea. Around 10% developed psychological side-effects like irritation and depression.[7]

By 2005 Eli Lilly had already received 10,998 reports of psychiatric reactions.[8] That same year the European Medical Products Agency issued warnings about Strattera causing hostility and emotional instability in children and there were other international warnings that Strattera increased the risk of suicide.

In 2006 the FDA issued a survey covering all reports of negative psychological side-effects to Strattera, they found 992 cases of aggression or violent behaviour and 360 cases of psychosis. In 90% of these cases there had been no previous history of this behaviour.[9] It is estimated that at the very most only 10% of drug reactions are ever reported, so the actual incidence may actually be higher.

Another FDA investigation (2004-2007) showed that 31 children and teenagers had died in the US while under Strattera treatment, including 19 who had committed suicide. In addition six children and teenagers were reported to have died in Europe. In same period 37 adults died in the US and Europe. Seventeen of them committed suicide. Altogether 78 persons treated with Strattera died within the 3 years.

Lack of Positive Effects of Central Stimulants

Central stimulants are not the only drugs that cause serious side-effects and death. These are common effects of many drugs and are tolerated by the medical profession provided more patients are believed to survive with drug treatment than without it. Also if the drug prolongs the life of most patients then a certain mortality rate is tolerated.

However, not even the most fervent promoters of central stimulants claim that ADHD is a life-threatening condition or that it shortens the life expectancy of the affected children. Therefore these promoters are forced to play down the severity of the side-effects and assert that they are relatively unimportant. In so doing, they also must pretend to be unaware of all the studies that show the opposite.

One thing they cannot deny is the result of the latest follow-up study of children treated with central stimulants. Remember the MTA study from 2007 showed that after 36 months of treatment there were no positive effects whatsoever, quite contrary to what the promoters had expected. According to one of the leading researchers nothing indicates that drugs are better than no treatment at all in the long term. Furthermore the study demonstrated that central stimulants are connected with more aggressive and antisocial behaviour and increased risks of future criminality and drug abuse.

In spite of these results the prescription of central stimulants continues to escalate, increasing the profits of the pharmaceutical companies and harming a growing number of children.

Another Way to View ADHD: An Impaired Maturing of the Brain

The idea that ADHD is a genetically determined biological disorder is a scientifically unproven assertion which justifies a ruthless abuse of an ever-increasing number of children. Sooner or later such destructive ideas must become obsolete and be replaced by more constructive concepts, which will make it possible for children with challenges to get real help.

This is my reason for undertaking this book. RMT is a safe way of working with people with challenges. It is not a quick fix. However with practise and consistency positive changes take place. This has been my experience, and the experience of others. I believe that the reason it works is that it is based on replicating what babies do naturally to mature the brain and lay the foundations for development.

When the motor development of the infant is impeded in some way the maturation process of the brain may be impaired or delayed. As we have seen there may be many reasons for such obstructed motor development: birth injury, microwaves, toxicity from heavy metals, genetic factors, cultural and psychological factors, etc. This delayed maturation of the brain may very well be the cause of the various challenges with motor function, attention, concentration, impulse control, learning, etc that many children have.

Chapter 4
A Comparison between Rhythmic Movement Training and Medication

Remember central stimulants cause brain damage, as shown by the experiments on monkeys I referred to previously. Treatment dosages for children with these drugs are as high on an mg/kg basis as those that caused brain damage in these animals. In monkeys the dopamine-producing basal ganglia and prefrontal cortex were especially damaged by the central stimulants. There is no reason to believe that children will not be affected in the same way.

There are many indications that in the long run RMT improves the functioning of the basal ganglia and the prefrontal cortex, and increases the supply of dopamine when the nerve nets are stimulated to develop.

Studies have shown that central stimulants obstruct learning and higher mental processes including flexible problem solving. Studies have not been able to show that central stimulants improve academic performance.

Peoples' experience of RMT shows that learning is facilitated, especially with reading and comprehension; however mathematics has also been shown to improve. In both the short and long-term academic performance will improve considerably.

It is known that central stimulants promote stereotyped, obsessive-compulsive, overly focused behaviours that are often repetitive and meaningless and suppress normal spontaneous or self-regulated activity, including curiosity, socializing and play.

The experience of RMT is that children become more extroverted and that their social ability improves including being able to make meaningful contact with other children. This is also the case with autistic children.

A 1993 scientific study of a group of chronic schizophrenic patients conducted by Lindquist and Pettersen from Umeå University, Sweden showed that RMT caused them to become more interested in people around them and more ready to take part in social activities.[1]

At the NIMH conference in 1998 a unique long-term study was presented which showed a significant correlation between stimulant treatment in childhood and later use of stimulants, e.g. regular smoking, cocaine dependence, and a lifetime use of cocaine and stimulants. Also the recent MTA study warns about increased risk of future drug abuse in children treated with stimulants.

RMT does not lead to any increase risk of future drug abuse.

Case-Study: Kalle

Kalle was 11 when he started RMT. He had taken central stimulants for 5 years and when I began to see him in August 2003 was taking 25 mg daily.

Kalle was an early developer and learned to walk when he was 10½ months. He was very defiant when he was 2 to 3 years of age and when he was six he had such severe challenges with hyperactivity, concentration and temper tantrums that he was medicated with amphetamine. The first two years of school he was provided with a personal assistant and he managed to stay in an ordinary class. In the third year he was moved to a special class with seven students and five adults.

During his first visit with me it was apparent that he was a very hyperactive boy who found it very difficult to sit still; his endurance was very poor and he was extremely impulsive and easily disturbed; he had severe temper tantrums nearly every day; found it difficult to play with other children, team sports being especially challenging; preferred to play on his own and was constantly busy playing Gameboy or similar games. It was very hard for him interrupt these activities and he could continue with them for hours. Kalle had several retained primitive reflexes: the Moro, Tonic Labyrinthine (TLR), Symmetrical Tonic Neck (STNR) and Spinal Galant were the most apparent. He had no problems doing the rhythmic movements and seemed to enjoy them.

Kalle had a number of goals, the chief one being to stop taking his medication, which he did not like at all. He also wanted to be able to go back to the normal class at school. He seemed to be very motivated to achieve these goals.

He was instructed to do passive and active rhythmic movements every day and exercises for the Moro and the TLR reflexes a few times a week. In addition his parents were encouraged to reduce his medication from five to four tablets a day. At his next visit his father reported that Kalle had not been motivated to do the active exercises every day but he had always enjoyed being rocked and had done the active exercises when he felt like it.

After a little more than half a year Kalle had become more motivated to do the rhythmic exercises himself and reported that he felt calmer and more harmonious. He had begun to seek body contact with his parents and wanted to sit in their laps, which he had never done before. His temper tantrums had diminished and his parents observed that he had become more reasonable and that he could follow a line of argument in a way he had never been able to do before. Also at school his changed behaviour had been noticed and it had been decided after the summer vacation that he should move a normal class, and that he would be provided with a resource person to assist him.

Before the summer vacation I had recommended to his parents that they reduce his medication by another tablet. However, when Kalle started back after the summer vacation the school protested strongly at the idea of this reduction and threatened not move him to a normal class if this happened. Therefore the parents had not reduced his dose.

After this it was more difficult to motivate Kalle to do the movements and only after constant reminding could they get him to do them, which happened only about every third day. It was now decided that his medication should be reduced by one tablet immediately and then again after his next visit to me if he had done the exercises at least five times a week.

At his next visit in November Kalle's behaviour was completely changed. Previously it had been difficult to interrupt his playing Gameboy in the waiting room. Now he romped and wrestled on the floor with his little brother whenever he had an opportunity. His parents reported that he had now taken responsibility for the movements and was doing them every day on his own. His parents only needed to remind him. He regularly took part in the reflex integration exercises assisted by his father.

When he had done rhythmic exercises for 1½ years his medication was reduced to two tablets a day. No one noticed any difference. He succeeded beyond all expectation at school. He continued to do the rhythmic movements on his own and the isometric exercises with his father. He had integrated his TLR, Spinal Galant and Moro reflexes.

He no longer had problems with endurance, concentration, attention or hyperactivity. His temper was even and he no longer had temper tantrums. Before the summer vacation he was getting nothing but praise from his teachers. He now reduced his medication by another tablet. In December, after doing the exercises for 2 years and 3 months, he took the last tablet. In February, 2½ years after his first visit to me he reported that he felt good and school was going well in spite of the fact that he had not done the exercises for several months.

A year later Kalle read in the newspaper that people who had been diagnosed with ADHD needed a psychiatric evaluation before they could get a driver's licence. He then made an appointment with the child psychiatric clinic that had initially labelled him as suffering from ADHD and prescribed him medication. He asked them to cancel his diagnosis since he no longer had any symptoms. After having done all the required tests they had to cancel the diagnosis.

Chapter 5
Infant Motor Development

The development of an infant follows a time schedule. There are many different basic movement patterns that the infant needs to move through sequentially to establish strong foundations and the ability to differentiate so that movement becomes easy, graceful and automatic. These developmental movement patterns are:

- Breathing – the foundation of all the patterns that follow as it gives life to movement.
- Mouthing – the mouth is the first part to reach, grasp, hold and let go.
- Navel Radiation (Core-Distal Connectivity) – connects all the limbs to the navel. A baby needs to develop a sense of his own centre before he can reach out into the world.
- Spinal Movement (Head-Tail Connectivity) – develops the ability to differentiate between the front and the back of the body which leads to the ability to attend and focus.
- Homologous (Upper-Lower Connectivity) – develops the ability to differentiate between the upper and lower halves of the body and leads to stability and grounding.
- Homolateral (Body-Half Connectivity) – develops differentiation between the left and right sides of the body which leads to mobility and the ability to move in all directions.
- Contralateral (Cross-Lateral Connectivity) – all the previous patterns set up this pattern which allows for the body to move efficiently and coordinates the opposite arm and leg to work together.

All babies are meant to grow and follow the same development pattern or stages. If they miss these stages, do not spend enough time or get stuck in a stage then we know that primitive infant reflexes will not be able to complete their job and it becomes difficult to establish the postural lifelong reflexes and obtain complete control of movements.

Important indicators for a baby to achieve are:

- head control
- rolling
- sitting
- crawling
- standing
- walking

Here is a brief list of the major milestones and abilities from birth to 2 years of age.

Newborns:

- Display automatic (reflexive) responses to particular stimuli
- Very little movement is truly voluntary as it is controlled by primitive reflexes

Neonatal period:

- Reaching is done without a real intention; it is done reflexively with no coordination of reaching and grasping
- Hands are kept in a tight fist. Grasping is only done when something is placed in the infant's hand
- Most objects are held by the entire hand rather than just a couple or few fingers

1 month old:

- Infant begins learning to control and lift his head

2 months old:

- May smile on purpose, blow bubbles and coo when you talk or play together
- Infant begins to mimic facial expressions

1-3 months old:

- Infant learns to support his head and upper body when lying on stomach
- Can stretch out legs and kick when on his stomach or back
- He learns how to open and close his hands and bring them to his mouth

2-3 months old:

- Infant can roll over from side to back
- Can support his head and shoulders on

his forearms
- Learns to grab and shake small toys and to reach for dangling objects
- Able to push his feet down on flat surfaces
- Able to follow moving objects with head and eyes

3-5 months old:
- Intentional reaching starts takes place

4 months old:
- Can sit with support

4-5 months old:
- Can roll over from back to side
- Starts to creep on stomach

4-6 months old:
- Become fairly successful at reaching for and grasping objects

4-7 months old:
- Learns to transfer objects from one hand to another
- Can support weight when held upright
- Explore objects with hands and mouth and using shaking and banging when playing with objects

5 months old:
- Can sit with hand support
- Grasp using whole hand

5-7 months old:
- Ability to coordinate vision and control reaching improves.

7 months old:
- Can sit without support

7-8 months old:
- Begins to crawl on hands and knees

8 months old:

- Most infants have developed the ability to pull themselves up to a standing position

9 months old:

- Infants develop the pincer grasp (ability to hold small objects between the thumb and forefinger)

10-11 months old:

- Most infants can stand up alone for a few moments

10-12 months old:

- Infants are typically able to hold a spoon in their hands and feed themselves, though their aim may be poor

11 months old:

- Reach and grasp are coordinated
- Can stand up alone well, and take some steps with assistance

12 months old:

- Most infants can walk alone
- Can stand up from a sitting position
- Places objects in and out of containers

13-18 months old:

- Refine walking abilities by learning to walk sideways and backwards

16-23 months old:

- Learns to walk up steps with help

14-24 months old:

- Learns how to run. By the age of 2 can run more smoothly

23-24 months old:

- Can jump in place

Chapter 6
The Brain Stem and the Cerebellum

The Neural Chassis and its Three Guiding Operators

Paul MacLean, who studied the development of the brain in amphibians, reptiles and mammals, has described how the different levels of the brain cooperate. The neural chassis he includes as the spinal cord, brain stem (medulla oblongata and pons) and midbrain "provides most of the neural machinery required for self-preservation and the preservation of the species. By itself the neural chassis might be likened to a vehicle without a driver. Significantly, in the more advanced vertebrates the evolutionary process has provided the neural chassis not with a single guiding operator, but rather a combination of three, each markedly different in its evolutionary age and development, and each radically different in structure, chemistry and organization."[1] These three operators that guide the neural chassis are the reptilian brain (in humans this is the basal ganglia), the mammalian brain (or the limbic system) and the neocortex.

The Development of the Motor Abilities and the Senses in the Foetus

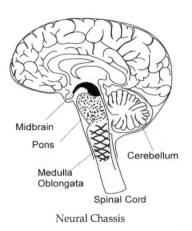

Midbrain
Pons
Cerebellum
Medulla Oblongata
Spinal Cord
Neural Chassis

In the foetus the brain stem (also referred to as the fish brain by MacLean) develops gradually and must function adequately for the newborn baby to survive. Like the brain of the fish the human brain stem receives signals from the vestibular, kinaesthetic or proprioceptive, visual and tactile senses and relays these signals to the motor system. In addition respiration, heart activity and other life-sustaining processes are directed from the brain stem.

In the foetus the senses mature gradually and at birth they are still to fully develop and are not yet well adapted to life outside the womb. The proprioceptive sense enables the foetus to keep track of different parts of its body. The foetus learns to perform well-regulated movements in the water environment of the womb and is able to move freely, suck his thumb and play with the umbilical cord when under stress. Under the new gravitational circumstances after delivery the baby loses these abilities and moves like a fish on dry land with slow movements mainly using the head, trunk and arms. A newborn baby is still a good swimmer. The vestibular sense develops early in the foetus and enables both the foetus and the newborn baby to keep his balance in water. However once on dry land a newborn baby has to develop the ability that is necessary to balance in gravity.

The motor abilities of the embryo are, at the very beginning, controlled from the spinal cord and involve simple reflex movements. As the brain stem gradually starts to function the more complex reflex patterns of the primitive reflexes are developed which help the foetus and the infant develop his motor abilities further, though at this stage voluntary motor abilities have yet to develop.

The newborn infant is faced with the task of programming his balance and proprioceptive senses and learning how to control his motor systems so as to move freely on land. In order for the baby to complete this programming he needs to be able to follow the inborn primitive reflex programme that allows him to perform spontaneous, rhythmic infant movements that form the basis of development.

The Brain Stem and Muscle Tone

All senses, except the sense of smell, send sensory signals to the Reticular Activating System (RAS) in the brain stem, which processes and integrates information from the senses and sends it on to higher levels of the brain. The vestibular nuclei which receive signals not only from the balance sense but also from other senses – especially tactile and kinaesthetic - are particularly important for developing muscle tone. If there is insufficient stimulation of the nuclei in the brain stem from these senses the result will be low muscle tone of the extensor muscles of the body.

Therefore it is essential that the baby is touched, hugged, rocked and allowed to move around freely, as it is this stimulation that sends signals from the senses to the vestibular system that starts the baby lifting his head and then his chest, activities that are so vital for developing muscle tone. Without this stimulation the vicious cycle of needing stimulation from the senses yet being unable to access it begins and slowly becomes more exacerbated as the child gets older. This low muscle tone means that he is more than likely going to develop problems keeping his head upright as he gets older and will have hunched posture. Another possibility is that his joints may be over-flexible. Because of the hunched posture he may be a shallow breather. He may very well get to the point where he is reluctant to move around and prefers to do activities that allow him to sit still.

Children with these tendencies will develop attention problems due to the malfunctioning of the cortex of the brain and be diagnosed as Attention Deficit Disorder (ADD) when they grow older. An over-flexible spine and joints make it even more difficult to maintain proper posture and breathing.

Rhythmic Movement Training gradually normalizes muscle tone and decreases the over-flexibility of the joints.

The Brain Stem and the Reticular Activating System (RAS)

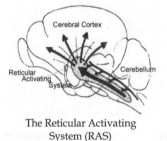

The Reticular Activating System (RAS)

The central part of the brain stem mainly consists of a dense nerve net, the Reticular Activating System, (RAS0. This system of nerve cells receives signals from the visual, auditory, vestibular, proprioceptive and tactile senses, and transmits the information to the cortex. The effect of these signals is to arouse the cortex which is necessary for maintaining attention and alertness. Without such an arousing influence on the cortex we are not able to maintain an awareness of external events.

My experience using RMT is that the movements are effective and can rapidly remedy a deficient lack of good signals from the balance, proprioceptive and tactile senses through the RAS to the cortex which results in ADD, poor muscle tone, hunched posture, a poor ability to stay alert, keep attention and focus. This is also true in the extreme cases of children who have so little arousal that they have very low muscle tone that leads to an inability to move around and lack the stimulation to be aware of the world around them and therefore habitually day-dream and hallucinate.

The Development of the Senses in the Foetus and the Infant

The development of the brain and neural system in the foetus and infant is dependent on stimulation from the senses. The senses which are first developed in the foetus are the vestibular, tactile and proprioceptive senses and these initiate the bulk of all sensory impressions to the brain of the foetus. They therefore play a decisive role for the development of the foetus and the infant.

In primitive fish the balance organs were hair like cells at the side of the head whose function were to react to vibrations and the gravitational force enabling the fish to know what was up and down and therefore being able to right itself. Eventually these hair cells were enclosed in the internal ear or labyrinth. In mammals the auditory sense developed out of the labyrinth through development of the external ear which also transmitted air vibrations to the internal ear.

In the foetus the vestibular sense is stimulated by gravity and from the mother's movement. The vestibular apparatus is fully developed by the sixth month after conception. The new-born child has a well-developed vestibular sense and is a good swimmer.

The foetus starts to move early thus stimulating the proprioceptive or kinaesthetic sense, which can be defined as the ability to know the position of your body parts and to be in charge of your movements. The foetus stretches and bends arms and legs, turns his head, etc. When he is able to put its thumb into his mouth or play with the umbilical cord his proprioceptive sense is well developed.

The pressure in the womb is higher than in the surrounding air and stimulates the tactile sense of the foetus. Also when the foetus moves and touches the womb wall the tactile sense is stimulated.

Reprogramming of the Senses is Necessary after Delivery

After delivery the movement ability of the baby changes completely. In the new gravitational conditions outside the womb the infant no longer knows the position of his body parts and can no longer command his body. He moves like a fish on dry land. The trunk moves slowly, arms and legs move jerkily and without control and his head is much more immobile than when he was in the womb.

The infant is confronted with the task of recapturing his proprioceptive sense that was working so well and now seems completely lost. This recapture is only possible if the baby can activate his inner programme of rhythmic infant movements.

However the baby also needs stimulation of the tactile and vestibular senses by being rocked and touched and turned around. Such stimulation affects the vestibular sense, strengthens muscle tone and is important for the baby's ability to lift his head and eventually get up on hands and knees.

When the position of the head is changed the hair cells of the labyrinth, which are partially responsible for balance, are affected by gravity. The vestibular sense relays information about the position of the head in the gravitational field but not about the position of the rest of the body. Therefore the baby must learn to coordinate signals from the proprioceptive and tactile senses with the vestibular sense to get a correct indication of the relationship between his head, his body and the world around him; to get an understanding of this relationship the small child experiments with his body and head in different positions.

For the tactile sense birth also entails a transformation since the pressure conditions change so fundamentally. Therefore the baby needs a lot of tactile stimulation or his motor ability and emotions will not develop normally. In former times (and still in some cultures) parents used to swaddle the baby to facilitate the change of pressure conditions before and after birth. For the mother to carry a baby on her body may also be a good way to stimulate both his tactile and vestibular senses.

When the baby learns to grasp things and put them into his mouth and eventually crawl around on hands and knees the development of the proprioceptive, tactile and vestibular senses continues while the baby simultaneously trains his visual skills such as binocular vision and accommodation.

The Primitive Reflexes

The motor activity of the foetus depends on the primitive reflexes. These are automatic stereotyped movements controlled from the brain stem. These reflexes emerge and develop during different stages of pregnancy and must mature and finally be inhibited by the basal ganglia and integrated into the whole movement pattern of the infant. By making movements that are rhythmical the baby inhibits and integrates these reflexes one after the other.

The most important sensory triggers for the primitive reflexes are stimulation from the balance, tactile and kinaesthetic senses. One of the earliest reflexes to develop is the Tonic Labyrinthine Reflex (TLR). When the head of the foetus is bent forward the spine and the limbs are also bent. After birth, when the baby extends his head backward, the TLR backward is developed and the baby begins to be able to stretch his body.[2]

When the foetus turns his head from side to side the proprioceptive receptor apparatus of the neck will be stimulated triggering the Asymmetric Tonic Neck Reflex (ATNR). This starts happening sometime between 18-20 weeks of pregnancy causing the foetus to stretch his arm and leg to the side the head is turned to. The mother then notices that the baby starts kicking.

The development of the Automatic Gait reflex into the mature adult walk illustrates the role that the maturing brain plays in the development of our motor abilities. The foetus starts to make walking movements very early, even before the brain stem and the spinal cord have been linked up. Such gait movements are controlled from the spinal cord.[3] At about the 37th week of pregnancy the primitive Automatic Gait reflex develops. This reflex is controlled from the level of the midbrain and is active when the baby is born. It can be triggered by holding him under the arms and lifting him into an upright position, leaning him slightly forward and letting the soles of his feet touch a flat surface. Then the baby starts making automatic walking type movements.[4]

When the baby is 3 or 4-months-old the Automatic Gait reflex should be inhibited and no longer able to be triggered. However it is not until the baby has learned to get up into a standing position and mastered the forces of gravity that he will be able to transform the Automatic Gait into the mature adult walk reflex, a postural reflex controlled from the basal ganglia.

The Importance of the Maturing of the Primitive Reflexes

If the baby is unable to inhibit his primitive reflexes at the appropriate time they will delay his motor development making it more difficult to follow the inborn programme. Consequently, there is a stumbling block to the maturing of his brain.

An infant whose primitive reflexes have not reached the proper stage of development and appropriate maturity when he is born will have more difficulties in inhibiting and integrating them at the time when they are due, than a baby whose reflexes are fully matured. This is especially the case for premature babies and babies delivered by Caesarean section.

In premature babies several primitive reflexes have not developed sufficiently when they are born. While in an incubator the baby does not get the necessary stimulation from the tactile, balance and proprioceptive senses from being in the womb. This delays the maturation of the primitive reflexes. If, on the other hand, the mother carries the premature baby around in a pouch on her chest, especially if there is skin-to-skin contact, he will get stimulation similar to being in the womb which will promote the appropriate maturing and integration of primitive reflexes and improve muscle tone and help the linking together of the different levels of the brain.

Many babies are now delivered by Caesarean section and therefore miss the normal delivery process. The birthing process is an important triggering and maturation stage for many of the primitive reflexes. Premature babies and babies delivered by Caesarean section run a greater risk of retaining their primitive reflexes into adulthood. Therefore, because there is an incomplete maturing of the brain, there is a greater possibility that they may acquire problems with motor ability, attention, concentration and learning.

Rhythmic Movements for Stimulating the Brain Stem

The foetus gets sensory stimulation from the mother's respiration, heart-beat, walking, running, etc. Such passive stimulation helps the tactile, proprioceptive and balance senses of the foetus to develop and stimulates the growth and maturing of the nerve cells of the neural chassis. All this sensory stimuli also promotes the maturing of other parts of the brain. When primitive reflexes are triggered in the foetus the motor responses cause stimulation of the neural chassis.

Another source of sensory stimulation for the foetus is all the movements he can do by himself such as turning his head from side to side, sucking his thumb, playing with his umbilical cord, etc. Playing with the umbilical cord stimulates proprioception which has a calming effect on the foetus.

Passive rhythmic movements are especially useful in stimulating the neural chassis for infants and also in children with brain injuries who are still neurologically on the level of infants. By passively rocking the child in different ways the neural chassis will be stimulated to improve muscle tone, mature primitive reflexes and stimulate spontaneous movements. When infants are slow to develop and do not easily move on from one stage of development to another, such as those who are not able to lift their head or who did not start to crawl on hands and knees then passive stimulation can be used to move development along.

In a child with severe brain damage who is stuck with his head turned to one side passive rhythmic stimulation may cause him to start turning his head from side to side in a reflex-like manner.

Case-Study: Olle

While I was following the work of Kerstin Linde I met Olle. He was 5-years-old when he started to do rhythmic movements. He had stopped developing during the previous year. I followed his progress for half a year during which time he made considerable progress.

When he was born he was quite floppy and limp and did not even have enough strength to cry. He developed slowly. When he was 8-months-old he was still lying on the floor but had learned to raise his head a little. His parents were not able to make eye contact with him. He was tired and sluggish.

When he was 11-months-old he learned to sit and at 18 months he began to rise up and even learned to be able to stand for short periods of time. However as he grew and got heavier he lost this ability. The medical establishment gave his parents no hope at all that Olle would improve. It was his parents' impressions were that the staff's attitude was that there was nothing that could be done to help Olle and they shrugged their shoulders at the whole thing. Olle's parents had the feeling that the physiotherapists were only fulfilling their legal responsibility by seeing Olle once a month. His parents felt that these people did not believe that they could ever help him.

Before Olle came to see Kirsten Linde for the first time he spent most of his time sitting quite still hardly making any sounds. His back was hunched and he had no strength to hold up his head. His legs were quite floppy. He did not meet his parents' eyes and hallucinated a lot. He was not interested in his surroundings except for those times when his parents played music or sang for him, which always animated him.

Olle was given the basic rhythmic movements to begin with. He was very positive about the movements and very diligent about doing them - kneeling on all fours, rocking backwards and forwards and crawling on all fours around the apartment. He started to pull things down and show an interest in his surroundings by putting things into his mouth. He suddenly wanted to eat by himself, something he had never done before.

He started to babble and make different sounds and to pay attention when he was called by name.

As his vision improved he began to look fixedly at things around him in a totally new way. Previously he had mostly shifted his gaze and only absentmindedly watched TV. He now started to watch TV more. He also discovered his hands which he started to examine and he became very interested at looking at himself in the mirror. For the first time he noticed the family dog and he started to play with it. When the family received visitors he showed interest and crawled up to look at them. His hallucinations decreased. He began to react when he hurt himself, also something he had never done before.

After a few months' training Olle's posture had completely changed and he managed to hold his head upright. His back was not as hunched and his legs were not so floppy.

Olle saw Kerstin once a month. However one or two days after every visit he used to be taken ill. After the first visit he had a fever and sore throat and he coughed up a lot of phlegm. After a couple of months' training there was a terrible rattle in his chest and his parents were very worried. However, suddenly he was able to cough for the first time in his life so he was able to cough up the phlegm by himself.

After a couple of months of training he started to have emotional reactions. He began to wake up at night and cry inconsolably. He also had a period when he was awake at night and was happily laughing and greeting people. He could show anger, which he had never done before and he began to form a will of his own. He learned to protest if he did not want some food, and then he could even shake his head, which was something entirely new. And if he wanted something he did not give up – he became very stubborn. Previously he had been absolutely indifferent and the parents had been able to stuff him with anything. He just opened his mouth and swallowed.

Five months after Olle started his training his physiotherapist noticed his progress and saw that his body had become much steadier. By this time Olle had not visited her for 3 months. Then she said that she wanted to see Olle more frequently. His parents did not dare to tell her that he was going to an alternative place for treatment. They made a choice to stop seeing Kerstin Linde and see the physiotherapist instead.

The Function of the Cerebellum

The cerebellum developed as a bulge from the brain stem. It receives signals from the receptors for the kinaesthetic and tactile senses that transmit information about touch and pressure. Between the cerebellum and the motor cortex there are important nerve connections which enable the cerebellum to play a fund-amental role in coordinating our movements.

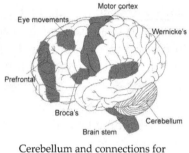

Cerebellum and connections for language, eye movements, attention, judgements etc

Along with the vestibular nuclei the cerebellum correlates postural and kinaesthetic information about the position of the body in the gravitational field. Its function is to make movement smooth, easy and coordinated, correcting deviation between executed and planned movement.

The cerebellum also plays an important role in coordinating the rhythms between the brain and the body. The rhythmic elements of spontaneous infant movements seem to have a special importance for stimulating the growth and maturation of the nerve nets of the cerebellum and the brain as a whole. During 6 to 12 months of age there is rapid growth of the cerebellum coinciding with the fast movement development of the baby.

Dysfunction of the Cerebellum in Attention and Learning Disorders

Some children have great difficulty making simple rhythmical movements in a coordinated way. This inability is usually not really apparent when a child is moving about in an upright position and therefore is mostly overlooked. However, when lying down these children are unable to make simple rhythmic movements in an active way. For example, actively rolling the bottom from side to side or actively sliding on the back may be very hard to learn for some children. Such an inability may reflect a dysfunction of the cerebellum which is likely to affect the function of many other parts of the brain, especially the cortex and therefore many areas of achievement. It may affect attention, planning, judgement, control of impulses and abstract thinking. It can also affect eye movements, reading comprehension, speed of information processing, working memory, learning and speech development.

The great impact of the cerebellum on all these functions can be explained by the strong connections between the cerebellum and those areas of the neocortex essential for these abilities. Such connections exist between the cerebellum and the prefrontal cortex[5,] responsible for attention, planning, judgement and impulse control, between the cerebellum and the speech areas of Wernicke and Broca[6] and between the cerebellum and the area in the frontal lobes responsible for pursuit eye movements or tracking. When these areas get insufficient stimulation from the cerebellum their nerve nets do not develop properly, which explains their poor functioning.

Rhythmic Movement Training and the Cerebellum

The strong impact on attention, concentration, control of impulses, abstract thinking, judgement and learning which is usually seen in RMT can be explained by various factors such as improved arousal of the cortex or increased stimulation of different areas of the cortex by the cerebellum. However, children who have difficulty doing rhythmic movements in a smooth, rhythmic way, due to a dysfunction of the cerebellum, do not benefit as much from the movements as children with no such difficulties.

It is therefore extremely important to teach these children to make the movements in a rhythmical way. Some of them learn quite quickly, within a month or so, but others may have to practise daily for more than a year before they can make the movements smoothly, rhythmically and effortlessly. Even then they tend to lose the rhythm when they are tired.

Rhythmic movements, that are made actively, are most important for the cerebellum. In addition, these movements have other effects such as integrating primitive reflexes and developing postural lifelong reflexes especially in small children. These movements also promote the linking together of different parts of the brain, for instance by stimulating the growth of nerve nets that are essential for the arousal of the cortex and the stimulation of different areas of the cortex by the cerebellum. All these effects are vitally important for resolving attention and learning difficulties.

It takes time to rebuild the brain in this way. It needs continuous and daily stimulation from active rhythmic movements for a long time, most commonly a year or more, before learning and attention problems can be completely resolved.

In children who are not able to do rhythmic infant movements due to a motor handicap, e.g. cerebral palsy or severe weakness of the muscles, as in Olle's case, the nerve nets of the cerebellum will not get sufficient stimulation. As a consequence the prefrontal cortex or the speech areas of the cortex will not receive sufficient stimulation. In such cases speech may not develop and there may be great problems with attention. When such children start to do rhythmic movements there may be a very rapid development due to the stimulation of the cerebellum.

Exact Movements

In order for the rhythmic exercises to be as effective as possible they must be done in a rhythmical, coordinated and smooth way. In addition they should also be done symmetrically. Movements that are not symmetrical are an indication that the primitive reflexes are still active. Subjectively we experience our movements as symmetrical even if we only move one half of the body, e.g. only rotate the head to one side and not to the other. Often you only need to call attention to the asymmetrical movement pattern to be able to correct it.

When we do rhythmic movements there must be no accessory movements of the mouth, feet, hands, shoulders, neck or hand. When the client's attention is called to these accessory movements either by pointing them out or by putting a hand on the body part that should not move, he will quickly learn not to make unnecessary movements.

Movements that are made in a rhythmic, smooth, symmetrical and coordinated way can be considered to be exact movements. Some can make these movements spontaneously while others may have to work hard to achieve them. The exercises need to be adapted to each individual so he can learn to do them more and more exactly.

Infants will learn how to do the rhythmic exercises exactly if they are able to and also if given the opportunity to move freely on the floor. When they develop a new movement it looks, at first, very tentative but gradually it will become more and more exact. Some children, however, will not give themselves sufficient time to develop a movement properly before they hurry on to do another one. Others may have some form of damage that prevents the infant movements developing exactly.

The more exactly the exercises are made, the more information they give the brain making it possible to adjust muscle tone in each moment and for the back and the joints to work in the best possible position and cooperate in the best possible way in the gravitational field. In many cases the spine or the joints may have become fixed in incorrect positions. For instance, the thoracic spine may have been locked in a hunch or the pelvis may be rotated. Such fixations need to be corrected before the rhythmic movements can be done exactly.

Case-Study: Eva

One of the most instructive cases I observed during the 4 years I followed Kerstin Linde's work was Eva. Not only was Eva's motor development extraordinary, she would more than likely have learned how to walk if it were not for the well-meaning yet nevertheless sadistic treatment she received in the rehabilitation ward of the hospital. Eva's speech development by following the work of Kerstin was also remarkable for a girl who doctors had predicted would never learn to talk. Her rapid speech development and motor abilities after she started seeing Kerstin intrigued me greatly and I was inspired to find a way to explain her progress.

Eva had just turned three when she visited Kerstin Linde for the first time. She was a small, lean girl with a thin face and small, cold feet, and looked as if she were squeezed and compacted together. She could turn from her stomach to her back but not the other way round. She could not sit up by herself and she had to be supported by pillows. She also could not eat without help. She could not speak a single word.

When Eva was 1-year-old it was established that she had cerebral palsy due to lack of oxygen at birth. After that she received extensive help from medical services. She had sessions with a speech therapist and a physiotherapist and she had her own assistant. Her mother told me: "She had the same physio-therapy programme all the time and her assistant made movements with her several hours every day for 2 years but nothing happened. Eva kept lying on the floor and could neither rise nor turn around." The doctors said that Eva would never learn to speak and it had been decided that she should take part in a project to learn sign language.

Eva's mother recalled their first visit: "Kerstin said that Eva's brain believed that she had only one leg and that it had to be informed that she had two. And then she took her two legs bending and stretching them as she said 'right, left, right, left'.

Then Eva was told to touch her right leg and then her left one. And she did it! I could hardly believe my eyes; she had never done anything like that before. I was asked to keep a diary about what happened with Eva. I thought that nothing much would happen. If nothing had happened in the previous 2 years I thought it would certainly be enough to write only once a week. However so much happened that I had to write a page every day."

In the evening when they got home after Eva's first visit she managed to sit up on the floor. First she lay on her stomach and then she rose on all fours and then she backed up and sat.

Not long after she started the training she began to use her hands so she could eat and drink by herself. After a year she was able to do jigsaw puzzles, dress and undress her dolls and switch the tape-recorder on and off. A couple of months after she started the training Eva began to speak, first occasional words, and then two word sentences and after a year up six word sentences.

Soon after she began the training her legs were quite relaxed and she was able to lie on her back and suck her toes and it did not take long before she could sit on the floor and occupy herself. Eight months after beginning the programme she had learned to rise up on to her feet supporting herself on furniture. Her vision had improved and she had to change her glasses.

Eva's training programme was described by her mother:

"In the beginning we had to work hard to get her relaxed. We took her by the feet and rocked her in the longitudinal direction of her body and then we rolled her legs. When she was relaxed we could start to do movements. She used to kneel on all fours and rock to and fro and then she used to lie on her stomach and make crawling movements with her legs. Soon she learned to use her arms to move on the floor and after some practise she learned to crawl on all fours."

After 8 months' treatment, just after she had learned to rise up on to her feet, Eva was admitted to the child rehabilitation clinic. Her mother reported:

"The opinion of the medical staff was that Eva would never learn to walk. They had to develop whatever could be developed. So she was tied to a board and had to stand up supported by the board or had to sit in a wheel-chair all day. She was not allowed to be on the floor. The physiotherapists said that it was no use working with her legs until she had an operation on them, but the orthopaedists did not think that an operation was required and refused to operate. Eva did not want to be tied up and was angry and protested. When I came to take her home they said that she was not at all cooperative, and even among the worst children they had treated. They advised me to consult a child psychologist and even gave me the address of one.

When Eva got home she had regressed totally. Her legs were quite stiff and she could not even rise from a prone position, something she had learned the first time she visited Kerstin. Not until we visited with her the next time did she get the help she needed so her legs could relax again."

Her mother reported her development after coming home from the child rehabilitation clinic:

"When Eva had learned to drive her wheel-chair she discovered how comfortable and fast it was. When she got home she did not want to be on the floor. She became much stiffer and the training became much more difficult. After she began sitting in her wheel chair she also got several urinary infections, something she had never had before. However at the same time Eva is so happy to be able to make her way more easily at home."

Needless to say Eva did not learn to walk.

Cerebellum, Motor Abilities and Speech

Eva's case illustrates how movement ability and speech are linked and how speech will only develop when motor abilities improve and the cerebellum is stimulated. Because of cerebral palsy Eva had not been able to move as an infant and her cerebellum had therefore not received the necessary stimulation to develop. When she started RMT the cerebellum started to develop and was able to stimulate the speech areas of the left hemisphere enabling speech to develop.

Chapter 7
The Reptilian Brain or Basal Ganglia

The reptilian brain, the first layer capping the neural chassis, corresponds to the new structures of the brain that reptiles developed. It was the first part of the triune brain to develop its function as a guiding operator of the neural chassis. According to MacLean in reptiles this part does not play a demonstrably important role in motor ability; rather it controls social interaction which is characterized by rituals, routines and strict hierarchical submission. The reptilian brain does not replace the neural chassis; however it does significantly influence it.

In man, rituals, routines and hierarchical dominance are also controlled by this part of the brain which in humans is called the basal ganglia. These behaviours however are not as important for man as they are for reptiles. As frequently happens during evolution a new function has been developed for an old structure.

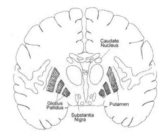

Cross-section of the brain showing the basal ganglia

This part has been modified so that in humans it works in cooperation with the motor cortex to control motor activity. The basal ganglia act as the intermediary between the brain stem and the cortex and control the motor cortex. Unlike the primitive reflexes the postural reflexes are governed to some extent by the motor cortex which permits voluntary movement to take place.

The Postural Reflexes

The motor activity of the newborn infant is controlled by primitive reflexes and is outside voluntary control. In order to control his motor ability voluntarily in the gravitational field the baby must inhibit and integrate his primitive reflexes and the lifelong postural reflexes patterns.[1] The postural reflexes are necessary for our stability and balance in gravity and they enable us to move automatically.

The basal ganglia receive signals from the proprioceptive, tactile, vestibular and visual senses and respond by sending signals downward to the neural chassis. These signals inhibit or modify the primitive reflexes transforming the stereotyped and "sweeping" movement patterns of these reflexes integrating them into the more precise and well-balanced movement patterns of the postural reflexes. Therefore, the basis of the postural reflexes is the primitive reflexes that are inhibited and transformed by the basal ganglia and integrated into the movement pattern of the infant.

This is brought about by the spontaneous rhythmic movements that a baby makes before he learns to crawl and walk. The main part of the inhibition and integration of the primitive reflexes need to be completed while the baby is still on the floor. Movements in an upright position and standing or walking at too early an age only allow the inhibition and integration of the primitive reflexes to a very limited extent.

The Importance of the Basal Ganglia for Automatic Movements and the Ability to Sit Still

Like the primitive reflexes, the postural reflexes are automatic and cannot be replaced by voluntary movements. When we move around we can't be aware of every single movement; we need to decide voluntarily when we want to start moving, where we are going and how fast, without the need to understand consciously the physiology of what is happening when we move.

When we are at rest, the basal ganglia are in full activity and have a strongly inhibiting effect on our movements. When we decide to start moving the motor cortex sends signals to the basal ganglia to decrease this inhibiting effect. The quicker we move the less inhibiting is the effect of the basal ganglia.

Small children who develop normally are usually over-active and move around more or less constantly, except when they are engaged in some very interesting activity. Like older children who are over-active they cannot be still on command. This is because the nerve nets of the basal ganglia are undeveloped in children who are still learning to master their balance and stability.

The basal ganglia control not only the automatic postural reflexes but all other automatic movement patterns that have been learned. They have therefore been called the "secretaries of the brain". In children whose basal ganglia are undeveloped, e.g. small children or those with the labels ADD/ADHD, the ability to learn to do things automatically is impaired. They must compensate for this problem by being conscious of what they are doing all the time which may contribute to their poor endurance and ability to maintain interest in tasks.

Basal Ganglia and Parkinson's Disease

Even when the postural reflexes have been established the original primitive reflex patterns remain at the level of the brain stem, although normally they should not be active. These reflex patterns reappear when the inhibiting effect of the basal ganglia end for some reason or other. This is exactly what happens in Parkinson's disease.

In 1967 the British neurologist Dr Purdon Martin published a report on 130 cases of Parkinson's disease caused by an epidemic of encephalitis between 1919 and 1925. He was able to demonstrate that late symptoms of the disease such as an inability to keep stability or balance, rise up and sit down and walk normally are due to a dysfunction of the postural reflexes and a consequence of the extensive death of nerve cells in the pallidum, one of the nuclei of the basal ganglia.[2]

Purdon Martin did not investigate what happens with the primitive reflexes in Parkinson's disease. However, my own experiences of treating patients with Parkinson's shows that the primitive reflexes are activated early, before the postural reflexes have been affected. By doing movements for integration of primitive reflexes and training of postural reflexes, motor abilities improve and the long-time impairment of motor ability that usually happens in Parkinson's will not take place.

It is not only in Parkinson's disease that the primitive reflexes may re-emerge. Old age, whiplash injury and other trauma are also able to reactivate the reflexes.

Motor Development of the Baby

The motor activity of the newborn infant is controlled by primitive reflexes. During the time a baby makes spontaneous rhythmic infant movements the primitive reflexes are inhibiting and the postural reflexes are developing. After birth the baby, while in a waking state, is busy exploring different movements one after the other. In the beginning these movements are fumbling and uncoordinated, however after some practise they become more accomplished until the baby then switches to another movement. If both the outer and inner requirements are satisfactory, the baby will learn to make these movements in an exact way before starting to make a new one.

In order to integrate primitive reflexes completely the baby must learn to do certain movements in an exact way. Sometimes there are inner obstacles to making certain movements, e.g. an inability to lift the head and low muscle tone. Sometimes adults may restrict the baby's ability to move freely, by doing things like not allowing babies to spend time on the floor or placing them in baby-walkers or keeping them in baby car seats even when not in a car.

When the baby is allowed to have tummy time he will follow the inner primitive reflex programme and exercise and strengthen the extensor muscles of the back and the neck thereby helping to integrate the TLR by beginning to lift his head off the floor. Thanks to the continued stimulation of the brainstem from this movement the chest then begins to rise off the floor when the head lifts then the legs also rise. When this happens the Landau Reflex has emerged and further strengthening of the spine continues. If the baby's muscle tone is so weak that he cannot lift his head there may be insufficient vestibular stimulation of the brain stem which causes muscle tone to remain low, thus jeopardizing motor development.

The baby also needs to roll his bottom from side to side while lying in a prone position. This prepares the baby for crawling on his stomach. Many babies do not crawl on the stomach but those who do it in an exact way will integrate the crawling reflex and also start to integrate the Babinski reflex.

Before he is 6-months-old the baby should have developed the rolling reflexes and be able to roll from tummy to back and on to the tummy again.

Between 6 to 9 months of age the Symmetrical Tonic Neck Reflex (STNR) is developed which assists the baby in being able to sit up, be on all fours and ready for crawling. When the head is bent backward the legs are flexed and the arms are stretched. When the head is bent forward the arms are flexed and the legs are stretched. He will now start to rock back and forth with slightly bent arms. In this way the STNR is integrated and it is not until he has made these movements for a sufficient time that will he be able to crawl on hands and knees. Crawling then allows the baby to practise crass-lateral movements, balance and stability which provides a better basis for rising up, holding on and moving along furniture and then walking.

Problems with the Linking Up of the Basal Ganglia

If the spontaneous movements of the baby are obstructed the primitive reflexes will remain active and the linking up of the basal ganglia will be negatively affected. This can result in ADHD, learning difficulties, dyslexia, Cerebral Palsy and other conditions.

There may be many reasons why the baby does not manage to make rhythmic infant movements satisfactorily. In cerebral palsy there is usually a brain lesion that has occurred during pregnancy or at birth. In some cases the baby may have contracted a serious disease at some crucial stage of his motor development. Some babies seem to be in a hurry; they develop early, skip stages such as crawling on hands and knees and learn to walk before 10 months of age. The cause can often seem to be hereditary. Other children are late to develop, they have low muscle tone, are sluggish and do not like to move and need stimulation and time before going on to the next stage.

The Effects of Restricting a Baby's Freedom of Movement

It is natural for parents to want to help their children develop their motor ability. When it comes to emotional development parents are guided by instincts and their own emotional experience from childhood. However when it comes to motor development parents are often not aware of what a baby needs to do in order to fulfil the inborn motor programme. Instead of letting a baby follow the programme at his own pace and develop his motor abilities by lying on the floor and using his own efforts parents will mistake the sound of effort for that of distress and sit him up into baby-walkers, strollers or car seat long before he is has the postural development and muscle tone to really sit up by himself. Therefore parents don't allow the practise he needs to work out how to move with balance and stability and to be ready to crawl and walk. What a baby needs is:

- Time to lie on his tummy in order to be able to learn to lift his head
- Encouragement to move around freely on the floor and gradually
    o develop movement patterns
    o master gravity
    o practice balance and stability
    o integrate primitive reflexes
- Let lie on the floor until he can sit by himself

By having the baby spend a lot of time in baby car seats and baby-walkers his motor development will be obstructed and there is a greater risk that he will develop ADHD or ADD, learning difficulties and emotional problems.

The Effects of Microwaves

The increase in attention and learning problems since the 1990s coincides with the evermore intensive irradiation from mobile masts, mobile phones and cordless phones to which foetuses and infants are exposed.

At the Swedish University of Lund researchers have demonstrated how the brains of young rats are damaged by microwave irradiation from being exposed to only 2 hours of a switched-on mobile phone. The irradiation caused a leakage of albumin through the blood brain barrier causing destruction in the brain cells of the neocortex, the hippocampus and the basal ganglia, areas especially important for learning and attention.[3]

In a 2008 Danish study more than 13,000 children born at the end of the 1990s were followed until the age of seven. Those children whose mothers used a mobile phone during pregnancy had a 54% increased risk of developing a behavioural disorder. They also showed a 25% increased risk of emotional problems, 34% increased risk of problems interacting with their playmates and a 35% increased risk of hyperactivity. In addition, if the child had also been exposed to irradiation from mobile phones as a baby the risk of behaviour disorder was 80%. Mothers only had to use their mobile phones two or three times a day for these effects to arise.[4]

Aspartame

It is well-known that sugar and food additives such as sweeteners and food colouring can cause the behavioural symptoms of ADHD. It is especially important to look at aspartame in this context, as the metabolites of aspartame are particularly harmful to foetuses and children. One of these metabolites is methanol. This is a deadly poison and amounts to 10% of the contents of aspartame. People who consume large quantities of aspartame may ingest 32 times the maximum daily quantity recommended in the US by the Food and Drug Administration (FDA).

Aspartame is broken down into formaldehyde, which can damage the foetus and cause cancer. According to reports from doctors the foetuses of mothers who consume great amounts of aspartame during pregnancy run an elevated risk of being damaged. When the manufacturer Monsanto sponsored a study of damage to newborn babies caused by the mother's aspartame consumption the grant was withdrawn when the preliminary results confirmed that aspartame was harmful to the infant.[5]

Other metabolites of aspartame such as phenylalanine and aspartic acid can accumulate in large amounts and may also damage the brain. Considering the extensive research and information available about the toxic effects of aspartame there is every reason to assume that the substance damages the brain and that it is best that children and pregnant women avoid consuming this sweetener.[6]

Mercury

Mercury is one of the most toxic substances there is and it is especially harmful to the brain and neural system. I believe that mercury from vaccines is one of the principal causes of the epidemic of autism which has arisen in the last two decades. Another cause is the rising levels of mercury in the environment due to coal burning. Mercury from the amalgam in the teeth of the mother will also be transmitted to the foetus and damage its brain. Brain damage due to mercury is probably a very important cause of ADHD.

The Environment Protection Agency estimates that 15% of American infants have been exposed to risky levels of mercury during pregnancy. In the US 1 child in 166 has been diagnosed with autism. In addition one child in six was estimated to have closely related neurological disorders that would probably cause many of the symptoms of ADHD.

According to a study from the Faroe Islands such adverse symptoms of mercury exposure are challenges with memory, attention, language and visual-spatial perception in children at 7 years of age.[7]

Examining Primitive Reflexes

In infants primitive reflexes are easy to test. The only thing you have to do is to stimulate the child in a way that will trigger the response. Different reflexes are triggered by different stimulation of the tactile, proprioceptive, vestibular, visual and auditory senses.

For instance the Tonic Labyrinth Reflex (TLR) can be triggered by gently bending the baby's head forward or back-ward. When the head is bent forward the baby will go into a foetal position and when it is bent backwards he will straighten and arch his body.

In an adult person the reflex can be tested by asking the client to stand in an upright position with his feet together, close his eyes and bend his head backward or forward. If the TLR is not integrated you may notice that the person loses his balance or starts swaying in this position. The person with a slightly active

TLR may be able to compensate for this reaction voluntarily so it will be hard to discover. If the test is repeated several times or is done for long periods the test person will tire of compensating and will sooner or later lose his balance. Getting feedback from the person about whether he feels the back of his body tensing, the knees locking, actually rising, or feeling as if he wants to rise, up on his toes, or even if he begins to hold his breath are other ways you can ascertain if this reflex may still be active.

If, on the other hand, the TLR has been integrated into the whole body movement pattern, he will stand firmly on the ground without any effort when his head is bent forward or backward. This means that the bending of the neck has become automatic on the level of the basal ganglia and that there is no need for compensation.

Another way to quickly ascertain with adults or older children if there is compensation or not is to use muscle checking.

Integration of Primitive Reflexes

Rhythmic movements to integrate primitive reflexes are an excellent method for children and can also be used with adults. The same exercise may integrate several reflexes which is very practical.

However, for older children and especially adults it may sometimes be a slow and trying procedure only to work with rhythmic movements. In such cases it could be helpful to supplement these movements with alternative ways of integrating primitive reflexes.

The British psychologist Peter Blythe has developed exercises that are similar to the reflex integration movements that infants spontaneously make. However, these movements lack rhythmical elements and therefore do not have the same impact on the RAS, muscle tone and the cerebellum as the rhythmic movements have. Although these exercises are helpful to integrate primitive reflexes, in my experience they are not more effective than rhythmic movements.

Another effective way of integrating primitive reflexes is taught by Educational Kinesiology's Paul Dennison[8], and Svetlana Masgutova[9] in Neuro-Kinesiology. The principle of this treatment is to reinforce the reflex pattern with a slight isometric pressure.

The client is asked to make a movement that imitates the pattern of the primitive reflex that needs some integration. He then uses only about 15-20% of his strength to push against the therapist's hands or their own hand, in this way activating the muscles that need to work in a different way and reinforcing the new pattern. The client needs to work up to being able to hold the activation for 6-7 seconds and between three to six times and often needs to be done two or three times a week for 3 months or more for a permanent change to happen.

This isometric repatterning of the reflex movement patterns is a very effective supplementation to the rhythmic movement programme, especially for older children and adults.

Chapter 8
Reflexes and ADD/ADHD

Intrauterine, Primitive and Transitional Infant Reflexes

From the moment of conception there is movement; cells start to divide and at certain times there are triggers to the embryo for new facets to start coming into being. Reflexes are an important component of these stages and triggers. Without them, first the embryo, then the foetus, and finally the baby, would not have the very foundations within himself to grow into full maturity.

The various reflex programmes lie at the very basis of who we are. They provide the triggers for movement that are essential for the development of neural connections and pathways which establish the basis of our ability to move, feel and think in the world as we mature.

The first set of reflexes is the intrauterine reflexes. These are thought to start appearing at 5 weeks in utero, when the embryo is only about 5mm long.[1] By nature these reflexes are withdrawal and freeze, and it believed that they provide the first survival patterns to the developing embryo enabling him to move away from stimulation. These reflexes appear to be responsible for establishing our most basic survival responses, and include the Dive, Smoke and, what has come to be known as the Fear Paralysis Reflex or Response (FPR). This set of reflexes start to be integrated[2] by the appearance of the first primitive reflexes at 8 t 9 weeks in-utero, the beginning of the foetal stage of development, and ideally they need to have stopped playing a primary role in our development by 12 weeks in-utero. The FPR is looked at more closely in the next chapter.

The emergence of the primitive reflexes at various times during foetal development allows a continuing basis for the foetus to move further into maturity. These reflexes lie at the foundation of the establishment of head control, posture and the ability to move through gravity with stability and control.

The transitional reflexes are those that are not present at birth; however they are also not postural and lifelong. They play a very important role in moving a baby from the time primitive reflexes form the basis of movement to the automatic movements of the postural lifelong reflexes.

There are many reflex patterns. In this, and other chapters I look at the reflexes I believe are the ones that remain most active in the system when there are challenges with attention, concentration, behaviour, emotions, mathematics, reading and writing.

While I look at these reflexes in isolation, it is important to understand that none of the reflexes act in isolation. They all emerge at various times, develop at a diverse pace and are integrated at different stages to bring the developing child to the time when the lifelong postural reflexes have the ability to become with practise, automatic, rhythmical, easy and graceful. The better our intrauterine, primitive and transitional reflexes have been able to go through their journey the better foundation the child has for the development of whole-brain access and learning at appropriate times throughout life. The more this happens the more able we are to move with intention and purpose creating opportunities and having the resources to live well.

Reflexes Active in ADHD and ADD

Children who have been diagnosed with ADHD and ADD always have retained primitive reflexes which effect posture, muscle tone, the ability to sit still and the ability to ignore distractions.

Cooperation between the back and front of the body is dependent on developing our ability to rise up from the floor, which is important for the strengthening of the muscle tone of the back and along the spine. In order to develop this cooperation the baby must first learn to raise his head and chest while lying in a prone position, then to straighten his back, afterwards to get up on to his hands and knees in order to crawl and finally to rise up and walk. Certain primitive and transitional reflexes are of basic importance for this development of posture and muscle tone. Primarily these reflexes are the primitive Tonic Labyrinthine Reflex, and the transitional Landau and Symmetrical Tonic Neck

Reflexes. Retained reflexes that are a contributing cause of low muscle tone of the extensor muscles and poor posture may also play a part in attention problems due to an insufficient arousal of the cerebral cortex by the RAS.

Hyperactive children who have problems sitting still and always seem to fidget and wriggle often have a retained Spinal Galant Reflex. Children who are easily disturbed and display difficulties in filtering out irrelevant sensory information usually have some level of retention combining both the Fear Paralysis Reflex (FPR) and the primitive Moro Reflex.

The following reflexes are the ones I think are usually active to some degree or other not only in people with ADD or ADHD, but also in those with other categories of learning challenges and motor problems.

The Tonic Labyrinthine Reflex (TLR)

In the womb the foetus lies in the Tonic Labyrinthine forward foetal position with his head bent forward and his arms and legs bent. The TLR forward emerges 12 weeks after conception and should be integrated between 3 to 4 months after delivery.

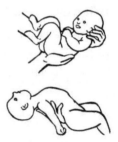

Tonic Labyrinthine Reflex (TLR) Forward and Backward

The Tonic Labyrinthine backward is developed at the time of delivery. In the TLR backward the whole body extends back and the tone of neck, back and leg extensors is increased when the head is bent backwards. The TLR backward does most of its integration by about 9 months, however it stays around in a less active form until about the age of three so as to help the child learn stability and balance in an upright position.

The TLR helps the infant adapt to the new gravitational conditions that exist after delivery and gives him an early primitive reaction to these forces. With every bending of the head forward the tone of the extensor muscles in the back of the neck, along the spine and legs decreases, while the tone in the muscles of the front of the body increases; at the same time with every bending of the head backwards there is an increase in the tone of the back of the body and a decrease in the front of the body. As the body is lengthened and stretched the proprioceptive sense is stimulated by the change in muscle tone and therefore the TLR gives the baby the opportunity to practise balance and develop his muscle tone and proprioception.[3] This is how the baby is meant to begin developing the ability of his body to get into an upright position with stability, balance and tone, without either the front or back playing a greater role than the other.

If the TLR is not integrated well into the whole body movement system then as the infant gets older every head movement backward or forward will continue to change muscle tone involuntarily, which confuses and stresses the balance centre as we become upright. As a result people with the TLR still active often end up having difficulties judging space, distance, depth and speed.

Behaviours and Challenges Associated with an Active TLR

People with an active TLR forward can have a combination of the following challenges:
- A difficulty holding the head up; it often bends forward or leans to the side
- Weak neck muscles
- Hunched posture
- Low muscle tone with over-flexible joints
- Problems lifting the arms up and problems climbing and brachiating
- Eye muscles that do not work efficiently with a tendency to be cross-eyed
- Balance problems, especially when looking down. A person may not like walking downstairs, or going down an escalator, or there could be fear of heights

Children with an active TLR backward can have a combination of the following:
- Tense muscles, especially in the legs, with a tendency to toe walk
- Problems with balance especially when looking upward. A person may find it very difficult to walk upstairs,

especially when there is no backboard to the stairs, and going up escalators can be very challenging

- Coordination challenges
- Spatial challenges
- Sequencing problems

If the TLR has not been integrated well in childhood there will also be other retained reflexes. If we injure our neck, back or head at any time, it is possible that a previously integrated TLR may be reactivated. Balance problems, and chronic pain in the back and neck may result.

Importance of Working with the TLR in ADHD and ADD

The TLR is usually active when there is ADHD and ADD. Children with ADD especially often have low muscle tone and poor posture due to a retained TLR forward. There is insufficient stimulation through the RAS to the cortex, especially the prefrontal cortex, which causes problems with attention and concentration.

If the Fear Paralysis Reflex or Moro Reflex is also still active the TLR may be impossible to integrate permanently until they have been addressed. A combination of an active TLR backward and FPR can result in hypertonic muscles in the back of the body causing the child to be a toe-walker.

The Landau Reflex

At the age of 4 weeks an infant lying in a prone position starts to lift his head from the floor. After another month or two the child will also lift his chest when the head is raised (Upper Landau). After the age of 4 months the child starts to extend his legs so they are raised from the floor while lifting his head and chest (Lower Landau). The Landau should be integrated by the age of three. When the reflex is integrated the child will be able to keep his legs on the floor while lying prone and lifting his head.

Landau Reflex

The emergence and development of the Landau is important for the integration of the TLR forward as it helps to increase muscle tone in the back and neck while the baby is lying in a prone position. This means that when the infant is able to lift his chest from the floor his arms become free so he can reach out and grasp things and bring them to his mouth. This helps with the development of near vision. The lifting of his head and chest also gives him a better view of his environment and an opportunity to practise his 3-dimensional vision.

If the Landau does not develop properly the TLR will not integrate. As a result the child will have low muscle tone especially in the neck and back. As he gets older the child may find it difficult to keep his head upright and things like swimming breaststroke are very challenging as the head and legs cannot work with the coordination needed.

If the Landau is developed but not integrated the child may be:

- Clumsy in the lower part of the body and may have tense legs which extend backwards
- An efficient cooperation between the upper and the lower part of the body will be difficult since the legs are extended when the head is bent backward
- When the Landau is not integrated the Spinal Galant may not integrate

The Importance of Working with the Landau in ADHD/ADD

The low muscle tone of the back and the accompanying poor posture that is the likely result of an inadequately developed and integrated Landau is also accompanied by insufficient stimulation of the cerebral cortex, and in particular the prefrontal lobes, from the RAS. This results in poor attention and concentration.

The Symmetrical Tonic Neck Reflex (STNR)

The STNR develops when the baby is about 6-months-old and should ideally have a short lifespan and integrate between 9 to 11 months. Therefore, like the Landau, it is not a genuine postural reflex but transitional.

The STNR is a very important step in the infant getting up on hands and knees and starting to crawl. In order to do this the two parts of the STNR pattern need to have been followed and become smooth, easy and rhythmical. One part of this pattern is when the baby is getting up on the hands and knees, the arms will extend and the legs will flex when the head is bent backwards, and the arms will flex and the legs straighten when the head bends forward.

Symmetrical Tonic Neck Reflex - Head Up

The STNR is important for the further integration of the TLR as it strengthens the muscle tone of the back of the neck and the back and is important for the development of proper body posture.

STNR
Head Down

It is important that the position of the arms and legs not be dependent on the position of the head in order for the infant to crawl well. If the STNR is not sufficiently integrated then instead of learning to crawl the infant will slide on his bottom to move around or just sit until one day he rises up on to two legs and walks. Children who never crawled on all fours have an active STNR.

When the infant is on all fours and rocking back and forth he is integrating his STNR which is so important for promoting proper body posture and developing strength in the upper arms. Another important component of this rocking is to train vision, especially accommodation - the ability to focus at near and far, and all positions in between.

An unintegrated STNR plays a role in the following:
- Poor body posture.
- The child may sit like a sack of potatoes
- When sitting at a table to write the child often ends up slumped and lying over the book. To prevent this from happening he supports his head with his hand
- Another thing that happens so he can keep himself upright is that he either sits on his legs or wraps his legs around the chair legs. When sitting on the floor he will often sit with his legs in a "W' position
- These children have difficulties focusing at far and near distances, which may cause problems in ball-games when

the child needs to follow the ball with his eyes. Therefore these children may have problems with binocular vision and will usually have poor hand to eye coordination

In children and adults with a rotated pelvis the STNR is nearly always active. If the reflex is integrated with isometric pressure the rotation usually decreases or disappears, depending on which other reflexes are involved.

Other common challenges for people with a retained STNR are:

- Weakness of the upper arms. So brachiating, climbing on monkey bars, doing push-ups and somersaults can be very difficult to master
- Doing the breaststroke and butterfly can be challenging because both strokes require good cooperation between the upper and lower body. Though swimming under water is usually easy, as the head does not have to move.

The Importance of Working with the STNR in ADHD/ADD

A non-integrated STNR causes bad posture making it very difficult to keep the back straight; therefore when the child looks down he hunches and leans over the desk which obstructs breathing causing insufficient stimulation through the RAS to the neocortex and prefrontal cortex, especially if the child is bored or under stress, resulting in problems with attention and concentration.

The Spinal Galant Reflex

Spinal Galant

The Spinal Galant reflex develops 20 weeks after conception and will normally be integrated sometime between 3-9 months after delivery. This reflex is considered to be important for both the conducting of body vibrations in the foetus and for the development of the vestibular system. It also helps the baby to move down the birth canal during delivery. If this reflex is not integrated it can be very difficult for the postural Amphibian reflex to emerge and develop which can lead to clumsiness in the lower part of the body and tension in the legs.

If the Spinal Galant is still active, then when you touch the area next to the spine on either side at the level of the waist, the hips swivel towards the side being touched.

Children with a non-integrated Spinal Galant can have challenges with some of the following:

- Restlessness and hyperactivity
- Tight clothing, belts or just leaning against the back of the chair can trigger the reflex and cause the child to fidget and wriggle
- Most children who have not integrated this reflex prefer to wear loose clothing
- May be a bed-wetter
- If the reflex is active only on one side there can be scoliosis

Spinal Galant Fashion

- Older children with an active Spinal Galant learn to fixate the lumbar spine, which may be a contributing cause to lower back problems later in life
- Fixation and rigidity of the spine at the lumbar level impairs the cooperation between the upper and lower body and may also cause problems in getting in touch with feelings and emotions
- Spastic colitis is a common condition in adults with an active Spinal Galant. This is because the muscles of the lower back have tightened up. These muscles, according to Applied Kinesiology and Touch for Health Kinesiology[4], have a relationship with the large intestine

The Importance of Working with the Spinal Galant for ADHD/ ADD

As a non-integrated Spinal Galant is responsible for fidgeting and distractibility, which are common challenges for children with ADHD and ADD, by working with this reflex we can improve the ability to focus and concentrate. When there is more integration of this reflex the vestibular is able to process more efficiently and there is improved muscle tone especially along the spine.

The Amphibian Reflex

The Amphibian reflex is a postural reflex that develops when the infant is between 4 and 6-months-old. The development of this reflex depends on the primitive reflexes coming before it, especially the ATNR

Amphibian

and Spinal Galant, having done most of their job which allows the infant to have an automatic flexion of the arm, hip and knee on the same side when the pelvis is raised. This means that the movement of the arms and legs are no longer dependent upon the position of the head, The infant has the development necessary to get into a position to roll over, creep and crawl, As he gets older he is able to walk, run, skip, etc with the freedom to use hip/leg and shoulder/arm with the choice of working independently of, or with, each other as needed. This reflex is first developed by the infant lying prone and then supine. As the Amphibian stabilizes it helps to further integrate the Spinal Galant and increase muscle tone especially in the lumbar region of the spine.

Adults who have not developed their Amphibian often suffer from clumsiness in the lower part of their body and tension in their legs.

The Importance of Working with the Amphibian for ADHD/ADD

As it is important for people with ADHD and ADD to learn to have smooth, exact, rhythmical and coordinated movement, having the postural Amphibian well-established is actually a vital component that indicates that there is readiness for independent and controlled movement coming from the core and therefore the neural pathways of the cerebellum, and its connection to the vestibular and prefrontal cortex, have been well-laid.

The Babinski Reflex

The Babinski reflex develops just after birth and remains active up to between 1 and 2 years of age, by which time it should be integrated.

Babinski Reflex

When you stroke along the outer lateral side of the sole of the foot from the heel to the little toe the big toe extends and the other toes spread if this reflex is still active.

The Babinski is important in preparing the feet for walking and influences the ability of not only the feet to move but also the maturity of coordination between the legs, hips and lumbar spine; therefore it is important for the development of muscle tone for the lower part of the body.

People with an undeveloped Babinski can:
- Be flat-footed, slow and not like walking
- Have a tendency to walk on the inside of their feet and consequently their shoes are worn off on the inside
- They may have loose ankles that are easily sprained
- In some cases children with an undeveloped Babinski have more of a tendency to walk on their toes and rotate their hips inward; this can be seen in some people with cerebral palsy and autism

If the reflex has developed yet not integrated the child can have a:
- Tendency to walk on the outside of the feet with the hips rotated outward
- Their shoes are worn off on the outside
- As they grow older these children develop tension in their feet and legs

The Importance of Working with the Babinski for ADHD/ADD

The Babinski is important for the development of the body's ability to have well-coordinated movement (especially through the hips and core). By working with this reflex, we are providing more stability to move freely for movements such as walking, running, sitting and getting up from a sitting position. When we have the ability to move rhythmically and smoothly we have more resources for the higher levels of the brain to work efficiently.

Case-Study: Tomas

Tomas was 11 when his mother contacted me. She was very concerned about him and had tried to get help for his motor problems and his learning challenges. Although a paediatrician had referred him to the rehabilitation clinic his problems were not considered to be sufficiently severe to justify a visit there.

Tomas was born after a protracted 3-day delivery. He was late in fixing his eyes on objects and his motor abilities were late to develop. He walked at the age of two and spoke when he was four. He learned to ride a bicycle when he was eight but he still had problems riding it. He was too weak to ride it uphill and used to have to get off the bicycle and push it.

On the whole, he was very weak and used to walk very slowly uphill, "as if he was 80", according to his mother. He never had the strength to carry anything heavy. His mother always had to wait for him when they were out walking. Tomas had not learned to swim or skate. He was clumsy and would often stumble and fall. He liked to wrestle but was very rough because he could not adjust his strength and therefore could not help hurting the people he wrestled with. He was restless and had difficulties sitting still. He easily lost his temper, and had poor perseverance. He had great difficulties reading and wore reading glasses. His handwriting was very poor and untidy and he wrote only in capital letters.

Tomas's First Visit

At his first visit Tomas was very dejected. He did not believe he could improve in any way and had no wish to get better at anything. Everything was boring, nothing was fun. He said he was tired of his mother's dragging him around to see people who ended up not being able to help him. He said he would no longer put up with it and he wanted to leave immediately.

I replied that I could understand why he believed he was a hopeless case and that he might be right to think so. However I would not be convinced of this unless he proved it to me. I offered to show him some exercises to do every day. If he did not notice any positive change doing these exercises for at least a month I would have to agree with him that he was indeed a hopeless case. Tomas reluctantly agreed to my proposal.

Before I showed him the exercises I examined his vision and reflexes. He had binocular problems with an esophoria at a reading distance which was corrected when he wore his reading glasses. He had a hunched posture with low muscle tone. Several primitive reflexes were not integrated; among these were the TLR, the Spinal Galant, and the STNR and ATNR. His Landau Reflex had not developed and he could hardly lift his head while lying in a prone position.

I showed him a few simple rhythmic exercises and told him to do these every day until his next visit in a month. He promised to do the exercises every day.

Tomas's Development during Rhythmic Movement Training

A few days before his next visit, his mother phoned and told me that Tomas had been doing the exercises every day and that he liked them. She had initially believed that the exercises were a joke on my part because they seemed so simple; however she now had second thoughts about them because she had already seen so great a change in Tomas that she now understood that they were indeed seriously meant.

Tomas continued to do rhythmic movements for a short time almost every day for more than a year. He visited me every month to adjust the exercises he was doing and learn new ones. He mainly worked with rhythmic movements to integrate reflexes. Not long after he started doing the movements he had a high fever for a few days. After a couple of months he had become more cheerful and his endurance improved. He no longer lost his temper so easily.

After 3 months he felt stronger and his mother had noticed that he was more focused and found it easier to sit still. She could reason with him in a new way and his abstract thinking had started to develop. Over the next few months he grew stronger and more active. His endurance improved and he did not get as tired as before. He could now ride a bicycle without problems even for 15 to 20 km. He could outrun his mother.

After 8 months of RMT his reading had improved and a visual examination showed that he now had good binocular vision at a near distance without his glasses; this meant that he did not need his glasses when reading any more. After a little more than a year he was very proud because he had just finished the last Harry Potter book. His handwriting was much better. He had learned to skate. He was cheerful and active; he had good endurance and no problems sitting still and concentrating.

Chapter 9
The Limbic System

The Limbic System or the Mammalian Brain

The brain evolved and became more complex as mammals emerged. The old mammalian brain, or limbic system, developed in mammals as an addition to the reptilian brain. The most important tasks of this area are regulation of emotion, memory and hormone control. The development of the limbic system reflects the importance of emotions for social organization and survival among mammals; in contrast to the relative unimportance of emotions among reptiles.

Reptiles lay eggs and, except for crocodilians, do not take care of their young who must manage completely on their own after hatching. The young of some species even need to be careful not to be eaten by their parents.

Unlike reptiles, mammals are warm-blooded. Their young are helpless and depend on being taken care of until they are ready to manage on their own.

Mammals developed mammary glands to breast-feed their young, which became a condition of survival. Another factor that developed was learning to protect offspring and come to their assistance when they were hungry, cold or threatened by outside danger. Being taken care of by the parents or the mother became a precondition for the survival of offspring and maternal affection became a central premise for the survival of the species. As mammalian young are generally born in litters family systems developed, and parents taught survival through sharing knowledge and experience. Through play the young learned social rules, the ability to get on, hunting skills and other abilities needed to manage and survive adult life.

The Function of the Limbic System

The limbic system is of vital importance for our survival. Firstly it regulates the inner environment through signals that are transmitted via the vagus nerve from the inner organs, such as the stomach, bowels and heart; and secondly, through receiving and relaying sensory information from the world around us. When we think we are threatened our limbic system is activated instantly. We either react fearfully and run away or aggressively stay to attack and fight. We only feel calm again when we reach safety.

Frank and Ernest

CANINE PSYCHIATRY — MY FATHER WAS A BOXER AND MY MOTHER WAS A GREYHOUND --- I'VE ALWAYS BEEN VERY CONFLICTED WHEN IT COMES TO THE "FIGHT-OR-FLIGHT" RESPONSE!

©2008 Thaves. Reprinted with permission. Newspaper dist. by UFS, Inc.

The inner environment activates the limbic system when we are hungry or thirsty which motivates us to eat or drink. So we go from feeling discomfort to feeling pleasure when full and satisfied.

Therefore the emotional information that is relayed through the limbic system from both our internal and external worlds can be vital for survival in certain situations. However thoughts also evoke feelings such as butterflies or chest pressure when we are worried, depressed or sad when thinking about unpleasant situations. Alternatively thinking of pleasant memories or upcoming events can make us feel happy and satisfied.

Overview of the Limbic System

The limbic system obtained its name from the limbic lobe or the cingulate gyrus, which is situated like a border around the brain stem and the reptile brain. According to MacLean an important function of the anterior cingulate gyrus is to regulate maternal behaviour and play.

The front part of the temporal lobe and part of the underside of the frontal lobes also belong to the limbic system. Two important structures in the temporal lobes are the amygdala, which lie in the front part of the temporal lobes and the hippocampus, which begins inside the temporal lobes and goes like an arch under the cingulate gyrus.

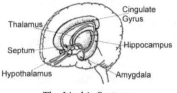

The Limbic System

The amygdala is of vital importance for the emotions of anger and fear; for defence and attack reactions; and for food intake and sex. The hippocampus is the seat of our episodic memory, i.e. our memory of events we have experienced personally; and therefore, is responsible for our experience of individuality. It is essential for learning as it is important for converting short-term memory into long-term memory. A very important function of the hippocampus is to form the stem cells which develop into new brain cells.

Since the limbic system is connected to the important nerve nucleus, the ventral tegmentum, in the midbrain, it will be stimulated by the RAS. From the ventral tegmentum nerve connections go to the limbic system then through to the prefrontal cortex. The transmitter substance between the neurons of this nerve pathway is dopamine. The limbic system must function as a unit with the prefrontal cortex in the same way as the motor cortex must function in close cooperation with the basal ganglia. If the limbic system and the prefrontal cortex are not closely connected our emotions will not be well regulated.

The hypothalamus is closely connected to the limbic system and functions as a controlling centre of the inner environment by regulating body temperature, the autonomic nervous system and the hormone system.

How Infants Handle Stress

The Moro Reflex is triggered when a newborn infant is frightened. The baby first takes a deep breath and flings his arms and legs out away from the body. Then the arms and legs are bent into the middle of the body and he starts to cry.

This second reaction makes up the next phase of the Moro and is also called the clinging reflex, and is just as essential for survival. The whining or screaming that accompanies this part brings the mother running and she will pick the baby up and hug him. The baby then clings to the mother and is rocked and carried until he calms down. In this way the Moro is integrated and the infant learns that there will always be a safe haven if necessary as he starts to reach out and explore his world.

However, if the FPR has not been well integrated it is possible that the rocking and hugging may actually trigger the reflex and rather than becoming calm the baby will, through the secretion of adrenalin, become even more sensitive to both tactile and vestibular stimulation and resist rocking and hugging making it impossible for the Moro to integrate well.

The Importance of Tactile and Vestibular Stimulation for the Emotions

In order for infants to feel safe enough to venture out into the world to explore and interact with the environment they must have adults around who can reassure and calm them when they become stressed and frightened.

The 1950s research of Dr Harry F. Harlow[1] with rhesus monkeys shows us the vital importance tactile stimulation plays in the development of our emotions. He took newborn rhesus monkeys from their mothers and raised them with artificial "mothers". There were two groups. In one group the "mothers" were plain wire, and in the other group the "mothers" were plain wire covered in terry towelling cloth. The monkeys with terry cloth mothers climbed, clung, hugged and became emotionally attached to them. These baby monkeys were able to venture out and explore their surroundings and when they were frightened they ran to their "mothers" and were reassured just by touching them. Even though these monkeys did not thrive and displayed emotional challenges shown through behaviour such as thumb sucking, they were able to interact with the world around them. In comparison the monkeys with "mothers" made of plain wire did not form any emotional attachment or develop any sense of security in relationship to their "mothers" even though they were able to feed from them. When put under stress these baby monkeys did not go running to the "mother" to seek reassurance, they sat in the corner rocking and scared.

For newborn mammals to develop self-confidence, pleasant tactile stimulation is not enough. Vestibular stimulation is also necessary. This stimulation comes from being carried around and rocked by their mothers. In further experiments a group of baby had "mothers" who were cloth covered and also rocked and swung, while another group had stationary, cloth covered "mothers". Monkeys from the stationary group were afraid to explore their environments and overreacted to unfamiliar and scary situations. Monkeys from the other group were curious and happy to explore.[2]

Attack and Defence Behaviour and the Tendon Guard Reflex

The Moro Reflex is a primitive reflex and as such is controlled from the brain stem. After it integrates, usually by the age of 4 months, it gets replaced by the startle response and the fight-and-flight pattern, which according to MacLean is directed by the amygdala[3].

When we get frightened and our amygdala is triggered, our blood pressure rises, and blood flow to the large muscles increases and adrenalin and cortisol are secreted. When we prepare to fight or flee we draw in our breath and hold it; the diaphragm is contracted as are the respiratory muscles of the chest and neck.

The Tendon Guard Reflex is a defence mechanism that is triggered to protect the tendons and muscles from too much tension when the fight-or-flight pattern is activated. When this mechanism activates body posture changes, the flexor muscles contract, calf muscles shorten, knees lock, and we rise up on our toes. At the same time the muscles of the neck and the back contract in order to keep the body upright.

We often don't want to be aware of these feelings of fear and aggression and so we repress them. However the body will still react. Persons who live in constant stress may react by having illnesses associated with one of their organs, and very tight muscles and problems that are associated with this such as tendonitis.

Wilhelm Reich, an Austrian-American psychiatrist and psychoanalyst, coined the term muscle armour describing how we contract our respiratory muscles and diaphragm when we repress feelings of anxiety and anger. When we contract our respiratory muscles the chest is expanded and the diaphragm is contracted. The widening of the chest and the secretion of adrenalin may cause hypertension in people who live in a state of constant stress.[4]

The Limbic System and Memory

We know that reptiles are able to do everything they need in order to survive from the moment they hatch. Mammals on the other are helpless when they are born and need to be taken care of. They have a lot to learn before they are ready to manage on their own. This learning takes place by imitating their parents and playing with their siblings.

In order to remember what they learn mammals have developed a new kind of memory, the episodic memory, which is located in the hippocampus. Many cases have been reported which show that damage to the hippocampus causes loss of memory, especially memories of events personally experienced. Because of this it has been postulated that the hippocampus, at least initially, plays a major role in developing our individual memories.

It is precisely these memories of personal experiences that make us the individuals we are. These memories represent what we have seen, heard and sensed of events going on around us that we can share with others. Of equal importance is that these memories also represent what we were thinking and feeling at that time.

The hippocampus receives input from the external environment by way of the visual, auditory, tactile, gustatory and olfactory senses and from the inner environment via the vagus nerve. It could be said that the hippocampus plays a major role in developing our sense of individuality by synthesizing all our inner and outer information and making it one.

The Importance of Play for Memory and Growth of Nerve Cells

When we interact with the world around us and store memories in the hippocampus our brain changes. The more signals our brain receives, the more the nerve nets and synapses between the nerve cells are developed.

Experiments conducted on mice show how important external stimulation is for the development of the brain. A group of mice was raised in poor conditions, alone in simple cages with very little sensory stimulation. Another group was raised together in a stimulating environment with labyrinths, treadmills, ladders and other exciting toys that were changed every day.

Psychological tests showed that the group of mice raised in a stimulating environment and allowed to play together was more intelligent than the other group. Their cortices were thicker and had more synapses and the nerve cells in the hippocampus also had more synapses. An important observation was that the increase of synapses could be seen only in mice who had actively participated in playing and not in mice who were only allowed to look at the stimulating environment.[5]

There is no reason to believe that the human brain does not react the same way. On the contrary there is a lot of evidence to suggest that it does. One important conclusion we can draw from these experiments is that children must be given opportunities to stimulate and organize their brains by playing and moving around. This is especially important for infants and small children. During infancy the nerve nets and the brain cells grow faster than during any other time. Parents cannot hope to develop the brains of their children by letting them sit for hours in car seats watching what is happening around them. Even more useless is to put them in front of a TV and turn on videos about Einstein or Bach in an attempt to make them "geniuses", in fact according to a study by Frederick Zimmerman of the University of Washington, the watching of these videos can be detrimental to language development.[6] For children to develop their intelligence they need to play and move around and be active in a joyful way. Children learn better when they play.

Stress impairs learning and memory. Stressed mice lose more cells in the hippocampus than mice that are not under stress. Under stress enkephalins are produced in the brain. These substances are neurotransmitters that diminish pain, increase hyperactivity and impair memory.

Play, Imagination and Inner Pictures

According to MacLean the cingulate gyrus is also important for regulating the ability of young to play and the mother's capacity to take care of her offspring.[7] When this part of the brain was removed in mice they started to behave like reptiles, the mothers stopped caring for their young, and young mice stopped playing.

The play of rodents and monkeys has many common features. It is often initiated by bouncing, followed by chasing and wrestling. These are similar features that you can see in the play of children, e.g. playing tag.

Children also play games of make-believe. Some children play more with make-believe friends than with children of their own age. Children play at keeping house and take on the roles of mother, father and child or they engage in other imaginary games. In such games they use their imagination. Like our emotions our inner images are created in the limbic system unlike the images we get from the outside world which we actually see.

When we read fairy tales to children we stimulate their ability to create inner images and experience emotions, thereby stimulating creativity. Many children have favourite tales that they ask parents to read over and over again. Some children love to tell stories in which they mix material from their imagination, dreams and fairy tales they have heard. The pictorial language of folk-tales is the language of the limbic system. It is also the language of dreams, psychosis and art. This inner language is the basis of the imagination and creativity of children and adults.

The Importance of Pleasure for Developing Motor Function

As the baby develops his motor functions and progresses from being helpless and totally dependent on his mother to becoming less dependent on her to meet all his needs, he starts to learn what is fun or what is unpleasant or even painful, and as a result he develops his ability to feel safe and explore the world.

The feelings of pleasure and discomfort are the motivation for the infant to move and experience. Feelings of pleasure are stimulated by breast-feeding and the care and gentle touch of the mother and being carried and rocked. When the motor functions of the child have developed, play and exploration of his surroundings become important for the feelings of pleasure, distress when he hurts himself, and later when he meets some obstacle and does not get what he wants, anger. Thus, the linking up of the limbic system is closely connected with the development of motor functions.

If the infant is depressed due to neglect and lack of tactile stimulation he will not feel like moving around, he will get even less vestibular stimulation, his motor functions will not develop and the primitive reflexes will not be integrated. In this way, the basal ganglia that is concerned with movement, will not link up properly, neither will the limbic system.

The Importance of Infant Movements for the Linking Up of the Limbic System

The maturing of the limbic system relies not only on stimulation of the tactile and vestibular systems it also needs the development of the baby's motor ability that is dependent on his making the inborn spontaneous movements in the best way possible.

By approximately the age of two the reptilian brain should be linked up. The child is then ready to begin to develop his individuality. This starts to take place during the assertive or defiant age, when the child learns to say "No" or "silly mother".

A child with severe motor handicaps usually doesn't go through this stage and neither do autistic children. The severely handicapped child remains in symbiosis with his mother while autistic children lose their ability to form emotional attachments. Children with fewer motor problems, who for some reason have not been able to integrate their primitive reflexes and develop their postural reflexes, will have at the very least some emotional problems due to an inefficient functioning of the limbic system. This is because the limbic system in these children does not get enough stimulation from the senses through the RAS. Therefore the dopamine system that allows the neural network transmission between the midbrain, limbic system and prefrontal cortex is not efficient.

Symptoms of Deficient Function of the Limbic System

There are children who do not seem to have motor problems and yet do not go through the defiant age. These children usually have retained FPR and Moro reflexes, which may explain why the limbic system is not properly linked up. Example of behaviours displayed by children can be:

- Extreme shyness
- A lifelong inability to assert themselves
- When older they can find it extremely difficult to say no
- Sometimes they have a compulsive need to please others
- A lack of curiosity about the world around them
- Disturbing the play of other children as they have difficulty understanding social interplay
- Unwillingness to be touched and handled roughly
- Either a lack of emotional responsiveness or impulsivity
- Bouts of depression or outbursts of anger

These children can sometimes be good at school and not display any actual problems with attention and learning.

Other emotional problems in children with insufficient integration of the limbic system may be that by the age of three they are showing exaggerated reactions of defiance with extreme temper tantrums. For some of these children the defiance syndrome continues throughout childhood and quite possibly into adulthood.

Motor Problems in an Inefficient Functioning of the Limbic System

As demonstrated in the case-study of Tomas, symptoms of depression may occur in children whose reptilian brain is poorly linked up such as when there is ADD or ADHD. Depressive symptoms can already be seen by the age of four and are not unusual at seven and by the age of 10 suicidal thoughts are not uncommon in children with ADHD. Listlessness and depression are often connected with general fatigue, poor posture, feebleness and low muscle tone. Problems with attention are also common in such cases.

Children with emotional problems have signs and symptoms of insufficient integration of the basal ganglia and poor arousal of the cortex. For example they may have retained active primitive reflexes and/or their muscle tone may be low. Rhythmic movements, both passive and active, will stimulate the growth of the nerve nets of the limbic system and improve its function. This may initially cause emotional reactions; however over time they will improve assertiveness and power of initiative and diminish impulsiveness and fits of emotions.

A motor problem that is often connected with emotional problems is shown in poor cooperation between the upper and lower body. Such children may not be able to move their lower body independently of the upper body and tend to involve their neck and shoulders in all their movements. This inability is often caused by problems in controlling the movements of the lumbar region.

Often the root of this is difficulty is a retained STNR which affects the muscle tone of the lower spine when the head moves back and forth which affects stability between the upper and lower body and results in poor coordination. Also people who find it difficult to be assertive usually have not integrated the STNR reflex efficiently.

Reactions on the Linking Up of the Limbic System

Children with severe motor handicaps do not receive enough stimulation for the limbic system to properly link up. Sometimes children with less severe motor problems may also have poor functioning of the limbic system and the prefrontal cortex. Emotional and physical reactions and dreams that occur in people doing RMT may be a manifestation of the training causing the nerve nets of the limbic system to develop and link up more efficiently. These processes cause changes in emotional responses, behaviour and even hormonal balance.

When children first start doing RMT it is possible they can have some of the following behaviours:

- Periods of defiance and regression
- Become demanding and also very babyish and start hanging around their mother wanting to sit on her lap
- Be afraid to sleep alone and can have horrible dreams or nightmares and sometimes difficulties falling asleep

- In rare cases fits of emotions will initially get worse
- They want much more attention and support than the parents are used to. This is especially true for children who did not go through the defiant age
- After a period of doing the rhythmic movements, start to protest and oppose everything and it may be difficult for them to take part in RMT for a while

These reactions correspond to crises in the emotional development of normal children. Such periods are succeeded by periods of emotional development when the children become more confident, calmer, happier, independent and less impulsive.

Adults can also have emotional reactions while doing RMT. Some may feel depressed and start crying without knowing why. It is also common to feel irritated or angry and some adults have reported that they feel as if they had entered the defiant age and want to protest and oppose everything.

Causes of Reactions to Rhythmic Movement Training

Some children with a retained FPR may be oversensitive to the vestibular or proprioceptive stimulation of the rhythmic exercises as the movements will trigger the reflex. These children may have severe emotional reactions such as temper tantrums, oppositional behaviour and compulsiveness. As will be explained in a later chapter the cause may be an activation of glutamate receptors with an accumulation of glutamate that causes an overstimulation of the cortex. In many cases intolerance to gluten and casein may worsen such symptoms. These reactions can be avoided or mitigated by undertaking a diet free from gluten and casein.

Reactions to the Easing of Long-Term Muscle Tension

These emotional reactions to doing RMT can also be caused by the easing of muscle tensions that we have acquired by long-term emotional stress and repression of our feelings of sorrow, anger or anxiety. When muscle armouring and defensive postures start relaxing we can react with irritation or depression as we start to release the repressed feelings.

When we get scared or angry we contract the muscles of our legs, hips, back, shoulders and neck, the physical aspects of the fight-and-flight response or startle reflex. Also the diaphragm and the respiratory muscles of the chest are contracted. With a release of these muscles respiration and circulation improve.

Long-term muscle tension and poor breathing often cause the body to accumulate toxins. With the release of tension the body can get rid of these toxins. Some of the physical reactions to the elimination of these toxins can be:

- Coughing up phlegm
- Flatulence
- Nausea
- Diarrhoea
- Skin rashes
- Itching

- Fever
- Colds
- Swollen eyes
- Headaches
- Fatigue
- Weakness

Our dreams can mirror the releasing of physical or emotional blockages. When we release muscle tension in the respiratory muscles or diaphragm and get in touch with suppressed feelings then dreams about reptiles and mammals are quite common.

The emotional reactions to RMT are caused by a combination of the above. A general rule of thumb is that the more emotional stress the individual has encountered, and the more feelings he has repressed, the stronger the emotional reactions. Strong emotional reactions are also expected where motor dysfunction has meant that a person hasn't received sufficient vestibular and proprioceptive stimulation to link up the limbic system well. When the FPR is retained intense emotional reactions are likely.

How to Handle Emotional Reactions to RMT

When a child experiences emotional reactions during the training he may start to protest and not want to continue the movements. During this time he needs to be given an opportunity to integrate his emotions and the new abilities and patterns of learning that are emerging. This is a stage of consolidation, when his brain needs to take a break from the movements that are providing a new and, seemingly, excessive stimulation, and it is often best to lower the demands and return to only doing one or two passive rocking movements and some massage, which will help the vestibular and tactile systems to settle.

These passive movements will continue to stimulate both the limbic system and frontal lobes, and usually the child will become more balanced and relaxed. It is important to exclude movements that have no rhythmical element or are working with releasing muscle tension of the back and hips, as these can exacerbate the emotional reactions.

After the child has been passively rocked for a while it may be possible to get him to restart doing simple movements such as windscreen wipers, sliding on the back or rolling the bottom. The growth of the nerve nets and the connection between the limbic and the frontal lobes will be stimulated by these movements and the regressive stage will end more quickly.

In some exceptional cases it does become necessary to pause the training completely for a while. If there is a retained FPR and the child is oversensitive to the vestibular stimulation of the movements then it is important that he be given a break to allow the system to get used to the new learning and calm down. After a little while it is usually possible to reintroduce rhythmic exercises for a couple of minutes a few times a week and gradually increase the frequency and period of the training.

Rhythmic Movement Training and Dreams

Our inner images are created in the limbic system. Dreams are the way that most people access these images and many people who regularly practise rhythmic movements report that they have more vivid and memorable dreams. In rare circumstances people practising the movements have reported that they experience accessing these inner images whilst actually doing the movements.

The symbolic patterns of dreams during RMT are usually similar to and characterized by symbols of folk-tales and myths. Such dreams during RMT usually come as a confirmation of physical and psychological development. Or they may throw light on unresolved psychological problems. Sometimes these dreams may be scary nightmares.

Children often find it difficult to separate their dream experience from their everyday life. It can be challenging for them to relate their dreams to others. Children may wake up in the middle of the night having had a scary dream, crying and not be able to tell you why they are so afraid or sad.

Sometimes the contents of the dreams can be reflected in a change with how children play. Suddenly they do not want to play with dolls or Lego, only with animals such as lions or crocodiles. Dreaming about or playing with animals signifies a change in emotional development and a more efficient linking up of the limbic system with the prefrontal cortex. The inner images of dreams may also become part of the fantasies and stories they like to tell.

Case-Study: Eva

Eva, whom I discussed in Chapter 6, suffered from cerebral palsy and could not speak, eat, sit or move around on her own when she started RMT at the age of three. After a few months she started to crawl, speak, eat and drink. It was not long after she started with Kerstin that she began to have emotional reactions. Her mother told me:

"After we had been with Kerstin Linde for a few days Eva started to behave so strangely that I was almost afraid. She abandoned her doll which previously she would never be parted from. She only wanted to play with animals. She had monkeys, tigers and lions in her bed and once when we entered a toy shop she absolutely insisted that she wanted a horse or donkey, so I had to buy her one.

After one visit with Kerstin Linde Eva kept smiling all the time, I think she even lay awake at night smiling. She seemed to be seeing things and I was afraid she had gone mad so I phoned Kerstin. She said that Eva was seeing images, probably of animals, and of a lot of things, that she had never seen before.

Eva also started to assert herself, protest and become defiant and say things like "silly mother".

Case-Study: Olle

Olle also had strong emotional reactions. Before he started the rhythmic training he was tired and sluggish and did not react when he hurt himself. He did not make eye contact with his parents and he hallucinated a lot. He was not interested in his surroundings except at those times when his parents played music or sang for him, which always animated him. He was absolutely indifferent to what he ate and his parents could stuff him with anything. He just opened his mouth and swallowed.

After a couple of months of the training he started to have emotional reactions. He began to wake up at night and cry and be absolutely inconsolable. He also had a period when he was awake at night and bellowed and shouted out a lot. He could show anger, which he had never done before and he began to develop a will of his own. He learned to protest if he did not like and want the food given to him, and then he could even shake his head, which was something entirely new. And if he wanted something he did not give up, he became very stubborn and persistent. When the family received visitors he showed interest and crawled up to look at them. For the first time he noticed the family dog and he started to play with it. His hallucinations decreased. He began to react when he hurt himself, also something he had never done before.

Both Eva and Olle are children who because of their motor handicaps had not been able to develop the limbic system and had never learned to assert themselves. When the rhythmic movements improved their motor functions the limbic system started to link up and they began having intense emotional reactions. A similar emotional development is to be expected in children with fewer challenges although I would not expect it to be so sudden and extreme.

Case-Study: Fred

Fred was 9-years-old when his mother brought him to see me. As an infant he had had severe sleeping problems and he still had to take Melatonin every night in order to sleep. He was very late starting to talk and for a long time he had problems naming things and he still had difficulties communicating using language. He also had problems socializing and playing with children of his own age. Just before his first visit he had developed tics. He was extremely sensitive to sounds and easily disturbed. His endurance was very poor, as was his balance. He had very low muscle tone and his upper arms were extremely weak and his posture was hunched. His handwriting was poor and he found it difficult to write. Fred had been evaluated by a psychologist and had been diagnosed with Attention Deficit Disorder (ADD).

Fred had some problems getting the rhythm when sliding on his back and rolling his bottom. I tested to see whether he had sensitivities to dairy and gluten products and found that he was sensitive for dairy. On my recommendation he stopped eating dairy products and his sleep improved considerably.

Fred did the exercises regularly every night and during the first months both his emotional responses and language regressed. He continued to do the exercises and work with his reflexes for a year, however without major improvement. His concentration and endurance was still very poor as was his ability to communicate. He never seemed to know what he was feeling, what was funny and what was boring. He seldom protested.

After a year, during which he had persistently and conscientiously done the rhythmic movements every day, I introduced the Pre-Birth exercises for the FPR. He did these exercises every day and liked doing them. Now he started to have strong emotional reactions. He upset his teacher by protesting vehemently at school and sometimes leaving the classroom. By his next visit 6 weeks later he had completely changed. He stated that he was too tired to do the exercises.

He had become articulate and could describe how he was disturbed by the neighbour's motorbike and could also articulate his inner feelings. When he found school too boring he would leave the classroom.

At his next visit five weeks later he did not even want to see me. He preferred to go out and play in the snow, which he did for 45 minutes. Meanwhile his mother told me that he now refused to do the rhythmic movements at home. However he still did the

Pre-birth exercises and did not mind his mother doing the passive movements with him. He woke up at night and wanted to sleep in his parents' bed. He had started to play in a new and more focused way.

Chapter 10
Reflexes for the Limbic System

The Fear Paralysis Reflex

The Fear Paralysis Reflex (FPR) is one of the early withdrawal reflexes that emerge during the embryonic stage early in the second month after conception. The withdrawal reflexes are characterized by a rapid-amoebic like withdrawal movement as a response to a tactile stimulation of the mouth region.[1] The pattern of the FPR has been described as a terrified rabbit, completely frozen on the spot unable to move. The FPR should be integrated into the Moro Reflex pattern by the 12th week after conception. If the FPR is not integrated both the Moro and TLR stays active. Balance problems are therefore common.

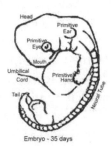

Emergence of the withdrawal reflexes at 5 weeks in utero

Children and adults with an active FPR have a low tolerance to stress and oversensitivity to one or more of the senses. Some-times there can be very great sensitivity to smell and taste. Persons with a strong vestibular sensitivity and a disposition to motion sickness may feel dizzy and sick when they do rhythmic exercises involving the head and these exercises may actually trigger the reflex in some cases. When the reflex is triggered there is a release of the stress hormones cortisol and adrenalin. In adults panic attacks and social phobias may occur and sometimes low or high blood pressure. Muscle tension in the neck and shoulder area is also common.

Some children with an active FPR may react with withdrawal, elective mutism or excessive shyness while others are more likely to act out. Some children have autistic-like symptoms and the reflex is normally active in autism. Symptoms may be poor adaptability and inflexibility or obsessive-compulsive behaviours. Some children show negativism, oppositional or aggressive behaviour. Temper tantrums are quite common.

It is usually stressful for children and adults with this reflex active to make eye contact. Some people have learned to compensate for this by staring intensely in people's eyes often without blinking.

One way of checking if this reflex is active is to see whether you can look the person in the eyes and walk toward him. Children will often look away. Adults and children who have learned to compensate for still having this reflex active may make eye contact, however it is usually done with stress which can be seen in tightly clenched hands and breath holding.

It can often be quite difficult to muscle check people with an active FPR, as the test can be stressful for them and they react by having a hypertonic muscle reaction, tensing the body which causes the muscles to over-compensate.

One way of helping the FPR to integrate is to use movements that are similar to those a foetus makes in the first few months after conception. Claire Hocking in Australia uses movements such as these in her work and in my experience a combination of these exercises is an excellent way to integrate the reflex if they are completed every day for at least a month or more. The fact that these exercises are effective indicates that similar early movements are important to integrate the reflexes of the foetus. If there are very stressful conditions for the foetus during the first months after conception the FPR may be constantly triggered and the foetus can spend large amounts of time frozen in immobility thereby preventing the reflex from integrating. Stress can include factors such as the mother's emotional or physical stress, irradiation from electromagnetic fields, microwaves from mobile phones or cordless technology or toxicity of the mother from heavy metals or other toxic substances.

The Moro Reflex

The Moro Reflex starts to emerge between the 8th to 9th weeks and should be fully emerged in the 30th week in utero and integrated about 4 months after delivery. When the FPR is not integrated the development and sub-sequent integration of the Moro Reflex will be obstructed. Therefore the Moro Reflex is usually active when the FPR is not integrated.

The Moro is triggered by a strong and unpleasant stimulation of the balance, auditory, visual, tactile or proprioceptive sense, e.g. a sudden change of the position of the head, a loud sound, a frightening visual stimulus, an unpleasant touch or a sudden change of position. The infant reacts in a characteristic way:

Moro Movement
First reaction – away from the body

- First by taking a deep breath and stretching his arms and legs out away from the body.
- Then the arms and legs are bent into the middle of the body and the infant starts to cry.

In the womb the Moro movement will help the foetus exercise his respiratory muscles. When the midwife initiates breathing in a newborn, e.g. by letting the head fall slightly backward she triggers the Moro response and the baby will start crying. In premature babies born before the 30th week this response may not be elicited because the reflex is not yet fully developed.

When the Moro is activated the defence mechanisms of the body are alerted. The sympathetic nervous system and the adrenals are stimulated and the stress hormones epinephrine (adrenalin) and cortisol are secreted. Epinephrine causes the senses to become oversensitive.

A non-integrated Moro causes many different symptoms from one or more senses:

- Visual sense: Dilated pupils that are slow to react to light which cause bad night vision and a hypersensitivity to light. There can also be a tendency to be cross-eyed at near and far distances. Some people have to wear dark glasses even when inside
- Auditory sense: Hypersensitivity to sound or specific sounds, difficulties to shut out background noise
- Vestibular sense: Hypersensitivity to vestibular stimulation, motion sickness, problems with balance

- Tactile sense: Hypersensitivity to touch

Both an integrated Moro and FPR may be reactivated in situations of great physical or emotional stress. These two reflexes are usually activated in cases of burn-out and chronic fatigue syndrome in adults.

Emotional Challenges due to a Non-integrated Moro and FPR

The constant inner stress children with an active FPR or Moro live with can have many effects:

- Withdraw and shut off external sensory impressions that they can't handle. Like the baby monkeys in Harlow's research they can be scared of unfamiliar situations and therefore afraid to explore the world
- Problems in having confident contact with children their own age
- Lack the inner security they need to be spontaneous and flexible and often react with anxiety and outbursts when there is a change of routine and things no longer remain the way they are used to
- Lack of emotional security and flexibility can result in a need to manipulate or dominate their playmates
- Oversensitive to sound, touch, light, visual stimuli or vestibular stimulation
- Become very tired after being exposed to excessive stimuli and may need to rest or even sleep after school

It is important to remember that some individuals with active FPR and Moro reflexes may be very sensitive to the rhythmic movements that stimulate the balance system. However, if they perform these movements very gently it is possible that they may be able to do them. If the FPR is active it should usually be integrated before the Moro Reflex to avoid unnecessary emotional reactions. The response of the FPR is to shut the system down whereas the Moro excites the system, so the reaction of the child to stress gives an indication as to what reflex is more prominent.

Chapter 11

The Prefrontal Cortex and the Limbic System

The outer layer of the brain is the cerebral cortex or the human brain. Like the lower levels of the brain its task is to process incoming signals from the senses and give adequate responses to this information. The cerebral cortex provides the most detailed analysis and interpretation of the sensory impressions and gives the most detailed responses. There are different areas of the cortex specialized in processing different sense modalities. The occipital lobes process visual information, the temporal lobes auditory information and the parietal lobes sensory information. The back part of the frontal lobe is in charge of voluntary motor functions.

The cerebral cortex also receives signals from both our inner and outer environments. The very front part of the cerebral cortex, the prefrontal cortex, functions as a coordinator between these environments and is closely connected to the limbic system. The prefrontal cortex has been defined as the areas of the frontal lobes which receive dopaminergic nerve connections from the midbrain and limbic system; that is to say the impulses of these nerves are transmitted by the neurotransmitter substance dopamine. These nerve connections are called the mesocortical dopamine system.[1] The prefrontal cortex has also been called the Chief Executive Officer (CEO) because it directs and organizes many of the processes of the brain.

This area of the cortex is important for many abilities such as making plans, judgements, motivation and impulse control. It enables our conceptual and abstract thinking and our ability to reason and change our conscious concepts and ideas.

The Linking up of the Prefrontal Cortex

The prefrontal cortex has important connections not only with the limbic system but also with the cerebellum, basal ganglia, and RAS of the brain stem. If there is insufficient stimulation of these parts of the brain the prefrontal cortex will not be linked up properly and the working of the whole brain will suffer.

Just as with the back part of the brain, the connections from various parts of the limbic system - hippocampus, cingulate gyrus, amygdala, hypothalamus, thalamus and dopaminergic nerve connections are also important to develop, as these all lead to a well-functioning prefrontal cortex.[2]

The frontal lobes of the cortex receive important stimulation from the cerebellum with connections going to both the prefrontal cortex and the Broca speech area in the left hemisphere. In cases of dysfunctions of the cerebellum these areas may not develop properly causing problems with speech development or difficulties with attention and the ability to make judgements, control impulses, motivation, and making sustained effort. The basal ganglia also have important nerve pathways to the prefrontal cortex.[3] Therefore when these two areas are not well linked we know that there are active primitive reflexes and insufficient establishment of postural reflexes, these in turn cause motor problems that will then be part of the basis for problems with attention and impulse control.

Retained FPR and Moro reflexes can also obstruct the efficient linking up of the prefrontal cortex. When these reflexes are triggered, the child will go into his survival pattern and become acutely aware of what is going on around him; therefore accommodation will be obstructed and he will not be able to focus his vision and attention and it is difficult to learn effectively. Instead of there being a stimulation of nerve cell growth into the prefrontal cortex there will be destruction of cells due to the constant release of the stress hormones adrenalin and cortisol.

Drive, Motivation and the Control of Impulses

We become aware of our inner drives when the information from the limbic system is processed in the prefrontal cortex. The amygdala and other areas of the limbic system responsible for emotions and drives such as hunger, sex and feelings of pleasure are closely connected with areas situated close to the cingulate gyrus. This part of the prefrontal cortex regulates motivation and drives. Damage or insufficient linking up of this area causes shallow emotional reactions, passivity, apathy and indifference.

In order for this area to function properly it must get sufficient stimulation from the RAS nuclei in the brain stem which is in charge of activation and arousal.

A child that has not developed the motivation to explore the world around him, because of disease, motor handicap or low muscle tone, lacks the necessary activation into the frontal areas of the brain that is necessary to be able participate and be interested in what is going on around him. In the most extreme cases of passivity the child remains sluggish and shows little or no emotion and develops neither his gross or fine motor ability.

The basal part of the prefrontal cortex plays a key role in our impulse control and ability to stay on track and maintain a consistent set of ongoing behaviour. Damage to, or insufficient linking up, of this part may cause impulsivity and aggressive outbursts, poor foresight, as well as a meagre understanding as to the consequences of actions taken.[4]

The Prefrontal Cortex Coordinates Thought and Feeling

Through experience we learn to imagine the consequences of our choices. We develop what Paul MacLean calls a "memory of the future", when we have learned what choices bring satisfaction and which bring pain and dissatisfaction.

In fact the prefrontal cortex has so many connections with the limbic system that there are some neuro-anatomists who classify it as a part of that system. It could be said that it is a comprehensive operational system, the task of which is to coordinate all our activities, talents and creative abilities in relationship to our surroundings and inner needs.

The prefrontal cortex is our highest level of coordination of thought and feeling and our survival depends on having a well coordinated process between these activities. We need to have an awareness of both our inner and outer environments to have a well formed ability to function and perform in the world.

The Linking Up of the Prefrontal Cortex during Childhood

When children begin school they are expected to:
* Sit still for periods of time and concentrate on tasks that are not always very exciting

- Focus their attention without being distracted or diverted by external or internal stimuli
- Check their impulses and function in a group
- Listen to and do what the teacher tells them to do

All these tasks presuppose a satisfactory linking up to the basal part especially of the prefrontal cortex. Children with ADHD have usually not linked up the prefrontal cortex sufficiently by the time they start school. Therefore they lack self-control and the ability to focus their attention. They may wander around the classroom disturbing classmates without understanding that their behaviour is considered thoughtless. They may have difficulties understanding how others feel and clomp about and break unwritten laws of social interaction.

These children find it very difficult to be able to control their impulses. They are talkative and interrupt others; they have aggressive outbursts and easily get into fights. They act on impulse without any reflection.

Between the ages of eight to nine children make another important developmental step in the linking up of the prefrontal cortex. Logical thinking starts becoming more prominent at the expense of symbolic imaginative thinking. Children begin to be able to imagine the future and to compare themselves with others. They understand that their parents cannot manage everything and are confronted by their own limitations and lose many of their dreams. At this age many children go through a crisis and can become depressed and passive or defiant and act out.

Children with ADHD can have special difficulties during this stage. It's as if they wake up and become aware of their problems, whether it is with motor planning, learning or social interaction and they can come to the conclusion that something is wrong with them. Often they have a combination of depression, dejection, defiance or denial. When asked if they want to improve anything they usually answer, "Nothing is wrong with me, I don't want to be better at anything". As in the case of Tomas you will often find that behind this attitude they have condemned themselves as hopeless failures.

The Disposition of the Limbic System to Sensitization or Kindling

When it comes to danger, whether external or internal, the limbic system can be compared to an amplifier in its ability to increase the intensity of the feelings that control our behaviour around the threat. The reaction to the initial event, even a trifling one, can be kindled by past events, or emotional or physical exhaustion into a full-blown inferno of overwhelming feelings. This happens in a split second, and before we know it we are in flight and running away or becoming aggressive and staying to fight. In extreme cases we become frozen to the spot unable to move in any direction, paralysed in our fear. When this happens we lose our ability to think clearly and see things in their proper perspective, which means that we have switched off the ability of the prefrontal cortex to handle external, objective reality.

Think about being on an overcrowded peak hour Underground train when there is an unexpected stop. Exhausted after a hard day at the office dealing with expectations and people, you can lose your cool over this unscheduled and unexplained stop. When you calm down you may not be able to understand how you could react so strongly. Next time you experience an unexpected stop on the Underground your reaction may be even more intense. It can get to the point that you only have to think about being on the Underground to start the reaction. This is called sensitization or kindling.

If the nerve nets between the prefrontal cortex and the limbic system are not sufficiently developed or if the prefrontal cortex is not sufficiently stimulated from the cerebellum or the basal ganglia we run a greater risk of switching off the prefrontal cortex and becoming overwhelmed by our emotions, causing fits of anger or anxiety. The greater the connections the more we are able to go into our rational survival brain, understanding the danger we are in and being able to overcome the fear we have. A wonderful example of this was demonstrated by the crew of the US Airways plane that had to ditch into New York's Hudson River in February 2009. Captain Chesley Sullenberg and his crew were able to control their fear and access all their resources, training and survival skills to save all on board in a terrifying and dangerous situation.

Small children have not developed the prefrontal cortex sufficiently and therefore can have violent outbursts of anger which may even end in convulsive fits. Children with ADHD and autism may also have violent outbursts of anger because of poor functioning of this area. If you have retained Moro and FPR reflexes you go into your survival pattern and can react either with paralysis or temper tantrums when stressed due to the shutting down of the connections into this area.

The Effect of Rhythmic Movement Training on the Prefrontal Cortex

RMT improves functioning of the prefrontal cortex by stimulating the RAS, limbic system, basal ganglia and most importantly the cerebellum to develop the nerve nets of these areas so that the prefrontal cortex may continue to receive enough stimulation for its proper operation.

In children with a retained FPR the rhythmic movements may, in rare cases, cause severe emotional reactions because the activated reflex causes kindling of the limbic system. Normally this doesn't happen because there is also a simultaneous stimulation of the prefrontal cortex by way of the cerebellum and possibly also the basal ganglia which will moderate and balance the tendency of the kindling of the limbic system.

There are many signs of improvement that start to happen for children with ADHD when doing RMT, usually within a couple of months of starting the training. These include:
- A decrease in impulsivity and emotional fits
- Attention and concentration become easier
- Being less distracted and staying on track more easily
- Able to reason more logically
- Mathematics is not as difficult as it used to be
- Increased self-confidence and self-esteem
- Become happier and more outgoing
- Have more friends

In some cases this development takes more time, especially with children who experience difficulties learning how to make the movements in a rhythmical, smooth and coordinated way. Consequently their prefrontal cortex gets less stimulation from the cerebellum than children who have no problem with the rhythm of the movements. Until the cerebellum catches up and is able to provide sufficient stimulation to the prefrontal cortex which is then able to moderate the activity of the limbic system, these children may have more emotional reactions, or even temper tantrums when they first start the training, however I have found that persistence pays off in the end.

Case-Study: Sam – premature

An occupational therapist who uses RMT in her work wrote to me about an 8-year-old boy whom I will call Sam. He was born prematurely at 30 weeks and spent a long time in an intensive care unit. Before he started the training Sam was very immature and did not function well at school either academically or socially. After a few weeks of passive rhythmic exercises from the knees, and in a foetal position and actively rolling the bottom he started to have enormous emotional reactions. His mother could not cope with the reactions and stopped the training. Gradually the bottom-rolling exercise was reintroduced and he could only cope with doing it one minute a week. After some time he could do it every day and after the foetal rocking was reintroduced for one minute twice a week. By then Sam had become a different child. He had grown in confidence and had started to assert himself and had made huge gains in school-work. However, he then started to lose confidence, saying he was stupid and he became tearful at the slightest thing.

Obviously the rhythmic movements helped Sam to link up his limbic system and assert himself. Also his prefrontal cortex was linked up enabling him not only to make huge academic progress but also to lose the innocence of childhood and get some perspective on his own limitations, which caused him to become depressed.

Sam's violent emotional reactions were most likely caused by the triggering of his FPR, and with the beginning of the integration of this reflex started to calm down. There is still further work to do with Sam to help him with coping with the developmental stages that have now started to emerge.

Chapter 12

Rhythmic Movement Training and Autism

What is Autism and How the Diagnosis Come into Existence?

In 1943 the American child psychiatrist Leo Kanner, in an article called *Autistic disturbances of affective contact*, described a new syndrome that had started appearing in children. The children he described had various symptoms including an inability to relate to people, poor or absent language skills, sensory sensitivity, repetitive behaviour and an obsessive desire to maintain things the way they are.

In 1980 the diagnosis "infantile autism" was included in the DSM III, the American diagnostic manual for psychiatric diseases with the following criteria:

- Onset before 30 months of age
- Pervasive lack of response to other people
- Gross deficits in language development or peculiar speech patterns

This definition was considered too restrictive and was modified in 1987. Now the criteria became abnormal social interaction, abnormal communication and narrowed interests or activities. This was exemplified using 16 separate criteria, of which a certain number were required for the diagnosis.

In 1994 the criteria for autism were modified yet again in order to narrow the diagnosis. Related disorders that did not fulfil all the criteria of autism, such as Asperger's syndrome were called Autistic Spectrum Disorder (ASD).[1]

Dramatic Increase of Children Diagnosed with Autism

Before 1980 autism was a rare disorder. Scientific studies consistently estimated the rate to be 2-5 per 10,000 people. In the following 25 years there was a rapid increase in the frequency of autism. In 2004 an official report from the US Center for Disease Control (CDC) established that the incidence of children with autism and ASD in the US were 1 in 166, and in 2007 it had risen to 1 in 100.

This development can be illustrated with what happened in California where there are regional centres to care for people with disabilities. About 75-80% of developmentally delayed children are enrolled in this system.

Before 1980 the number of enrolled children with autism was between 150 and 200. In 1987 this number had risen to 400. During the following 10 years there was a rapid increase. Between 1987 and 1998 there was an almost threefold increase in children diagnosed with autism. The number of enrolled children with ASD had increased almost 20 times. In 2000 more than 20,000 children with autism and ASD were enrolled in the regional centres as compared with 200 children with autism in 1980.[2]

Other studies have confirmed a similar increase in cases of autism in other parts of the US. The increase in Europe has been substantial but not as rapid as in the US.

What Caused the Increased Incidence of Autism?

According to academic medicine autism is a chronic neurological disability with hereditary genetic causes. However, an increasing amount of research during the last 20 years shows that children develop autism because their immune system and detoxification ability can no longer cope with the increasing environmental stress from vaccinations, heavy metals and other toxic substances.

Academic medicine has made great efforts to deny the increasing incidence of autism since an epidemic of a hereditary genetic disorder is considered to be impossible. However, a recent study has shown that autism may be caused by damaged genes that have not been inherited from the parents but originate in the sperm or eggs.[3] This discovery confirms the importance of the environment as a causal factor in autism.

Underlying Causes: Mercury and Vaccinations

It is a widely recognized theory that children who develop autism have an impaired ability to cleanse the body of mercury and other heavy metals which accumulate in the brain and inner organs. Mercury is one of the most toxic substances in existence and is especially harmful to the neural system and foetuses. One important source of mercury is amalgam which releases mercury into the body. There is evidence that pregnant mothers will pass on mercury from amalgam to a foetus that will then accumulate in his developing neural system. A recent study of 100 women has shown that if a mother has more than eight amalgam fillings her child runs a more than four times increased risk of developing autism than children of mothers without amalgam.[4]

Another source of mercury is vaccinations. In the beginning of the 1990s the number of vaccinations given to children containing Thimerosal increased in a drastic way in the US. Thimerosal is a preserving agent containing mercury widely used in vaccines. According to a 2005 article in the Boston Globe[5] by Robert Kennedy, Jr., "one of the fathers of Merck's vaccination programmes, Dr. Maurice Hilleman, in a 1991 memo, warned his bosses that 6-month-old children administered the shots on schedule would suffer mercury exposures 87 times the government safety standards. He recommended that Thimerosal be discontinued and complained that the US Food and Drug Administration, which has a notoriously close relationship with the pharmaceutical industry, could not be counted on to take appropriate action such as that taken by its European counterparts.

"Dr Hilleman's warning went unheeded and the vaccination programme was allowed to continue causing an enormous epidemic of autism. In 10 years the autism rate in American children increased from 1 in 2,500 children in 1995 to 1 in 166 or 1 in 80 boys in 2005. In addition one child in six was diagnosed with a related neurological disorder."

The Harmful Effects of Thimerosal

Numerous scientific studies have been conducted that point to Thimerosal as a culprit in this epidemic. Autistic children have been shown to have higher mercury levels than children without autism.

Many symptoms of autism are similar to the symptoms of mercury poisoning. A study by an FDA scientist, Dr Jill James, found that many autistic children are genetically deficient in their capacity to produce glutathione, an antioxidant generated in the brain that helps remove mercury from the body.

After the year 2000 drug makers ceased using Thimerosal to produce vaccines so as to avoid liability. However vaccine stocks with Thimerosal were not destroyed and continued to be sold until 2004. Health authorities are still defending the use of Thimerosal in vaccines. Robert Kennedy, Jr. concludes his article: "Government officials who continue to champion Thimerosal should recognize...that they are depriving vulnerable populations from being identified to avoid Thimerosal. They also cannot escape responsibility for their failure to warn international health agencies and governments who, based upon American assurances, are now injecting the developing world's children with this brain-killing chemical."

The MMR Vaccination

Another devastating effect of vaccinations is damage to the immune system of the intestines caused by the MMR (measles, mumps, rubella) vaccination. Statistics from California show a significant increase of autism after the introduction of the MMR vaccine in 1978. Three years after Californian children started to receive this vaccination the number of children diagnosed with autism trebled.[6]

The British scientist Andrew Wakefield has demonstrated a connection between the MMR vaccination and autism. Such vaccinations can cause swelling of the lymph nodes in the bowels and impair the assimilation of nutrients; the swelling can also cause constipation. Wakefield and his colleagues have been able to isolate the same measles virus as in the MMR vaccine from the intestine of autistic children with bowel symptoms. Other research teams later confirmed Wakefield's results.[7]

Wakefield's findings have been corroborated in a study from Japan published in 2000.[8] This study isolated the measles virus from the blood samples of a small group of autistic children. They found that in every case the RNA sequence was consistent with the vaccine strain.

Another study presented at the International Meeting for Autism Research (IMFAR) in June 2006 by Walker et al, found that the measles virus was present in a high percentage of biopsy tissues from autistic children with enterocolitis with Ribonucleic acid (RNA) sequences consistent with vaccine strain measles.[9]

Dr. Bryan Jepson in his book *Changing the Course of Autism* discusses many other published studies that have confirmed the presence of vaccine strain viruses in bowel tissue, blood and cerebro-spinal fluid of children with Autism and gastrointestinal disorders.[10]

In the UK more than 2,000 families claim that their children developed normally until they were given the MMR vaccination between the ages of 12 and 18 months. In many cases the child came down with a fever after the vaccination and suddenly regressed, stopped talking and playing as before and developed typical autistic symptoms. The British Health Department and the British Medical Association claim that the vaccine is safe citing numerous statistical studies.

However, having heard so many parents relate how their child became autistic immediately after the MMR vaccination I am convinced that this is just another instance when statistics are used not to reveal the truth but to conceal it.

Intolerance to Gluten and Casein in Autism

In the beginning of the 1990s a colleague told me about a Norwegian doctor and researcher, Karl Reichelt. He had met Dr Reichelt at a medical conference where he had presented his research about treating autism and schizophrenia with a gluten and dairy-free diet. He theorized that an impaired functioning of the bowels prevents the breaking down of casein (milk protein) and gluten and that peptides rather than amino acids are formed. These peptides produce exomorphines, which have an effect similar to morphine. About half the children with autism have been found to secrete such peptide chains in their urine.[11]

In autistic children these peptides affect play and social interaction and may cause reduced sensitivity to pain as well as self-mutilating behaviour. These exomorphines are highly addictive and often cause children to limit their diet to dairy products and wheat.

For people with autism another harmful effect of this gluten and casein intolerance is that is produces cytokines - substances that cause inflammatory reactions especially in the cerebellum.

Treating Autism with a Gluten and Casein Free Diet

I travelled with my colleague to Oslo to see Dr Reichelt to discuss his research and experiences and was very impressed with his results in treating autistic children with a gluten and casein free diet. Back in Sweden I introduced the diet as a treatment in the anthroposophical boarding school where I was a school doctor. The students were youths, many of whom had been diagnosed with autism or Asperger's. This school had its own cows and produced its own milk which was served at meals. Many of the students suffered from severe constipation. Impulsivity and severe temper tantrums were also a big problem. When dairy products were excluded the problems with constipation and temper tantrums decreased and there were dramatic changes in some students.

Case-Study: Carl

I especially remember a 17-year-old autistic boy, Carl. He was a student at another anthroposophical boarding-school. He had deteriorated severely during the previous months and had stopped talking. He did not go to classes, he refused to go for meals and spent his days in his bed, not communicating and scratching himself until he was bleeding. I was called in to do RMT with him. When I asked what he ate I was told he survived on milk and biscuits which he took from the kitchen at night. He did not eat anything else. I told the staff to exclude all gluten and dairy from his food before I was willing to start the rhythmic training.

After a couple of months I was asked to give a lecture on RMT at the school. The staff informed me that Carl had recovered dramatically after they had managed to change his diet. He now went to school and had stopped mutilating himself and talked and communicated as he did before his condition had deteriorated.

Carl continued his diet for as long as he stayed at the school and got along fine. Then he moved to a group home. They needed a doctor's certificate confirming that he had intolerances to gluten and dairy products which I was asked to write. However, before I sent it I was informed they did not need it any more. He had been given bread and milk from the very first day and now he was eating it without a problem. I was very surprised and asked if his health had been affected after he moved to the group home. I was told that he became psychotic within a week, had to be admitted to hospital, where he was heavily medicated with neuroleptics. He was still on medication.

Gluten, Dairy Products and Psychosis

This episode reminded me about something Dr Reichelt had told me. He believed that neuroleptics not only affect the brain but also the intestines and that they might decrease the assimilation of peptides, which have a similar effect to morphine, and may cause psychosis.

During my work as a school doctor I time and time again learned that becoming psychotic is not an occasional incidence but rather what normally happens at a certain age to a certain group of people. Young men diagnosed with autism or Asperger's, especially those who also have bowel problems such as constipation or loose stools run the risk of becoming psychotic at around the age of 18-20, sometimes before. In many of these cases I have established by muscle checking that they do not tolerate gluten and casein and although some of them have been able to exclude the latter from their diet their motivation had not been sufficient to exclude gluten. However, experience has taught me that, provided they get a moderate dose of neuroleptics, these patients can go on eating gluten and in many cases do not relapse into psychosis. And in some severe cases of constipation it seems as if the bowel problems also improve by taking the medication.

Electromagnetic Fields (EMF) and Microwaves

To my knowledge no studies have been conducted about electromagnetic fields from mobile phones, cordless phones or wireless networks as being a contributing cause of autism. But there is extensive evidence that such irradiation may cause the very kind of damage that is common in autism.

According to the large REFLEX[12] study commissioned by the European Union (EU) such irradiation is the cause of free radicals that may damage the DNA and the cell membranes and cause cell death.

In 2007 a group of 14 scientists published the *Bioinitiative report* which was an investigation based on 1,500 studies of the effects of electromagnetic irradiation. They found that genes are becoming damaged below accepted safety standards and extensive evidence showed that electromagnetic fields cause inflammation and allergies and weaken the immune system.[13]

Considering the fact that many men have a tendency to carry their mobile phones in the front pockets of their trousers the findings of damaged genes causing autism are easily explained. Foetuses, whose genes are already damaged before conception, will then be exposed to even more irradiation from wireless networks and their mothers' talking on mobile or cordless phones. Knowing that all this irradiation may damage cell membranes, kill brain cells, damage the immune system and cause inflammation of the brain and the bowels then it is easy to understand why many children are so weakened when they are born that they develop autism especially when they are exposed to additional environmental stress such as vaccinations, virus infections and heavy metals, to say nothing of continuing micro-wave irradiation.

When a cell is exposed to electromagnetic irradiation it produces stress proteins which make the cell membrane less penetrable and reduces the active transport of toxins and heavy metals over the membrane. Elimination of electromagnetic irradiation is therefore necessary to give the child a basis to detoxify the cells from heavy metals and other toxic substances.

The Glutamate-to-GABA Ratio

Glutamate is the most common transmitter substance of the synapses of the brain. It has a stimulating, excitatory effect and causes cellular toxicity if it accumulates too much. Glutamate is converted into GABA, the function of which is to inhibit the firing of the nerve cells. Several studies have shown an imbalance between glutamate and GABA in autism due to a deficient ability to convert glutamate into GABA.[14]

An accumulation of glutamate and a lack of GABA will trigger uninhibited firing of the nerve cells which will cause inflammation and eventually cell death. When the level of glutamate increases GABA will diminish which may cause the child to stop talking.

When the brain of an autistic child gets too much sensory stimulation, physical activity, psychological stress or peptides from the bowels the accumulation of glutamate may cause the child to become overstimulated and hyperactive and have great difficulties in being able to calm down. Because of the accumulation of glutamate the neurons of the brain continue firing causing self-stimulating behaviour and inflammation of the brain and eventually brain damage.

Such reactions are considered to cause similar brain damage seen in Parkinson's disease, Multiple-Sclerosis (MS), and Amyotrophic Lateral Sclerosis (ALS) as well as in autism. Accumulation of glutamate has also been linked to epileptic seizures that are common in autism.

Self-Stimulating and Symptoms of Inflammation of the Brain

Self-stimulating behaviour, or stims, indicates that there is an accumulation of glutamate in the brain. Common stims include hand flapping, body spinning and rocking, lining up or spinning toys or other objects, perseveration and repeating rote phrases.[15]

Uncontrolled firing of neurons due to elevated levels of glutamate causes inflammation and injury to nerve cells. As stated, peptides from the bowels may also cause inflammation of the brain. Symptoms of inflammation can be epileptic seizures, obsessive-compulsive behaviours, aggressiveness, temper tantrums, depression, anxiety, psychosis, insomnia.[16]

RMT in Autism - Passive Movements

Passive rhythmic movements usually work very well for children with autism causing them to become calm and relaxed. However, if the brain becomes over-stimulated by the exercises they will become restless and anxious. Such reactions are also sometimes seen in children with ADHD and ADD. Children that have either autism or ADHD may have a reduced ability to filter sensory impressions in the brain stem due to a retained FPR causing over-stimulation of the cortex and activation of glutamate receptors and accumulation of glutamate. This may cause the child to squirm and struggle to get away. Autistic children may also react with self-stimulating behaviour.

If this happens you need to do the movements very gently and stop immediately when the child starts to wriggle. You may be able to repeat them just a few times and gradually increase them over time. In this way the child will learn to tolerate the exercises for longer periods without negative side-effects. This possibly happens because the movements improve the filtering ability of the brain stem or because the passive exercises stimulate glutamate to convert into GABA. It may also be effective to rock the child gently when he is asleep.

Rhythmic Movement Training, Autism and Seizures

Epilepsy is not uncommon in autism. Seizures are a symptom of inflammation of the brain which may be caused by excessive levels of glutamate. As we have seen, an accumulation of glutamate and inflammation of the brain may be caused by intolerances to gluten and dairy. According to Reichelt's research a diet free from gluten and dairy will reduce seizures. Other causes of accumulation of glutamate in the brain are food additives like monosodium glutamate (MSG) and aspartame, which are common in processed food. Both MSG and aspartame are notorious for causing seizures. Seizures may also be triggered by electromagnetic irradiation.

In order to avoid triggering seizures when doing rhythmic movements it is essential to prevent an accumulation of glut-amate. Therefore a diet free from dairy and gluten, MSG and aspartame is advisable in autistic children and of course also in all children with known epilepsy. It is also very important to avoid self-stimulating behaviour by doing the exercises very gently in the beginning and gradually increasing the rhythm, duration and frequency. Elimination of electromagnetic irradiation especially in the child's bedroom is also of great importance to preventing seizures.

Rhythmic Movement Training and the Cerebellum in Autism

Most children with autism are more or less unable to do simple active rhythmic movements when they start RMT. They cannot do them automatically and I have found that they have to use a lot of effort for every turn to the right or left when they roll the bottom from side to side. Unlike other children with problems of the cerebellum they do not lose the rhythm when they do these exercises - they simply have no rhythm at all. This inability is caused by a dysfunction of, or damage to, the cerebellum.

Many studies have shown that damage to the cerebellum due to inflammation or toxic processes is very common in autism. The Purkinje cells that use GABA as their transmitter substance are especially damaged. Moreover the cerebellum in autism is often smaller than normal, as is the dentate nucleus deep within the right hemisphere of the cerebellum, which is linked to the speech areas of the left hemisphere by an important nerve pathway. When this nucleus is damaged language will be affected. Consequently lack of speech, deficient speech or late speech development is common in autism.

RMT usually has a very positive effect on language development in autism. The active movements stimulate the Purkinje cells and GABA. The movements also indirectly stimulate the speech areas of the left hemisphere. The rhythmic movements therefore improve both language comprehension and spoken language provided the harmful inflammation process of the cerebellum has been brought under control. In some children the cortical speech areas of the left hemisphere are also damaged. In such cases language will be slower to develop.

Simple rhythmic exercises such as the windscreen wipers or rolling the bottom are excellent for stimulating these areas of the brain. When children learn to do these exercises in a rhythmical way the cerebellum will be able to stimulate the function of the prefrontal cortex thus improving impulse control, endurance, judgement and empathy.

Rhythmic Movement Training and the Limbic System in Autism

The passive and active rhythmic movements stimulate the limbic system by way of the ventral tegmentum in the mid brain. When the limbic system is stimulated by the exercises emotions will develop. Children will usually begin to show emotional attachment to their parents and for the first time ever they may want to sit in their lap or to be hugged. Compulsive symptoms and ritualistic behaviour may diminish and they usually begin to show emotions of defiance and self-assertion. They often start to play in a different way, as well as initiating play with other children, and many parents report that they begin expressing empathy.

Some children, especially after puberty, can find it difficult to handle the feelings of assertion, defiance and aggression that can occur during RMT. Sometimes aggressiveness and temper outbursts may increase, especially in children with developmental delay. Such reactions are usually caused by excessive glutamate levels and aggravated by intolerance to gluten and casein in the way that has been explained. These reactions can be avoided or mitigated by again implementing a diet free from gluten and casein and by eliminating as much electromagnetic irradiation from the environment as possible.

Retained Stress Reflexes in Autism

Most children with autism or ASD have senses that are over-sensitive and easily overwhelmed by sensory stimulation due to retained FPR and Moro reflexes. An active FPR often causes vestibular sensitivity and may cause the child to become nauseous doing passive movements. The vestibular, tactile and proprioceptive sensitivity may also contribute to stims when the brain is over-stimulated by the exercises. It is therefore very important to integrate this reflex in order to be able to continue the movement training.

As stated the FPR starts to develop in the fifth week after conception. At that age the foetus is spending a lot of time busily moving his recently developed arms and legs. When the foetus is exposed to stress the FPR is triggered which means that it withdraws, stops moving and freezes to the spot.

The reflex is not a primitive reflex, since neither the senses nor the neural system has been sufficiently developed to generate any reflex pattern. Instead the reflex pattern is created by direct transmission of information via electromagnetic frequencies between all the cells of the foetus.

The FPR is triggered when the cells of the foetus are exposed to stress. Unicellular organisms react to stress by withdrawing from the source of danger, be it a toxic substance or some other threat. However the cells of the foetus do not have that option, they must stay where they are. Instead they shut off the environment by producing stress proteins that make the cell membrane hard to penetrate and diminish the active transport over the membrane. This stress is one that causes the foetus to withdraw and stop moving.

Other sources of stress that may prevent this reflex from integrating include stress in the mother due to things such as depression, illness or drug abuse. Environment stress such as being exposed to mercury or other heavy metals, toxic substances or electromagnetic fields are factors that can bring on the response.

When the FPR is not integrated then the Moro reflex also will not integrate. It is likely that it is important to integrate the FPR before starting to integrate the Moro; however this is not always the case and there are times where working with the Moro first is a priority.

Many Symptoms of Autism are also Symptoms of a Retained Fear Paralysis Reflex

Many symptoms of a retained FPR are also common symptoms of autism, including low tolerance to stress, oversensitivity to sensory stimulation such as sound, light, smell and taste. The reflex will be triggered by eye contact and poor eye contact is a common symptom both of autism and a retained FPR. When the reflex is retained the child needs to withdraw from challenging stimuli and situations which are perceived as threatening. Children with autism tend to shut off the world around them and stop communicating. Other children may become very shy. Other strategies to avoid challenging situations are things such as obsessively sticking to routines, poor adaptability and refusal to accept change, all common symptoms in autism. When the child is not able to shut out the world severe temper tantrums are common reactions.

Integration of the Fear Paralysis Reflex

Since the FPR is a cell reaction to stress the cause of the stress must be dealt with in order to integrate the reflex. If the reflex is constantly triggered by electromagnetic irradiation it cannot be integrated until the electromagnetic stress has been reduced. Likewise, if the reflex is caused by toxicity in the environment or the body or food intolerance these causes must also be taken care of. In autism you need to reduce electromagnetic stress, heal the bowels by providing a proper diet, cleanse the body from heavy metals, etc. In ADHD and ADD you may also have to deal with such issues, especially electromagnetic stress and intolerance to casein and gluten.

Active and passive rhythmic movements also contribute to integrating the reflex as do the Pre-birth exercises. The latter movements are similar to the movements the foetus makes in the womb. These exercises can be very powerful for some children and can actually trigger the reflex and cause negative reactions. That seems to be especially true if there is a lot of environmental stress. In such cases this stress should first be taken care of before continuing with the movements.

Chapter 13
Rhythmic Movement Training and Psychosis
Increased Activity in the Limbic System in Psychosis

When a person lies in the heavy salt water solution in a completely dark and silent floatation tank he may, after a while, start to react with intense anxiety or visual and auditory hallucinations. Under these conditions of sensory deprivation the cortex of the brain receives no stimulation. There is no awareness of outer stimuli and the mind instead focuses on the inner processes of the limbic system. When the activity of the prefrontal cortex decreases the limbic system increases due to the kindling effect, which explains the hallucinatory symptoms.

A 1974 Swedish study, by David H. Ingvar and Goren Franzén, revealed that people diagnosed with schizophrenia have decreased activity especially in the left prefrontal cortex. The blood flow in the brain of healthy individuals when at rest is concentrated mainly in the prefrontal cortex. However, in a person diagnosed with schizophrenia the blood flow to these areas is conspicuously absent. Instead the blood flow is increased in the parts of the temporal lobes which belong to the limbic system.[1] When this happens it becomes impossible for the prefrontal cortex to regulate the activity of the limbic system.

When a person experiences strong emotional stimulation, e.g. falling in love or the death of a close relative, they can lose contact with reality and experience more or less frightening symbolic inner images as outer reality. In more extreme cases a catatonic condition may develop where the person loses the ability to react to external stimuli at all and their consciousness becomes totally focused on inner images, or hallucinations. This is what happened to Olle before he started rhythmic movements. As we have seen Olle suffered from a severe lack of sensory stimulation to his brain which resulted in a decreased activity in his prefrontal cortex.

When a person no longer reacts to external stimuli he has developed a condition of total inner sensory deprivation. In spite of normal outer stimulation the prefrontal cortex does not have sufficiently activation to be able to maintain its activity.

Intolerance to Gluten and Casein in Schizophrenia

As stated in the previous chapter the limbic system may also be triggered by peptides that arise in the bowels due to intolerances to casein and gluten in combination with a lack of peptidase. Reichelt has shown that a diet without gluten and casein will improve symptoms in schizophrenia.[2]

The recognition of the connection between gluten and casein intolerance and schizophrenia is not new. Research started in the 1960s and led by the American psychiatrist F.C. Dohan found that gluten intolerance was much more common in schizophrenic patients than would be statistically expected. They studied schizophrenic patients who were given a cereal and milk free diet after being admitted to hospital due to a deterioration of their illness. They were able to demonstrate that the patients who received the diet recovered more quickly and could be discharged in half the time when compared to a control group without this diet. Additional studies showed that patients who had recently fallen ill benefitted most from this kind of diet while chronic patients who had been ill for many years only improved in exceptional cases.[3]

I am sometimes consulted by young people who have recently been treated for psychosis and are looking for an alternative to medication. They, or their parents, may have heard or read about RMT. I normally recommend that they exclude gluten and dairy from their diet, especially if I have established that they do not tolerate these foods. I explain that they will benefit more from RMT if they change their diet not only because gluten and milk products may cause psychosis by themselves but may actually trigger stronger emotions because of the intolerance. Such strong emotions may trigger a psychosis if the function of the prefrontal cortex is insufficiently developed. The rhythmic movements will stimulate this area to develop but may also trigger strong emotions. Gluten and casein can also cause inflammation of the brain, which will worsen the disorder in the long term.

I therefore discourage these young people from stopping their medication when they first start the training. As the movements start developing the nerve nets into the prefrontal cortex more efficiently it then becomes possible to start decreasing the levels of medication until it gets to the point where it is safe to stop taking it completely.

Negative Overshooting Feedback

It is possible to understand the cause of inner sensory deprivation in psychosis by looking at the role of the brain stem in maintaining the activity of the limbic system and the prefrontal cortex.

The dopamine producing nerve cell nuclei of the midbrain have nerve pathways into the limbic system and prefrontal cortex. One function of the mesocortical dopamine system is to regulate the activity of the limbic system. This regulating activity can be compared to the ventilation system of a house, the function of which is to keep an even and stable temperature in all rooms. Feedback to the system will affect the thermostat enabling it to increase or decrease the temperature according to need. When the temperature in one or more rooms rises the ventilating and heating system will cause a decrease in other rooms, so as to keep a balanced environment throughout the house.[4]

If we use this model in schizophrenia we can appreciate how an activation of the limbic system combined with a disorder of the prefrontal cortex may trigger psychosis. When the limbic system is kindled and fed, by psychotic delusions, hallucinations and intense emotions the compensatory regulation will be activated. By way of receiving feedback from the limbic system the nerve nuclei of the midbrain will decrease their activating signals to the limbic system and the prefrontal cortex. However, due to kindling, the activity of the limbic system will not be affected. Only the activity of the prefrontal cortex will diminish, creating a vicious cycle: the more the limbic system is kindled the less activity there will be in the prefrontal cortex. The person will lose the basis of his reality and rational thinking ability and will become prey to distressing emotions. The more the limbic system is activated the more the activity of the prefrontal cortex decreases, which may eventually lead to a catatonic state.

Rhythmic Movement Training in Acute Psychosis - a Case-Study

The hyperactivity of the limbic system in psychosis can be treated with neuroleptic drugs that block the function of dopamine, which diminishes hallucinations and delusions after a few days. However, neuroleptics also block the activity of the prefrontal cortex causing side-effects such as mental and emotional blunting.

A different strategy to treating psychosis is to increase the activity of the prefrontal cortex in order to create a better balance between it and the limbic system. This can be done by rhythmic exercises and in cases of acute catatonia you can have a positive effect very quickly, and I have found that changes can happen within a very few days.

Case Study - Lisbeth

One of my patients, whom I will call Lisbeth, had developed increasing anxiety and delusions after an emotionally traumatic experience. She did not want to take neuroleptics because of their debilitating side-effects and decided to start doing rhythmic movements which she initially did every day. Her condition improved during the first months but then she stopped doing the movements and her condition deteriorated. She became bed-ridden and catatonic and lost her ability to communicate with her family. After a couple of days being in this condition she was brought to hospital.

I met Lisbeth in the ward soon after she was admitted and before she had been given any medication. I could not establish any contact with her and so I started to do some passive rhythmic movements with her. After a few minutes she was able to do the movements on her own and after about 15 minutes of rhythmic exercises she was sitting up and talking to me freely.

She told me that during the previous 2 days she had had intense and frightening hallucinations about war and her house being bombed. I continued to help her to do rhythmic movements in the ward every day. She was also prescribed a very small dose of neuroleptics.

Lisbeth recovered rapidly and could be discharged after a couple of weeks. She continued the rhythmic movements and could soon discontinue the medication and after a year she had recovered completely and started working again. Lisbeth worked without further psychotic incidents for another 15 years until her retirement.

The Mode of Action of Rhythmic Movement Training in Psychosis

The rhythmic movements have a strong arousing effect on the cortex, especially the prefrontal cortex, by way of the RAS. However this is not the only reason why the movements have an immediate effect on delusions and hallucinations. In all probability the rhythmic movements also affect the prefrontal cortex by way of the cerebellum, thus shortcutting the limbic system.

Research has demonstrated that the cerebellum plays an important role in increasing the activity of the prefrontal cortex and decreasing psychotic symptoms such as hallucinations. In 1977, an American scientist, R.G. Heath, published an article about treating a group of severely ill schizophrenic patients who had been hospitalized for many years and had not responded to any treatment.[5] He inserted a pacemaker into the cerebellum of each member of this group. The patients in the study could self-regulate the activity of the pacemaker. When they started to hallucinate they only needed to turn the knob to increase the stimulation and the hallucinations would subside. Most of the patients improved conspicuously and several could soon be discharged. Since the rhythmic movements, to a great extent, stimulate the cerebellum it can be concluded that they have a similar mode of action as the pacemaker, in that they stimulate the prefrontal cortex by way of the cerebellum.

In another study Heath and his co-workers showed that between 33-60% of people diagnosed with schizophrenia suffered from atrophy (decrease of cells) of the vermis area of the cerebellum which has important pathways to the prefrontal cortex.[6] Impaired functioning of the vermis can explain why the prefrontal cortex gets insufficient stimulation. A common cause of atrophy in the vermis is heavy metal toxicity. The atrophying of the vermis and the impaired functioning of the prefrontal cortex in schizophrenia can explain how inner sensory deprivation can be so conspicuous in some cases of schizophrenia.

Positive and Negative Symptoms in Schizophrenia

Psychotic symptoms such as hallucinations and delusions are called positive symptoms and are caused by negative over-shooting feedback triggering a hyperactivity of the limbic system and a shutting down of the prefrontal cortex. The impaired functioning of the prefrontal cortex in schizophrenia also causes negative symptoms such as emotional blunting, passivity, in-difference towards others, and poor judgement. Such negative symptoms are common among schizophrenic patients who have been ill for a long time.

RMT may actually improve the symptoms of psychosis in different ways. In acute cases with severe positive symptoms the hallucinations and delusions may decrease because the rhythmic exercises stimulate the activity of the prefrontal cortex creating a balance between it and the limbic system. In chronic schizo-phrenia with severe negative symptoms the stimulation of the prefrontal cortex will usually improve the negative symptoms and cause the patients to become more interested in other people, less withdrawn, more active and more involved.

Psychosis as a Language Disorder

An important contributing factor to the long-term recovery of psychosis is that anxiety decreases when frightening psychotic delusions are taking shape while a patient dreams during RMT. The dreams help patients learn to discriminate between inner symbols and outer reality, which helps to reduce anxiety. When anxiety decreases then the limbic system stops being un-controllably activated making it possible to retain inner balance and harmony and avoid psychosis.

A psychotic person has more or less lost his ability to dis-criminate between inner and outer reality and often perceives his inner symbolic world as outer reality. Such inner symbols can be a manifestation of inner blockages or malfunctions on a physical or emotional level. In psychosis such inner symbols come to the forefront. Kerstin Linde used to say that psychosis is a condition when the person has turned his eyes inwards and uses symbolic language to explain his problems to himself and those around him.

RMT allows physical and emotional blockages to take shape in dream symbols. This will permit a dialogue between the language of the cerebral cortex, i.e. spoken language that has been learned, and the inborn symbolic language of the limbic system. When a psychotic person has a dream in which his delusions are taking shape he may understand that the delusions he has been fostering are not outer reality but only inner dream symbols. This can come as a great relief since the experienced reality in psychosis may be so much more frightening than the dream experience that we wake up from. By means of this dialogue between the symbolic language of the limbic system and the spoken language of the cerebral cortex the psychosis may heal.

Case-Study: Lotta

The case of a patient I treated in the 1980s may illustrate the healing effects of dreams during RMT.

Lotta was a woman aged around 30 who had been suffering from severe delusions for a couple of years. She was afraid of being murdered and there were times when she did not dare go out. She thought that someone had come into her apartment and pressed her down onto her bed. She also formed the idea that she would be cut into pieces. In addition she was afraid that her former boyfriend would come into her apartment and kill her.

Over a 2 year period she had cut her wrists three times and taken pills once. She had been hospitalized 10 times. At hospital she had been treated with neuroleptics and quickly discharged but she stopped taking medication regularly at home and she had refused outpatient contact. The last time she was hospitalized she believed she'd heard on the radio that she ought to kill herself and she had cut her wrists so deeply that the sinews of her wrist had to be sewn up and her forearms put into plaster.

Lotta agreed to start RMT and I saw her in the ward to show her the movements. She started to do them every day and when she was discharged she told the ward physician that the exercises had helped her to escape her thoughts and she was in better contact with herself. She continued to do the exercises two to three times a day for nearly 2 years and had regular therapy sessions with me. She did not need to be hospitalised again, at least during the next 2 years when we ended our sessions because I resigned from the hospital and went into private practice.

Lotta's Dreams during RMT

Lotta had intense dreams while she was doing the rhythmic movements. After 3 months her dreams became quite violent and she felt very angry. One dream was that her former boyfriend was dead and that she attended his funeral. Because of this dream she started to contemplate suicide and wanted to be admitted to the psychiatric clinic; however she changed her mind and a few days later she felt better after having had a dream about war where people were wounded and killed.

In another dream she was bitten by a snake. A few months later she dreamed that a man tried to rape her in a church. She killed him, cut him up into pieces and put him in a plastic bag which she carried around.

After having done the rhythmic movements for 7 months she dreamed that her former boyfriend had murdered the former Swedish Prime Minister Olof Palme and that she would be publicly disgraced when this was known. She therefore decided to commit suicide and was assisted by a doctor who cut her wrists and put on a bandage. After having told me this dream she added that the last time she cut her wrists she had believed that her former boyfriend had killed Olof Palme and therefore she had decided to kill herself. During the next few months she felt good and had several pleasant dreams about being with her mother.

After doing the movements for a little more than a year she suddenly got worse and started to feel frightened. She had a number of dreams about people breaking into her apartment and strangling or shooting her. These dreams reminded her of what she experienced when she was psychotic and she could now tell me how she used to crouch in a corner waiting for someone to come in and kill her.

After these dreams she felt much better and started to dream about being the manager of a big company that was very successful and in which everyone got on very well.

Dreams as Confirmation of Recovery from Psychosis

A psychotic person's prefrontal cortex is disconnected and this is expressed symbolically by the idea that the king, the prime minister or the father has died. This is one of the most common delusions in psychosis. Lotta was only one of many of my patients who soon after the murder of Olof Palme had the delusion that they had killed him. She believed that her boyfriend had killed Olof Palme and therefore decided to commit suicide.

It was not until she dreamed about this after having done the rhythmic movements for 8 months that was she able to tell me about this delusion. The dream permitted a dialogue between the symbolic language of the limbic system and the spoken language of the cortex and she was able to gain a perspective on her misconception.

After the dream about Olof Palme, Lotta had several pleasant dreams about being with her mother; these indicated that Lotta's feelings were less characterized by fear and guilt than they used to be before she started RMT. The dream about being the manager of a very successful, big company where everyone got on very well is a clear indication that her prefrontal cortex was now able to exert inner leadership and that she felt much better emotionally. She confirmed this when she said that she had not felt so good for many years.

Lobotomy as a Treatment for Chronic Schizophrenia

In the 1930s experiments were conducted on chimpanzees where the connections between the prefrontal cortex and the limbic system were severed. For one chimpanzee the operation had a dramatic effect, as before he suffered from severe temper tantrums and after the operation he became meek and mild.[7] In a time before there were any effective antipsychotic medicines some doctors wanted to see if this method could be as effective, as it was in the chimpanzee, in treating severe psychotic conditions.

The first human lobotomy was conducted in 1935. The method became increasingly popular among psychiatrists as hallucinating and violent psychotic patients were turned into manageable, apathetic and passive persons without will power of their own. In 1949 the initiator of this treatment, the Portuguese neurologist Egas Moniz, was awarded the Nobel Prize.

During a period at the end of the 1940s there was a steady stream of lobotomies carried out in Swedish mental hospitals. Altogether 4,500 Swedish schizophrenic patients were to fall victim to this treatment. It is estimated that one in six of these patient died from the operation. It was not until 1951 when a Swedish doctor raised an outcry about the deaths of six patients from a series of 21 operations that there was a debate in the media. Lobotomies were still being routinely conducted in the 1960s.[8]

Gradually the devastating and incurable effects of these lobotomies were recognized. A lobotomy causes personality changes in patients, and relatives found that these people now behaved like children. Their interest span was short and they were easily distracted. Some became extremely indolent, whereas others showed a lack of self-control and would explode over nothing, and also have periods where they could not stop talking or laughing. They lost their ability to be empathetic and feel, and also lost interest in social affairs, politics and books.

The Swedish psychiatrist G. Rylander conducted a study with patients who had been lobotomized. He found that the more introspective patients were aware that they were unable to feel as before, that something had died within them. An operating room nurse who had undergone the operation commented on her loss of sympathy with patients. In his study Rylander interviewed relatives of the patients. A mother described how her daughter had lost touch with her deep feelings and become hard. There was a general agreement among the relatives that lobotomy results in an indescribable personality change.[9]

By Means of the Prefrontal Cortex We "Remember our Future"

We need to ask how an operation that disconnects the prefrontal cortex from the limbic system is effective as a treatment for hallucinating violent psychotic patients. This does not seem to square with the theory that schizophrenia is caused by an impaired function of the prefrontal cortex. This apparent contradiction can however be easily explained. In psychosis the patient more or less shuts off impressions from the world around him and focuses on inner images and emotions, which often are charged with anxiety. After a lobotomy the situation is quite reversed. The patient has lost much of his contact with his emotions and inner images and is mainly affected by outer stimuli.

It is by means of the prefrontal cortex that we can imagine our future on the basis of our present situation and our previous experiences of similar situations. It has been said the prefrontal cortex enables us to "remember our future". Thanks to this ability we can act in a long-term rational way to achieve what is important to us and avoid unwanted consequences of our actions. We do not need to be ruled by our impulses like small children. Instead we can imagine and reason about alternatives actions and their consequences and examine them against the feelings they arouse.

In stressful situations we may lose this ability of rational planning and decision-making. We may get scared or anxious if we feel threatened. This is not necessarily based on any real or noticeable threat. All it needs is for us to feel criticized, ignored or a worthless failure. If the situation also reminds us of previous similar traumatic experiences our feelings may be kindled to a degree where the prefrontal cortex is more or less disconnected and we can lose our judgement and clear thinking. Under these circumstances it very easy to become panic-stricken or have temper tantrums.

After some time we will normally calm down and nothing more will happen. However if we have a predisposition to psychotic disease such reactions can actually trigger psychosis. When the kindled limbic system sends signals to the dopamine-producing nuclei of the midbrain to reduce activity it mainly decreases it in the prefrontal cortex and then the person easily loses his basis in reality.

However the lobotomized patient no longer feels as frightened, anxious and threatened as before because the connections between the limbic system and prefrontal cortex have been severed by the operation. And since he has lost his ability to "remember the future" he can no longer kindle his limbic system with frightening thoughts. Often his feelings are completely blunted but in some cases the patient may still react emotionally in concrete situations. Such emotions however, will quickly pass.

Release Phenomena

After a lobotomy the limbic system is released from the regulating influence of the prefrontal cortex. The effect of this is to cause what are called release phenomena - such as tactlessness, poor judgement, emotional lability and changeability, euphoria, and, temper tantrums - to activate and become dominant.

Symptoms of emotional immaturity, difficulties with concentration and focusing attention are also release phenomena due to the fact that the prefrontal cortex can no longer govern the activity of the limbic system.

After a lobotomy the patient functions more like a child, unable to plan and take any responsibility. What becomes prominent is the inability to imagine the future and therefore to have an understanding of the consequences of his actions all accompanied by a serious lack of judgement that becomes very difficult for relatives and others to handle.

Rhythmic Movement Training in Chronic Psychosis

In the beginning of the 1990s I was invited to treat a group of severely psychotic patients in a Swedish mental hospital with RMT. Most of these patients had been hospitalized for 10 years or more and were heavily medicated. They showed many negative symptoms such as indolence, passivity, little interest in those around them and emotional blunting. Most of these patients agreed to do the exercises daily assisted by the staff.

Due to very fortunate circumstances we had the opportunity to conduct a scientific study of the patients who did the RMT. There was also a control group of similar patients who did not do the exercises. Unfortunately the study did not start until a couple of months after the treated group had begun the exercises and the initial changes were therefore not registered.

Despite this, an evaluation after 2 years showed that the treated group had improved in several aspects compared to the control group. The patients, who had done RMT, showed more interest in those around them, were more involved in social activities such as occupational therapy and doing different chores in the ward; they also had a greater sense of well-being and were less irritable.[10]

The results confirm the positive effect of RMT on the function of the prefrontal cortex and negative symptoms which are so prominent in chronic schizophrenia.

Chapter 14
What is Dyslexia?

The Expert Definition of Dyslexia and Reading and Writing Difficulties

In 2003 a group of 22 Swedish dyslexia researchers issued a consensus statement declaring that a distinction needs to be made between dyslexia and general reading and writing difficulties. They expressed the belief that the basis of dyslexia is an inefficient functioning of language biology that often has a genetic basis and those children with dyslexia "do not succeed in managing the sounds of the language in reading and writing"[1]. On the other hand they believe that reading and writing difficulties are caused by a deficiency in achieving the requirements for developing language that are meant to be gained from the child's family and school as opposed to problems with language biology.

All other theories about dyslexia were promptly brushed aside. "Widespread ideas about dyslexia as a consequence of visual disorders, defective motor development, lack of certain nutrients or deficient interplay of the ability of the brain to process sound signals have no support among the consensus researchers."[2]

How Best to Help Children with Reading and Writing Difficulties

An ever-increasing number of Swedish children finish the 9 years of compulsory schooling without having learned to read and write properly and do not obtain a pass in either Swedish or English. One important cause of this, according to the researchers, is the incompetence of the teachers who do not know how to teach children to read. However, the measures that the researchers propose, i.e. intensified reading instruction, have so far not been effective and the problem is becoming more and more acute. In 2008, 11% of the students in year 9, the final year of compulsory schooling, failed to do well enough to pass into senior high school.

When schools fail to teach children to read, many parents have chosen to seek assistance outside the school system and discovered that this help may be both quick and effective. By way of movement training, reflex integration, massage or sound stimulation many children have improved their reading ability enabling them to keep up with their schoolwork.

The statement by the 22 dyslexia researchers must be seen in this context. In the worst academic tradition they are entirely focused on proving the correctness of their own theories and dismissing alternative methods which in practice are effective. It appears that they want to prevent what they see as unorthodox methods being used in Swedish schools. In my experience they have been successful in preventing school leaders from trying these alternative methods that could easily help many children with reading and writing difficulties.

In this and following chapters I comprehensively deal with the causes of dyslexia that the researchers have so hastily dismissed. My purpose is to explain why both motor training and reflex integration work are so much better in helping reading difficulties than intensified reading instruction and speech training.

The Sensory Process

Reading and writing are complicated activities that require many subordinate processes to work together. In order for us to be able to read and write there must be a sensory process that receives impressions (letters, words or signs) and transfers them to specific areas of the brain, especially in the neocortex, to be processed and understood. By means of the perception process we become aware of and understand this sensory input. Many different areas of the neocortex must work together in a neural network in order for the reading process to function.

For the sensory process to function properly our sensory organs and brain have to work adequately. A proper functioning of the eyes is not enough for good vision. The eyes must be able to work together (binocular vision) and move properly and also change the focus of vision from near to far (accommodation). All these abilities are controlled from different centres at various levels of the brain, which have to collaborate. As will be shown our motor abilities are fundamental for visual skills such as accommodation, binocular vision and eye movements to work well.

The Perception Process

The perception process depends on the functioning of the sensory process. Impressions from the senses have to be processed in different areas of the neocortex in order for us to become aware of them.

Visual impressions are processed in the occipital lobes, auditory impressions in the temporal lobes and sensory impressions in the front part of the parietal lobes. If the sensory process does not work properly the corresponding parts of the neocortex will not be sufficiently

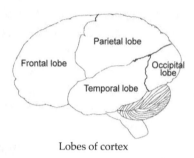

Lobes of cortex

stimulated which will obstruct the proper functioning of these areas and affect the perception process.

The perception process also depends on our alertness and the arousal of our neocortex. When we listen to a boring lesson the arousal of our neocortex will decrease and we may start daydreaming. We no longer perceive the stimuli from the world around us; instead we are more aware of memories and spend time daydreaming, letting our limbic system take over. We may hear the lecturer speak but we don't know what he is saying.

In similar ways we may be reading a book and suddenly discover that we have been thinking of something else entirely and haven't a clue about what we've been reading. In this case the reading process has been entirely automatic.

If we listen to a lecture in a foreign language or on a very complicated abstract subject we can have great difficulties under-standing it. Although we try to stay focused and concentrate we soon tire and give up attempting to understand what it is all about and start daydreaming or thinking of other things.

To be Able to Read Means that Reading has Become an Automatic Process

A child who has not learned to read properly is in a similar situation. The reading process, decoding letters and words and perhaps sounding out the words laboriously requires so much of his attention that he really hasn't got a clue what the text is about. In the practised reader this part of the reading process is completely automatic and his perception can instead focus on understanding the text.

There is a great deal of difference between the adult, who is thinking of something else when reading, and a child who hasn't as yet learned to read properly and is struggling to understand the meaning of what he is reading. The adult reads totally automatically but does not grasp the meaning because he is thinking of something else. The child, who has not learned to read properly and is struggling to understand the text, has not yet learned to coordinate the neural network of reading and the automatic reading process.

Most children gradually learn how to read by more or less diligent practice as most people learn how to drive a car by practise. Some children, however, have great difficulty in coordinating all the processes required for reading and therefore do not attain the level of automatic reading.

The Causes of Reading and Writing Challenges are Different for Different Children

What is common to all children with reading challenges is their inability to make reading an automatic process in spite of intensive practise. In the past there have been many theories proposed about the causes of this inability. However these theories are now thought to be obsolete and currently among many dyslexia "experts" there is thought to be only one factor. This is a weakness in the sound aspect of language or a phonological disability. According to Swedish experts, who share this outlook, nothing can be done about dyslexia except to intensify the practise of reading.

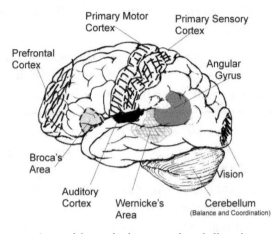

Areas of the cerebral cortex and cerebellum that
Work together to read successfully

However I think that it is more important to work out the specific challenges of the individual child. Modern research has shown that the various centres in the neocortex and at other levels of the brain must cooperate in a neural network for the child to be able to read and write. There is no simple answer to the question as to why this network does not work properly in a child with a reading disability. The causes are different for different children. Using various methods it is possible to understand the under-lying causes that obstruct reading and writing and how to stimulate these abilities, rather than putting it down to just one cause.

Without using sophisticated methods to evaluate the activity in various parts of the brain, such as PET scans (measuring the blood flow of the brain) or an fMRI, we must draw conclusions in other ways about the causes of a reading disability. First and foremost it is important to conduct a thorough interview to get an understanding of the nature of the reading disability, how it manifests and what subjective symptoms there are. By examining motor ability, reflexes and vision, which can be done by simple means, and making an audiogram it is possible to reach an understanding of the nature of the reading disability and how to proceed to stimulate the neural processes in order to improve reading ability.

Various Theories about the Causes of Dyslexia

There are dyslexia researchers who look at dyslexia as more than just phonetic problems, and they have found various groups of dyslexic children. By analysing the ability of reading and spelling in dyslexic children Elena Boder[3] classified dyslexic children into three groups.

The most common problem for many does seem to be difficulties with phonetic analysis. Children in this group read words as whole images. Their spelling skills are poor and since their reading is based on recognition they have great trouble reading unknown words and they often make wild guesses when reading. According to Boder these children have what she calls dysphonetic dyslexia. They constitute nearly 2/3rds of dyslexic children.

Children who manage phonetic analysis but have poor visual memory belong to a smaller group, around 10%. They sound out the words laboriously as if they are seeing them for the first time. They spell poorly especially if the spelling is irregular. This group's challenge is called dyseidetic dyslexia.

A third combined group constitutes the hard core of dyslexic children. They have challenges both with phonetic analysis and visual memory. They frequently have difficulties in learning the names of the letters and memorizing their appearance. They often make transpositions and reversions of letters. Their reading and writing challenges often remain into adulthood, unlike the other two groups whose prognosis is better. Audiovisual dyslexics constitute about 20% of all dyslexic children.

A similar classification has been made by Gjessing.[4] He distinguishes one group with auditory challenges corresponding to the dysphonetic group of Boder. These children have challenges in distinguishing similar sounds such as "b" and "p" and they may guess frequently when they read. He labels this group as having auditory dyslexia.

Gjessing also distinguishes a group with visual dyslexia corresponding to the dyseidetic group of Boder. They have challenges in perceiving the words as images and completely rely on sounding out when they read. They spell the words according to how they sound and they omit silent letters.

Sequential and Simultaneous Processes

The classification of dyslexia according to sense modalities has been criticized. Critics emphasize that rather than dyslexia being a problem with the senses it is more a matter concerning two different processing modalities, sequential and simultaneous.

In the simultaneous, words are perceived as images or visual totalities. The sequential is characterized by phonetic analysis. Spoken language is organized sequentially and written language simultaneously. Both these processes must operate in order for reading to be fluent and automatic. We use the simultaneous process to perceive the meaning of the word image and the sequential process to understand the meaning of the text.

In alphabetic languages there are two ways of perceiving the meaning of a word. If we are familiar with a specific written word we can directly understand its meaning by recognizing the word image. If not, we can analyse the syllables phonetically and sound the word in order to hear if we recognize it.

In a language like Chinese, where each word corresponds to a pictorial sign it is impossible to analyse the words sequentially and words must be memorized as images.

Aaron[5] has demonstrated that children who are diagnosed with dysphonetic dyslexia have challenges with the sequential process and children with dyseidetic dyslexia have challenges with simultaneous processing.

The Specialization of the Hemispheres of the Brain

The two hemispheres of the cortex specialize in different tasks.[6] It has long been known that the left hemisphere, in the vast majority of people, specializes in linguistic tasks, such as analysing the sounds of language (phonetic decoding), speaking and understanding spoken language and the ability to use grammar and understand the meaning of language. The right hemisphere specializes more in comprehending context, under-standing metaphors and perceiving intonation and emotional undertones.

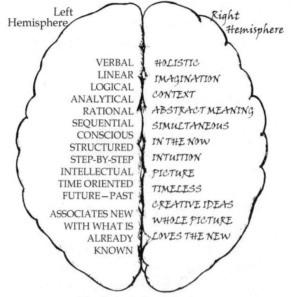

Hemispheric Specializations

For visual skills the right hemisphere specializes in seeing the whole picture, e.g. faces, and in seeing details within their spatial context. Individuals with a right hemisphere injury may draw an object with all the details but not in any coherent way so that it may be impossible to work out what has been drawn and they will have difficulty in represent-ing any 3-dimensional aspect of the object.

Two areas are especially important for language, the Broca's area in the left frontal lobe and Wernicke's area in the left temporal lobe. Injuries to the Broca's area may cause an inability to speak; this is called expressive aphasia. Such injuries also impair the ability to utilize and understand the grammatical structures of language. Injuries to Wernicke's area make it difficult to have meaningful express as well as being able to understand the meaning of spoken language.

Studies have shown that 96% of all right-handed people have their speech centre in the left hemisphere. In the terminology of the researchers that means that the left hemisphere is dominant. For 70% of left-handed people the speech centre is situated in the left hemisphere making this the dominant hemisphere for them as well. In 15% of left-handed people the speech centre is to be found in the right hemisphere and in the remaining 15% there is no preference, i.e. both hemispheres are considered to be equally dominant.[7]

Traditionally it has been thought that sequential processes are primarily processed in the left hemisphere and simultaneous processes primarily in the right. However recent research has thrown new light on the specialization of the hemispheres.[8] Using PET scans it has been shown that unfamiliar phenomena, be it a word, an object or a symbol, activate both the right and left hemispheres. The more times the experiment is repeated the less the right hemisphere activates, while the activation of the left remains unchanged.

The same thing happens when we are exposed to faces, commonly thought to be processed in the right hemisphere. Experiments have shown that every time we see an unfamiliar face both the right and left hemispheres are activated but for every additional exposure the activation of the visual cortex of the right hemisphere decreases, while that of the visual cortex of the left hemisphere increases.

From this research we can draw the conclusion that simultaneous processing takes place in both hemispheres. When we are exposed to unfamiliar phenomena the right hemisphere is more important than when we are exposed to the familiar.

The specialization of the hemispheres serves an important purpose in enabling different parts of the brain to fulfil various tasks, such as those described above, as this increases the efficiency of the brain. If there is poor specialization of the brain then the neural processes are more global and complicated, and processes like reading and writing require more effort. As a consequence poor specialization of the brain may be one cause of reading and writing difficulties.

Chapter 15
Visual Challenges and Dyslexia

Visual Challenges and Reading Challenges

Modern theories about dyslexia define it as a problem caused by phonological and auditory processing challenges rather than visual challenges. However, as seen in the previous chapter, researchers who have investigated the relationship between reading disability and visual challenges estimate that visual challenges are an exclusive or contributing cause of reading disability in at least a third or more of cases. In spite of this there are still many optometrists and opticians who do not believe in the relationship between visual challenges and reading disability, and because of this many children whose reading could easily be improved or remedied by wearing suitable glasses do not get appropriate help.

I think it is unreasonable to make a distinction between children with either phonological or visual challenges, especially as children with difficulties in both areas are the ones who find dyslexia most difficult to overcome. It is also important to note that a child who is both left eye dominant and right-handed may actually develop phonological challenges when learning to read.

Development of Vision and Visual Skills

Vision is the ability to identify, perceive, interpret and understand what we see. However this is not an inborn skill. It is one that is developed and learned from infancy up to the age of 12. The development of vision and motor ability is interrelated. It is through the innate programme of baby movements such as grasping, putting things into the mouth, lifting the head, crawling on the stomach, crawling on hands and knees, etc. that the baby learns to develop his visual skills. An infant who does not learn to grasp and put things in his mouth does not practise eye-hand coordination, binocular vision or fusion. A baby who does not creep and crawl doesn't practise moving his eyes from far to near and may develop challenges with accommodation. Binocular vision, accommodation and eye movements are all important skills that need to be well established in infancy so as to learn how to read easily and well later on.

Cooperation between the hemispheres of the cortex is also crucial for the establishment of our reading abilities. This means that the corpus callosum is well myelinated. The first step towards this is through the integration of the Asymmetrical Tonic Neck Reflex (ATNR), followed by creeping and crawling. This is further reinforced with the walking, running, skipping, etc that a toddler practises as he learns to move well in the world. It is between four to five years of age that the corpus callosum has matured enough for the child to start working in the midline; however it is not until the age of seven or eight that the eyes have the ability to continuously follow a moving object across the midline without twitching or jerking, and total eye dominance is not established until 11 or 12 years of age.

Binocular Vision

Vergence, or the ability to direct our eyes to look at an object, is one aspect of our ability to use our two eyes together. Since the eyes are a little apart the images of an object that end up on the fovea, or absolute centre of vision, are somewhat different. The eyes see the object from different angles. Fusion is the ability to integrate the slightly different visual images from our two eyes into an accurate 3-dimensional image in the visual cortex.

Phorias

Phorias are when the direction of one or both eyes at rest will change. The eyes are still able to work together when needed however they do so by making far more effort. If the phoria is large it can lead to headaches or eyestrain; as the eyes have to work hard at keeping aligned, to avoid double vision. Esophoria is where the eye will be directed inwards; exophoria directed outwards; hyperphoria directed up; and hypophoria directed down.

Esophoria

Exophoria

Hyperphoria

Hypophoria

When there is a strabismus (squint or

crossed eyes) and the eyes are misaligned or do not move normally then binocular vision does not work. However it does still work with phorias, even if it does require a big effort. If a child hasn't yet made reading automatic they not only have headaches and irritated eyes, they also easily lose concentration, read slowly and with great effort, and have challenges understanding and remembering what they have read. Sometimes the demands on the eyes are so great that they develop double vision or suppress one eye. Phorias can be found in both near and far distance vision.

Accommodation and Myopia

Our vision is constructed to have good acuity at a far distance. In evolutionary terms it was necessary for us to be able to see long distances so as to hunt well and be aware of threats around us. Our vision is not constructed to work for long periods at a near distance. However our modern culture makes quite different demands on our vision. From an early age our eyes must get used to working at a near distance and in some cultures children as young as five, or even younger, are taught to read and write, both of which require near visual skills.

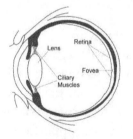

Cross-section of lens and ciliary muscles of the eye

When we look at something at a distance the image ends up on the retina. In order to move the focus of our eyes from an object at a distance to one close up we must accommodate, which occurs by the lens changing its form and becoming more spherical. The lens is elastic and suspended by thin threads on the surrounding ciliary muscle. When the ciliary muscles are relaxed our vision is normally adjusted for vision at a distance. When we accommodate the ciliary muscle will contract and the lens will change its form and become more spherical. In children the lens is still very flexible but after the age of 40 it loses its plasticity and does not change its form in the same way when the ciliary muscle is contracted. Then our power of accommodation will diminish and we may have to get reading glasses.

In accommodation, when the ciliary muscles contract and the lens becomes more spherical the pressure within the eyeball will increase. If there is recurrent accommodation due to frequent work of the eyes at a short distance (such as in reading) the ball of the eye will grow longer due to increased intraocular pressure. Such an adaptation in a way is appropriate since it demands less accommodation and strain on the eyes and especially on binocular vision during work at near distance. However we have to pay a price for this adaptation because when we look at an object at a distance the image will no longer end up on the retina but in front of it and therefore it will be blurred. In this way we develop myopia and have to correct our impaired vision by using concave minus glasses when we want to see clearly at a distance.

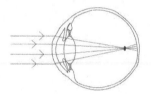

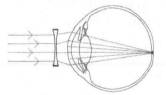

Near-sightedness (myopia) eyeballs too long. Focus falls in front of the retina

Correction of myopia with concave minus lenses

A contributing cause of myopia is an inability to change the focus of our eyes instantly from near to far and back again. For a child with this problem it might take 10 to 20 seconds or even longer before they can see clearly when looking from the white-board to his desk. The more a child with delay accommodates when reading or working at a near distance, the less opportunity the ciliary muscles will have to relax. This problem might even cause the ciliary muscle to go into spasm creating a condition of pseudo-myopia. In this case the myopia is not caused by the prolongation of the eyeballs but by the constant accommodation of the lenses.

The adequate treatment of this condition is to give the child reading glasses to relax the ciliary muscle, thus preventing the development of myopia.

Myopia does not occur in peoples who do not have a written language.

Hypermetropia, Accommodation and Convergence

Small children are normally slightly long-sighted (hypermetropic). This means that the eyeballs are by nature a little too short so they have to accommodate slightly when looking at a distance in order for the image to end up on the retina and not be blurred. Usually this is of no practical importance since small children have a good ability to accommodate. However, some small children may be very long-sighted causing the image to end up behind the retina and become blurred even if they accommodate as much as they can. Then they will need convex plus lenses at both long and short distance in order to see clearly.

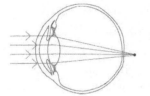

Long sightedness (hypemetropia)
eyeball too short,
focus falls behind the retina

Correction of hypermetropia
with convex plus lenses

We don't really know the cause of such striking long-sightedness. One explanation could be that these children, because of some form of motor dysfunction, have not been able to use their hands enough to practise hand-eye coordination, and because of this the natural tendency to focus more at far distances takes over. It may very well be that the practise of playing with the fingers and toes in the mid-visual field is necessary to counteract our innate long-sightedness. If, in addition, accommodation is slow, which will certainly be the case for most motor-handicapped children, it takes more effort to accommodate which adds further stress and diminishes the inclination even further.

When we accommodate there is an automatic physiological change in the direction of the eyes by means of the outer eye muscles causing the eyes to be directed inwards or converge, so called accommodative convergence. The more we accommodate the greater will be the convergence.

Children with slight long-sightedness manage to see clearly at a distance if they accommodate to compensate for the prolongation of the eyeballs. When these children look at a near distance they must accommodate even more, therefore straining not only their accommodative faculty but also their convergence.

When the vision of these children is examined using instruments there is usually a more or less marked esophoria at a reading distance because of the accommodative convergence. This esophoria is usually corrected if the child is given reading glasses, which decreases the accommodation and therefore also the convergence.

Summary of the Signs of Accommodation Problems

Dr David Cook in his book *When Your Child Struggles*[1] discusses many of the myths surrounding vision. According to him accommodation problems are shown when a child:

- Tires quickly when reading and the longer reading continues the more reading comprehension reduces
- Avoids reading or reads as little as possible
- Gets headaches or irritated eyes when reading. He may start to rub his eyes after reading for a while
- Blinks excessively when reading or looking at things like street signs in order to see more clearly
- Complains that the text becomes blurry
- Holds his book too close to his eyes or moves the book or his head closer and farther as if to clear things up
- Moves the book back and forth
- Makes careless errors when reading or copying from the board. Little words such as *of, as* and *is* or small beginnings and endings of words are misread while long words like *hippopotamus* are recognized

Causes of Poor Accommodation

Incomplete accommodation may be seen in children who never crept and crawled and therefore never integrated the STNR. Integration of this reflex is very important for the ability of the eyes to focus precisely on the text whether it is close or far away.

If this ability is deficient the child may experience blurred vision when reading.

Accurate accommodation is not only dependant on the integration of the STNR; the FPR and Moro reflexes are also very important. The ciliary muscles which control accommodation are innervated by the parasympathetic nervous system which needs a tranquil and relaxed frame of mind to function well. Under stress, e.g. when the Moro Reflex is triggered, the sympathetic nerve system will take command and obstruct contraction of the ciliary muscle. When the ciliary muscles relax the lens will become flat and the eyes will focus at a far distance. When the FPR is excessively triggered and a person becomes unable to move, the ability to see clearly even at a far distance may cease and everything becomes blurry.

Some people with an active Moro Reflex and a severe sensitivity to light find that the contrast between very bright white paper and black text obstructs their accommodation and causes the text to become blurry and the letters to move.

Examples of blurred and distorted text

Eye Movements

When we read the eyes move along the line by small, jerky saccadic eye movements. With every jerk the eyes move from one fixation point to the next. An unpractised reader makes more and longer fixations than a practised one. In addition unpractised readers will often move backwards along the line. The same is true for dyslexics. However, there is no sure causal connection between poor saccadic eye movements and dyslexia. It is more likely that lack of reading practise causes the poor saccadic eye movements.

Pursuit eye movements, also called tracking, are the ability to follow a moving object with the eyes. The pursuit eye movements should be gentle and continuous without accessory movements of the head. This can easily be tested by asking the client to follow a pen with his eyes. When you draw a big H, circle or X in the air, you should especially notice if the eye movements are jerky or twitch or stop in the midline. The other thing to notice is whether the eyes can move without the head moving. The ability to track in a smooth and continuous way usually develops at the age of seven or eight. Good connections to both the frontal lobes and the cerebellum are important for pursuit eye movements. There does seem to be a causal connection between poor pursuit eye movements and a reading disability.

Eye movements are controlled in an area of the frontal lobe that has important connections to the cerebellum. For some children difficulties with pursuit eye movements are connected to a dysfunction in this relationship. In such cases just doing eye exercises will not help as the cerebellum needs to be stimulated through rhythm to establish the connections more effectively and therefore improve tracking. This will then lead to better reading, writing and understanding.

Eye Dominance

When we are faced with a choice we prefer to use one eye over the other. It is easy to decide which eye is dominant by holding the hands stretched out in front one hand  crossed on top of the other leaving a small hole to see through. Stand about 3-5 metres away and ask the child to look at you, notice which eye he is looking at you with, this is the dominant eye for far vision. Now come closer and get the child to bend his arms a little and look through the hole at a book or pen, notice which eye he is looking with, this is the dominant eye for near.

In dyslexia it is important to decide which eye is dominant since this affects how the two hemispheres of the brain collaborate when we learn how to read. The part of our visual field to the right of the midline fixation point ends up in the left hemisphere. Since the right eye is usually considered to be dominant for the right visual field the left hemisphere will mainly process information from the right eye and the right hemisphere will process information from the left one.[2]

As the dominant eye is not completely established until 11 or 12 years of age, it is important that the necessary hemispheric cooperation through the corpus callosum continues to strengthen so as to allow the different specializations to be used and practised. The child who does best when learning to read is the one who can consciously change eye dominance. By reading with the left eye, i.e. the right hemisphere, he sees the word as a whole image and learns to recognize it. When he meets totally unfamiliar and difficult words he changes to the right eye and left hemisphere and analyses the words sequentially and phonetically.

A child who for some reason has developed a strongly dominant eye before learning to read will have challenges. If the right eye is strongly dominant he will be able to learn to read by sounding out the words but will find it difficult to learn to read fast, since he does not easily learn to recognize the words as pictures because the right hemisphere is not stimulated when he is reading.

If the left eye is significantly dominant only the right hemisphere will be stimulated. This child will find it difficult analysing words and learning to read by sounding out words, therefore he will develop phonological challenges. He easily learns to recognize words but has challenges decoding unfamiliar words.

When good connections between the hemispheres have developed by the age of 11-12 years, then hemispheric co-operation comes about more by communication through the corpus callosum than by changing eye dominance. It is usually at this age that normal eye dominance is established. A child who has formed strong eye dominance before this age will now be able to use the strengthening of the corpus callosum to start overcoming his challenges, and his reading abilities may now develop quickly.

Moreover the dominant eye controls how the eyes follow lines. The right eye naturally moves from left to right while the left eye moves from right to left. Learners who have a dominant left eye will start to look at the right side of the page first and will have more challenges reading languages that are written from left to right, such as English. These learners have a tendency to make reversals of letters and mix up "b" and "d" and other letters. Sometimes they find it easier to turn the page upside down when they are reading.

Challenges with Binocular Vision that Affect Eye Dominance and Reading Ability

One effect for children who are long-sighted and struggling to use both eyes together can be this development of strong eye dominance. On the other hand, some children do not develop a strong dominance. Instead they use alternate suspension and have rapid changes in eye dominance and become confused when reading. The text jumps and is unstable when the eye dominance constantly changes. Therefore these children will tire easily and find it very difficult to understand what they read. A considerable number of children with dyslexia have these challenges which if resolved can considerably improve their reading ability.

If one eye is permanently suppressed, such as in strabismus, reading ability will be less affected. In these cases the necessary cooperation between the hemispheres will be handled by the corpus callosum. When the child no longer needs to use most of his energy to maintain binocular vision the stress will diminish and the child will be able to read more easily and will eventually be able to make the processes required for reading automatic.

Visual Perception

According to Dr Cook visual perception includes the ability to compare things and see how they are different. In order to be able to learn the letters a child must be able to perceive the difference between a circle, a square and a cross. In order to tell the difference between "b" and "p" the child must have some understanding of concepts such as *top* and *bottom*. And in order to tell the difference between "b" and "d" the child must understand what is right and left.[3]

Visual perception gradually matures during the first 4 or 5 years of life. This maturing can be promoted by doing rhythmic movements that will stimulate the cortex and consequently perception. Visual perceptions can also be practised by letting the child draw figures like circles, squares, straight lines, etc. Perceiving the difference between "b" and "d" may still be a challenge for some children when they start school and many of these may develop difficulties with reading and writing. Challenges with left and right may also cause frequent reversals of letters in reading or writing, e.g. *saw* becomes *was*. Such difficulties are usually linked to a retained ATNR, a reflex that is of fundamental importance in dyslexia.

Visual Challenges Need Not Affect Reading Ability

Certain children with marked visual challenges may still be able to read quite well in spite of their difficulties. This is the reason some dyslexia researchers, optometrists and opticians deny the connection between visual challenges and dyslexia. It is certainly not easy to tell just from a visual examination if a child has a reading disability. However studies comparing groups of good and poor readers have demonstrated which visual challenges lead to a predisposition to have reading difficulties. Challenges with accommodation, long-sightedness, suppression of one eye working at a close distance, poor binocular vision with alternate suspension and poor tracking are significantly more common in poor readers than in good ones.[4] However many children do not experience any trouble and are able to read without getting tired in spite of one or more of the above mentioned challenges. These children have diligently practised and learned to make reading automatic and have adequately compensated for their visual challenges.

The consensus statement issued by the 22 Swedish dyslexia researchers categorically denied that visual problems could have anything to do with dyslexia. They based their opinion on extensive studies showing that binocular problems are no more common among people with dyslexia than normal readers. This argument not only shows how little these scientists know about the challenges of dyslexic children, it also demonstrates how they have left behind all common sense in order to pursue their phonological theories.

If they were not so limited in their outlook they would understand that children find it difficult to read and easily get tired when they experience irritation or smarting of the eyes, headache, blurry or jumpy text. If they would just ask children about the challenges, including visual ones, they are facing instead of just assuming that there is one cause, they would find out that many children have one or several of these visual challenges. If no one asks a child about the challenges he faces he will not complain. He will just continue to think that the headaches, irritated eyes, double vision or jumping text are normal. To recommend increased reading practise to this child, as the experts do, is nothing less than an insult and in many cases cruel and heartbreaking. Reading practise will rarely improve this child's reading. All it really does is to stress him even more and convince him that he really is hopeless.

The Development of Binocular Vision during Infancy

As has been mentioned the development of vision and motor abilities are interrelated. An infant learns to develop his visual skills by means of the inborn programme of baby movements such as grasping objects, putting them into the mouth, lifting the head from a prone position, crawling on the stomach, getting up on hands and knees, rocking and crawling on hands and knees etc. Children who, because of motor challenges, do not make these movements adequately usually have many challenges with vision.

By means of the outer eye muscles we can see in different directions. In order for us to have functioning binocular vision we must be able to direct our eyes so that the image of the object we are looking at ends up on the central visual field or fovea of both eyes. This ability implies cooperation between the two eyes. Since the eye muscles that direct the right eye are controlled from the left hemisphere and vice versa the two hemispheres must co-operate in order for binocular vision to be possible.

In newborn babies the hemispheres do not yet cooperate. This is due to the homolateral ATNR movement pattern of the newborn infant which means that the body halves do not cooperate but move separately. When the infant turns his head to the right the right arm and legs are stretched while the left ones are bent. Likewise the left arm and leg will stretch while the right ones will bend when the baby's head is turned to the left. During the first weeks of life the infant spends 80% of his time in such an ATNR position. It is an advantage if the head is turned to the left because in this way right ear dominance is naturally established.[5]

When the infant lies on his back or stomach with his head in either direction and learns how to fixate his eyes on his hand or an object, how to grasp the object and bring it to his mouth then eye-hand coordination and binocular vision is being developed. Later the baby will learn how to move the object from one hand to the other, which indicates that the hemispheres are learning to cooperate.

While the ATNR is the most important primitive reflex for developing these visual skills, other reflexes are also significant. The Grasp Reflex also enables the baby to grasp and to release things and move them to the other hand. When the baby grasps something with his hand the Hand-Mouth Babkin is activated. Sucking movements of the mouth will stimulate the baby to put the object in his mouth and the Hands Pulling Reflex will help to bring it to his mouth. All these reflexes belong in part to the group of reflexes that develop cooperation between the hemi-spheres, the body halves and the eyes, and which allow us to form the ability to cross the midline and work in the midfield or the lateral dimension.

If these reflexes have not developed and integrated normally and have not been properly integrated there is an increased risk of developing strabismus, poor eye pursuit or other serious challenges with binocular vision.

The Importance of Integrating the ATNR in Dyslexia

In light of the above it is not difficult to understand why integrating the ATNR is so central in overcoming reading and writing difficulties. The integration of the ATNR is important because it:

- Stimulates the myelination of the corpus callosum

- Improves the communication between the hemispheres
- Increases the speed of transmission for the neural network of reading
- Improves binocular vision and tracking eye movements
- Improves the motor ability of the hands and arms therefore improving writing ability

The February 12, 2000 issue of *The Lancet*[6] journal published a report of a study on the effect of a retained ATNR in dyslexia. A group of children with a retained ATNR integrated the reflex by means of motor exercises. Results showed that the treated children improved their reading ability in a significant way compared to an equivalent control group that did not do any exercises to integrate the reflex and in which it remained active.

Another study from Belfast[7] published in 2007 of 739 children demonstrated that a retained ATNR deteriorated both reading and spelling ability significantly. The authors question the notion that dyslexia is a limited phonological phenomenon and instead emphasize many studies that point to different causes.

Development of Convergence and Accommodation

During the first couple of months the baby spends much of its time in the ATNR pattern with his head turned in one direction. After that the baby develops the symmetrotone reflex pattern with his head and hands in the midline of the body fixating his hands, playing with an object or sucking his toes.[8] This pattern is suggestive of the second phase of the Moro reflex when arms and legs are drawn to the midline of the body. Each time the Moro is triggered the baby will activate this symmetrical pattern. Normally the Moro is integrated into the symmetrotone reflex pattern by the age of 3 or 4 months.

By means of this symmetrotone pattern the infant will have an opportunity to practise focusing on an object at a near distance in the midline. In order for the picture to get to the fovea of both eyes the baby must direct both eyes towards the object in the midline, i.e. converge. In order for the image to be clear he must accommodate, i.e. change the shape of the lens. By lying on his back, fixating his hands, grasping objects and moving them from one hand to the other or putting his toes into his mouth the baby gets a basic training of both accommodation and convergence.

As a baby lies on his stomach and starts to lift his head and chest he begins to focus on objects at a distance and eventually he starts crawling on his stomach, then on hands and knees to reach what he sees; when doing this he is practising changing focus from far to near. When he learns to sit up and then to crawl and finally rises and walks his focus changes to his natural ability of focussing at far. Later, when he learns to read and write, work at a near distance will become more important.

Before the baby is able to lift his head the Tonic Labyrinthine reflex (TLR) must be integrated at least to some extent. The Landau must develop for the baby to be able to lift his head and chest from the floor. Before the baby is able to crawl on hands and knees the STNR must have been sufficiently integrated.

Working with Reading Challenges Due to Visual Imbalances

Reading disabilities that have visual components can be remedied using various methods: visual correction with glasses, movement training and reflex integration and exercises that improve visual skills.

First of all have a visual examination preferably by a behavioural optometrist. Often this kind of reading disability improves considerably if proper glasses are prescribed. Long-sightedness that cause challenges with accommodation and binocular vision, such as changing eye dominance or suspension of one eye, are among those challenges that might be easily remedied by using proper reading glasses.

Regrettably, not all opticians and optometrists believe in the connection between visual challenges and reading Therefore, they do not make a thorough examination of binocular vision and limit themselves to examining for errors of refraction. Many children with slight long-sightedness do not get appropriate reading glasses or the necessary assistance. Or if incorrect glasses are prescribed, such as when there is pseudo-myopia caused by ciliary muscle spasms, and the child gets concave minus lens for myopia, it can aggravate the spasms instead of relaxing them, potentially causing serious harm.

Behavioural optometrists understand the relationship that can exist between vision and reading challenges, they not only take into account possible refraction errors but also make a thorough examination of all visual factors that can cause reading difficulties and make a comprehensive assessment of the situation for each individual.

It is also important that a child be given the opportunity to improve his vision by RMT and reflex integration. This will allow the underlying lack of motor integration that has contributed to the challenges with vision to improve. Another advantage of movement training and reflex integration is that it not only improves vision but allows the necessary integration for other aspects of dyslexia to be resolved as well.

Exercise of the pursuit eye movements is part of motor training. Training of other visual skills such as accommodation and fusion may also be considered. However this training needs to undertaken after movement training and reflex integration has been more or less completed.

Checking of Primitive Reflexes in Visual Challenges

Many children with active FPR and Moro reflexes have marked esophoria, often at both near and far distance. If there is only esophoria at a near distance that improves if he uses reading glasses, then we can draw the conclusion that there is long-sightedness and/or impaired ability of convergence due to an unintegrated STNR.

Impaired ability of accommodation is a definite sign that the STNR has not been integrated. In long-sightedness impaired accommodation and an active STNR is usually seen. The STNR is usually active when there is short-sightedness.

In children with strabismus or difficulties with pursuit eye movements the ATNR is usually active, often more in one direction than the other. The Grasp, Hand-Mouth Babkin, and Hands Pulling reflexes are also often active as well as other reflexes associated with the lateral dimension.

Reflex Integration and Motor Training in Visual Challenges

Reflex integration and RMT are often very effective methods in assisting with visual challenges. In many cases it is possible to remedy challenges with accommodation and binocular vision quite quickly by integrating the STNR and ATNR and combining isometric reflex integration with focusing on a point at a distance. There are times when challenges with binocular vision show up when doing isometric pressure integration. What happens is that the client starts experiencing transient double vision while focussing at a distance at the same time as doing the isometric movements. The double vision often disappears before the integration activity is completed. The client may also experience blurred vision or strain of the eyes during these exercises.

When the degree of phoria and the ability of fusion are examined with an instrument, such as a bernell-o-scope, before and after the STNR or ATNR is integrated it is quite possible to find significant changes have taken place within even a single session. After a few sessions of integration balancing challenges with binocular vision at a near distance can even be completely resolved.

It is also very important to integrate the FPR and Moro reflexes not only to correct esophoria but also to reduce the inner stress and light sensitivity that obstructs accommodation and causes blurred text.

Chapter 16
Phonological and Writing Challenges

Dyslexia and Phonological Challenges

Many people with dyslexia have phonological challenges. It is thought that there is impaired auditory perception, i.e. challenges in perceiving sounds, with understanding the sound structure of words, poor short-term memory for words, indistinct articulation, poor short term memory for sounds, and difficulties in storing new names and words as well as repeating complicated words.

There are two factors that may cause phonological challenges – impaired hearing and poor articulation. Both hearing and articulation can be improved by different methods. Hearing can be improved by auditory stimulation and motor training and reflex integration can improve articulation.

Ear Dominance and Dyslexia

Sounds that we hear with our right ear predominantly go to our left auditory cortex and vice versa. In about 90% of all people the language centre is situated in the left hemisphere. In most people the right ear is the dominant one, which is practical since, in this case, most sounds of the language primarily go directly to the speech areas of Wernicke and Broca in the left hemisphere.

The Danish psychologist and dyslexia researcher Kjeld Johansen[1] has shown a connection between dyslexia and left-ear dominance. He found that more than half of a group of dyslexics he studied were left-ear dominant. This dominance usually makes it more difficult to perceive spoken language since sounds from the left ear must make a detour to the right hemisphere before they reach the language areas in the left auditory cortex where they are processed. In such cases the hearing process will be delayed and the individual will have difficulties catching on to what is being said.

In another study Johansen discovered that many dyslexic children had suffered from recurrent ear infections when they were babies. These infections temporarily caused insufficient stimulation of the auditory cortex and occurred at critical times for the development of the ability to discriminate between sounds which lead to impaired hearing. This inability persisted even after the infection had healed. The study showed that right-ear inflammation was more serious since it made it more difficult for the right ear to become dominant.

Sound Stimulation for Dyslexia

Phonological ability is not only dependent on hearing. The Russian scientist Alexander Luria noted that in sensory cortex disorders of the left parietal lobe the sounds "b" and "p", which are pronounced with the same lip movements, are easily mixed up. He also found that this disorder leads to difficulties in discriminating between the sounds "d" " e" "n" and "l". This indicates that phonetic analysis is not only dependent on hearing but also on articulation.[2]

Our articulation is dependent on our ability to control the fine motor ability of the lips and tongue. What is less obvious is that it is also closely connected to the fine motor ability of our hands. There are many indications that movements of the mouth and hands are connected. Dyslexics often move their lips and hands when they write or cut with a pair of scissors or do other fine motor tasks. Many also have to move their lips and trace their finger across the line to read silently.

A similar pattern can be found in a newborn infant. When he is sucking he can be seen opening and clasping his hands. Later when he begins to investigate his surroundings the connection between hand movements and mouth movements is of great importance. As he grasps an object he begins to make sucking movements and puts the object in his mouth. The sensory cortex in the parietal lobe is then stimulated from the signals coming from the baby's tactile and kinaesthetic senses.

It is no coincidence that the nerve connections from the hands and the mouth/tongue region go to two areas of the sensory cortex that are very close to and take up considerable space next to each other. The connection between movements of hands and mouth is due to the hand–mouth part of the Babkin Reflex (hereafter referred to only as the Babkin).

If the Babkin is not integrated the voluntary fine motor control of hands and mouth will be impaired. It may also cause tension in the jaw and teeth grinding and challenges with articulation. An active Babkin may also cause poor motor ability of the hands and fingers, challenges in doing up buttons, tying shoe-laces and poor handwriting. Low muscle tone and over-flexibility of hands and fingers are common signs of this reflex being active. Involuntary movements of the mouth when writing or playing an instrument are reliable signs that the reflex has not been integrated.

Due to these difficulties with articulation the corresponding area of the sensory cortex of the left parietal lobe is not properly stimulated, which can explain the impaired phonological ability and difficulties perceiving sounds. Motor training and integration of the Babkin articulation will generally improve phonological ability.

Writing Challenges

Writing difficulties are not only caused by retention of the Babkin, other primitive reflexes are also involved, primarily the Grasp and the Hands Pulling reflexes. The Asymmetrical Tonic Neck reflex (ATNR) is also involved when there are writing challenges. When these reflexes do not integrate well there can be a lot of tension in the shoulders, forearms, hands and fingers, making it difficult to maintain appropriate pressure when writing. If one or more of these reflexes is active it is difficult for the child to achieve the ability to write automatically and he will have to focus consciously on the laborious writing process instead of focusing on what he wants to express. It is difficult for him to write essays because of the effort it takes to just focus on the mechanics of writing leaving little left for the flow of ideas.

Effects of Rhythmic Movement Training in Cerebral Palsy

Children with Cerebral Palsy (CP) often have speech challenges. If they start talking at all their articulation is usually poor. Such problems are seldom caused directly by a brain lesion but are rather a consequence of the impaired motor development due to the CP. I have found that speech in small children with these problems (which is also often accompanied by vision challenges - especially strabismus or refraction disorders) usually improves considerably when their motor abilities are developed by RMT. Two short case-studies illustrate this.

Case-Study: Eva

Eva, whom I wrote about previously, was three when she started RMT. She could not sit on her own without being supported and she could not use her hands. She had not started to talk and the doctors had concluded that she would never do so and that she should start learning sign language. She was long-sighted and wore strong glasses.

Not long after she started the training Eva learned to use her hands and also to eat and drink on her own. After a few months she began to speak, first occasional words, then two word sentences and after a year up to six word sentences. By then she had also learned to do jigsaw puzzles and dress and undress her doll. Her vision had improved considerably and she was able to start wearing much weaker glasses.

Case-Study: Lisa

Lisa was four when she started RMT. She was hemiplegic, with a quite pronounced paralysis on one side. She could speak a few words however her pronunciation was poor and only her parents could understand what she said. She also had a severe strabismus in one eye; could not sit up on her own; and, when lying down her arms bent into her chest and her hands clutched.

A few weeks after starting the rhythmic movements her arms were more relaxed and she started to grasp things with her hands. After a few months she learned to sit on her own supporting herself with one hand. By then her strabismus had improved considerably and after a year it could only be observed when she was very tired. She had learned how to draw and paint and loved it.

Her speech developed considerably as did her articulation. After 4 months she could tell long fantasy stories about princes and princesses. After a year it was no longer difficult to understand what she said although her articulation was still not perfect.

How Rhythmic Movement Training Improved Vision and Articulation

It was through the rhythmic training that Eva and Lisa were both able to start using their hands.

Eva started using her hands when after her first visit to Kerstin Linde she was able to sit up on her own without being supported, this meant that her hands were free and for the first time she was able to use them and create her own world. By rocking on hands and knees and crawling her Symmetrical Tonic Neck reflex (STNR) was integrated, which also improved her accommodation and decreased her long-sightedness.

For Lisa, it was far more challenging to learn to sit without being supported and therefore it took more time for her to learn how to use her hands and to draw and write. It was when her fine motor ability improved that her articulation became clearer and her strabismus started to disappear.

Rhythmic Movement Training, Cerebellum and Speech

Research has shown that challenges with the cerebellum can cause speech difficulties. Individuals with lesions of the cerebellum often have poor articulation.[3] The cerebellum is not only important for articulation but affects most aspects of spoken language. In Chapter 12 I told you about the smaller than normal dentate nucleus in the right hemisphere of the cerebellum in people with speech delay, especially in autism.[4] This nucleus has important pathway connections to the Broca and Wernicke areas

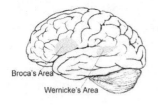

Broca and Wernicke Areas

in the left frontal lobe. These areas are important for language and speech. Broca's area is important for being able to analyse and understand spoken language and Wernicke's area for using grammar and speaking in a comprehensible way.

Children like Eva and Lisa who have never been able to carry out rhythmic infant movements do not get sufficient stimulation of their cerebellum. Their speech areas therefore do not receive adequate stimulation leading to slow speech development. When these children start RMT the cerebellum gets the necessary stimulation and speech develops rapidly. This is the most likely reason why there was such rapid speech development with both Eva and Lisa.

In autistic children late or no speech development is more likely to have been caused by a lesion or a dysfunction of the cerebellum as evidenced by their apparent inability to do the movements in a rhythmic way. However even though it may take longer with persistence speech will develop as the rhythm becomes more accessible. Progress depends on other circumstances such as the extent of damage to the cerebellum due to heavy metal toxicity and/or inflammation of the brain, and how effectively these can be eliminated.

Most children with late speech development have challenges doing the rhythmic movements in a coordinated and rhythmic way. Speech usually improves concurrently with the ability to do the rhythmic exercises. The more time it takes to learn to do the exercise rhythmically the slower speech development will be.

The Importance of the Cerebellum in Dyslexia

Many children with dyslexia have challenges doing the rhythmic movements in a coordinated, rhythmic, effortless, smooth way, which indicates a dysfunction of the cerebellum. If the cerebellum is not working well, it will cause challenges with the eye muscles and therefore with reading, in addition to the existing articulation and phonological difficulties. All these will improve when the cerebellum is stimulated by the rhythmic exercises.

We know that the cerebellum is very important for the functioning of the prefrontal cortex. Improving the functioning of the cerebellum will improve the working of the prefrontal cortex making it easier to learn to read, understand, write and communicate.

Case-Study: Hanna

Over and over again I am amazed by the effectiveness of RMT in overcoming late speech development. In my work as a school doctor I met a girl, Hanna, who was in second form. Her speech development was such that she had been placed in a class for children with special needs. She did not want to speak with me but her teacher informed me that Hanna never seemed to understand the topic of conversation and her answers would be constantly inappropriate. In addition her incorrect grammar and syntax made her speech difficult to understand. She had been diagnosed with late speech development and autistic syndrome with a question mark.

I showed her three simple rhythmic exercises, the windscreen wipers, sliding on the back and rolling the bottom from side to side, which she did with some difficulty. I told her mother that Hanna needed to do these exercises every day in order to improve her speech.

After a year I met Hanna again. She was now speaking fluently and comprehensively and answered my questions well with correct grammar and syntax. Upon questioning her mother told me that Hanna had done the exercises every day for 8 months during which time her speech had continuously improved. Then she had taken a break and had not started again.

Her teacher confirmed that her speech problems had gradually disappeared and concurrently many of her autistic symptoms had also gone. However she had not yet learned to read.

Chapter 17
The Neural Network of Reading and the Chief Executive Officer of the Brain

The Neural Network of Reading

As we have seen in order to read the brain must be able to efficiently use and coordinate many different senses and abilities. The visual, auditory and proprioceptive senses all contribute to the decoding of the text. If the sensory processes are not functioning adequately, corresponding areas of the brain do not develop properly. If we had challenges in hearing as infants the auditory cortex may not have learned to discriminate different sounds. If vision does not function properly the visual cortex might not develop properly. Challenges with the fine motor ability of our hands might cause challenges of articulation and challenges with articulation might cause a malfunction of the sensory cortex of our parietal lobe. If the cerebellum does not get adequate stimulation due to an inability to perform rhythmic movements; there might be a lack of stimulation of the frontal lobes, especially in the areas that are essential for language. If our body halves cannot cooperate due to motor challenges the nerve fibres through the corpus callosum that connect the body halves will not get sufficient stimulation. There will be insufficient myelination of these fibres obstructing the cooperation of the body halves and eyes.

Stimulating the auditory cortex with specific frequencies and sounds can improve hearing. Prescribing the correct glasses can take care of refraction errors which in turn can help improve reading ability. However, by stimulating the brain through motor training the areas responsible for our vision, phonological abilities, articulation, eye movements, etc are better able to develop the networks which are necessary for easy learning. Movement training is also important for developing the co-operation between the hemispheres which is of vital importance for allowing reading and writing skills to be learned, practiced and made automatic.

This neural network of reading[1] has been measured using PET scans that show several areas of the neocortex that are activated when we read. The visual cortex of the occipital lobes, areas of the temporal lobes and the frontal lobes that are in charge of grammar and phonetic analysis, areas of the motor cortex of the frontal lobes that control motor speech ability and eye movements are all essential for the neural network of reading. Each of these areas must be sufficiently developed and linked together in both hemispheres in order for the function of reading to work without challenges.

Neural Network of Reading

1. Speech motor skills   5. Eye movements
2. Motor coordination   6. Reading comprehension
3. Syntax   7. Visual processing
4. Phonetic analysis of sounds

If the corpus callosum is not thick and well myelinated the exchange of information between the hemispheres will be impaired. In spite of the fact that language and speech centres are situated in the left hemisphere blood flow measuring shows that both hemispheres are equally activated when we read.

Since the areas of the neocortex that are activated during reading are situated far from each other the transmission speed of the nerve signals is of crucial importance. If the transmission is slow, reading will be impaired. The speed is dependent on the myelination of the nerve fibres that are involved. Transmission time is also dependent on how often the pathways are used. The more reading is practised the more myelination there is which in turn leads to faster reading times.

Various kinds of cross lateral-movements also stimulate the myelination of the corpus callosum as do exercises that develop fine motor abilities and eye-hand coordination.

The Prefrontal Cortex – The Chief Executive Officer of the Brain

The prefrontal cortex also plays an important role in reading. Elkonin Goldberg who calls this area the Chief Executive Officer (CEO) of the brain says:

"The prefrontal cortex plays the central role in forming goals and objectives and then in devising plans of action required to attain these goals. It selects the cognitive skills required to implement the plans, coordinates these skills, and applies them in a correct order. Finally, the prefrontal cortex is responsible for evaluating our actions as success and failure relative to our intentions."[2]

When we are learning how to read the task of the prefrontal cortex is to mobilize and direct the neural network for reading and the various centres that take part in the reading process. If these centres are not developed enough, or if the lines of communication do not work properly, the prefrontal cortex cannot fulfil its task to direct the learning process and the child can very easily develop problems with reading.

Reading Comprehension and the Prefrontal Cortex

Once we have learned to read, the prefrontal cortex no longer plays a central role in the reading process. However to comprehend what we read it must work adequately. Reading comprehension is dependent on our ability to create something in our consciousness that cannot be found in the text. Let us call this ability our personal home video.

For example when we read a cook book with recipes of our favourite dishes the text evokes memories and sensations of the images, tastes and smells of past enjoyments.

To a large extent our reading comprehension is dependent on the memories of our experiences, which are stored in various places of the brain. The prefrontal cortex has to produce the memories that correspond to the text and make them available to our consciousness in the reading process. It needs to do this in real life as well. When we want to wear our shoes, we know where to look for them; if we have a memory of where we put them and we engage the prefrontal cortex to make that information available. If it does not function as it should, we may not know where to look for our shoes and we might even end up putting on a cap instead of a pair of shoes.

It is the same thing when we read. If the prefrontal cortex does not work properly we will not be able to play the relevant home video corresponding to the text and when we read our cook book, we will not see the images and feel the smell and taste of our favourite dishes.

Dyslexia and the Prefrontal Cortex

In dyslexia the CEO of the brain does not work properly thus impairing reading, learning and comprehension. And as we have seen this can happen for many reasons, especially lack of stimulation from the RAS, cerebellum or any area involved in the neural network of reading. Brain lesions can also have an effect. A lesion in the prefrontal cortex can have an effect on the functioning of the whole brain. Alternatively lesions in other areas can very well have repercussions in the prefrontal.

Research has shown that the blood flow of the frontal lobes will decrease if there are lesions in other areas of the brain.[3] It is easy to understand the relationship between the prefrontal cortex and the rest of the brain if we compare it to the relationship between a commander and his army. If the commander is wounded the lower units will not get proper guidance and chaos may follow. If, on the other hand, the lower units are dis-organized or the lines of communication do not work, the ability of the commander to give relevant orders will diminish.

Dyslexia and Challenges with Attention

Attention and concentration are also affected when there is a lack of stimulation from the RAS and cerebellum into the frontal areas of the brain. Therefore many children with dyslexia also have challenges with being able to focus. The other common cause of these challenges with attention is that the FPR or Moro reflex is retained and this leads to increased distractibility.

Once children with attention challenges have learned to read they will not have great challenges in decoding the words if their neural network of reading is functioning reasonably well. They may even be fluent readers, especially if they have integrated the ATNR; however they often still have problems understanding what they read. This is because the neocortex is insufficiently activated, and the prefrontal lobes cannot direct the personal home video. In some ways it's as if the child cannot switch on his video. Even if he can read perfectly well nothing happens, there is no understanding.

Rhythmic Movement Training, Reflex Integration and the Prefrontal Cortex

If the prefrontal cortex does not work properly, the child may have challenges learning to read. During the learning of reading, the prefrontal cortex plays an essential role as the director of the neural network of reading. Once reading has been made an automatic process, we will be able to read even if the frontal lobes are damaged, however reading comprehension will suffer.

It is important to help children with reading challenges improve the functioning of the prefrontal cortex. RMT and reflex integration provide many ways in which these improvements come about:

- Enhancements in muscle tone and posture, which in turn provides more stimulation of the neocortex via the RAS
- Stimulating the myelination of the nerve pathways of the neural network of reading
- Better connections from the cerebellum to the speech areas of the frontal lobes and prefrontal cortex, which allows it to do its job of CEO of the brain more easily
- Visual skills, articulation, and fine motor abilities are developed which also help to strengthen the neural network of reading

Different Causes of Dyslexia Demand Different Approaches

Some people with reading challenges are easy to help. Individuals with poor reading comprehension, who read fluently, will benefit rapidly from doing rhythmic movements and integrating primitive reflexes. Most commonly they need to work on the TLR and STNR, and often the Fear Paralysis and Moro reflexes. In such cases the ATNR and other midline reflexes are usually adequately integrated which also explains why these people usually had no problems learning how to read.

Children without attention problems who have problems learning to read because of visual challenges may start reading rapidly as soon as their vision improves. In such cases the priority would be to work with the visual challenges by integrating the ATNR, STNR, FPR and Moro reflexes. This can be done both by rhythmic movements and isometric integration exercises as illustrated by the following case-studies.

Case-Study: Maria

The case of Maria illustrates the results of stimulating the neural network of reading and the frontal lobes by motor training.

Maria was 12 when she started RMT. Her condition resembled a slight cerebral palsy, although she had never been diagnosed. Her hips were noticeably rotated inwards and she stumbled when she tried to run. She did not lift her feet when walking and had a shuffling gait. Her articulation was indistinct and she visited a speech therapist regularly. She had poor fine motor ability and had not developed a correct pen grip. She had a hunched back, her arms were very weak, it was difficult for her to keep her head upright and her balance was unstable. She found reading difficult and could only sound out single words as the text jumped about on the page. She had been prescribed reading glasses but didn't like wearing them.

A visual examination showed marked esophoria at both near and far distances. There was no fusion and sometimes she suspended the use of one eye. When Maria used her glasses her esophoria at a near distance was almost normal and there was fusion. Her pursuit eye movements were very poor.

All reflexes that relate to developing the ability to work in the midline were active - the ATNR, Grasp, Babkin, Hands Pulling, Babinski and Leg-Cross Flexion. The two latter reflexes were strongly active and may explain her inability to run. Her articulation challenges can be explained by the Babkin and Grasp reflexes. These two reflexes also explain her poor fine motor ability and absence of a correct pen grip.

Affecting Maria's ability to focus was the retention of the TLR, STNR and Spinal Galant, which were all active. The STNR and TLR explain her hunched posture, weak arms and inability to keep her head in an upright position. The TLR explains her poor balance and STNR her long-sightedness and tendencies of suspension which made the text jump when she did not use her reading glasses. She had also an active Moro Reflex that contributed to her esophoria.

Maria started RMT and reflex integration. She did not get a lot of support from her parents, though her grandmother used to help her at times. Besides rhythmic movements great stress was laid on isometric integration of her primitive reflexes which her grandmother helped her with. After a few months her reading improved. After half a year of training Maria had learned how to run. Her balance improved, she straightened her back and was able to keep her head in an upright position. Her articulation improved considerably. After a year of training she could read quite well without reading glasses. An examination of her vision showed that her esophoria had improved especially at a close distance, where she had good fusion without tendencies of suspension. She began to play basketball and became a good basketball player.

Case-Study: Agnetha

A 12 year-old girl, Agnetha, had never been able to read more than one or two sentences, because the text always jumped and was blurred when she read she was always exhausted. She did not have severe attention problems and from the start and could take part in the isometric exercises without any problem. While doing the ATNR integration exercise focusing at a point at a distance she experienced double vision and some irritation and tension in her eyes. She was asked to do rhythmic exercises every day and the isometric integration of the ATNR three times a week. After a couple of months her reading progressed as the visual symptoms improved. She was able to read a page before her eyes got tired, the text got blurry and started to jump. She said that this happen sooner if having to look at what was written on the board.

Testing Agnetha for the STNR revealed that she also had a rotated pelvis. As she did the isometric integration exercise the point in the distance she was looking at started to move and her vision became blurry. Before the isometric integration was finished the point had stopped moving and her pelvis was no longer rotated. She was told to go on doing rhythmic movements every day and the isometric exercises for the STNR and ATNR twice a week. When I saw her a few months later her reading had improved dramatically. During the summer vacation she had been able to read three books without any visual problems.

Rhythmic Movement Training in a Swedish School instead of Remedial Teaching

One Swedish school was having challenges with many of their third grade students in the months before they were to move into the fourth grade. Nine of the students were such poor readers that their teacher estimated that the school needed to employ a half-time remedial teacher to work with them. The remedial teacher tested the students with second grade material and the results showed that their reading was so poor that they actually needed remedial teaching at that level. Instead of hiring a half-time teacher it was decided to try RMT and reflex integration.

In February the group started reflex integration and RMT activities once a week. My colleague Lars-Eric Berg tested all the students and gave them each an individual training programme. The remedial teacher was present and learned how to work with motor training during her classes. The parents were instructed on how to help their children with rhythmic movements every day. No additional remedial education for reading was started.

After three months the remedial teacher re-evaluated the reading ability of the children. All students, except one, were now normal readers for third grade. In 3 months the group had made up for one year of reading development *by using only motor training*.

The parents also reported many positive side-effects of the training. The motor ability of some of the boys had improved to such a degree that they now qualified to play in the football team where they rarely had been admitted before.

One girl who had kept to herself and had no friends started to invite other children home and joined the scouts.[4]

Contradictory Expert Opinion on Motor Training in Dyslexia

According to the 22 Swedish dyslexia experts who released the consensus report and believe that the only cause of dyslexia was a phonological problem, reading problems should only be treated with intensified reading practise and better reading instruction. Any positive effects of motor training on dyslexia are flatly denied. The experts even claim that all efforts that focus on anything other than the linguistic development of the student will have negative effects "since they reduce the scope for efforts that by evidence will lead to improved reading and writing development".

However, if we look beyond the backwater of Swedish dyslexia research, we find that this conviction is not shared by dyslexia researchers internationally. During the past 10 years or so a number of published articles show that children with dyslexia can have problems that go beyond only language related difficulties. A 1997 study by Stern and Walsh pointed to impairments with visual processing[5]. Witton and colleagues found impaired auditory processing in the temporal lobes in 1998.[6] Other studies have shown that poor motor skills and balance, suggesting a dysfunction of the cerebellum, underlie many of the challenges of dyslexic children[7]. The 2002 study by Rae et al.[8], using neuro-imaging on adults with dyslexia showed abnormal activation in a number of brain areas of, including the cerebellum. There are also many pointers to the interconnection between reading difficulties, attention challenges and motor co-ordination problems that exist for many dyslexic people, as demonstrated by the 2003 Visser study[9] and research by Iverson et al. in 2005.[10]

All these finding have caused scientists to question the idea that dyslexia is a limited phonological phenomenon. According to the researchers behind the study from Belfast these results support an understanding that is becoming more widespread: "the development of literacy is dependent on a complex inter-action of cognitive, environmental and biological factors over time".

Chapter 18
Primitive Reflexes Involved in Reading and Writing Difficulties

All children with reading and writing difficulties have retained primitive reflexes that may hinder the cooperation of the hemispheres of the brain and the cooperation between the eyes and binocular vision.

The movements of the newborn infant are mainly homolateral, i.e. the baby moves one body half independently of the other. The cooperation between the hemispheres is slight and the nerve connections between the hemispheres through the corpus callosum are yet to develop. The corpus callosum is stimulated when a child learns to use both hemispheres simultaneously, such as when crawling on hands and knees.

The left and right hemispheres are specialized in different functions. Even though the language and speech centres are located in the left hemisphere it does not mean that it is more important than the right when we read. Brain scans have shown that both hemispheres are equally activated. Good reading ability is therefore dependent on a working exchange of information between the hemispheres through the corpus callosum.

It is important to integrate the reflexes that have an effect on working in the midline. Chief among these is the Asymmetrical Tonic Neck Reflex, however several others are important as well - the Spinal Galant, Babinski and Hand and Arm reflexes.

The Asymmetric Tonic Neck Reflex (ATNR)

The ATNR develops about 18 weeks after conception and should be integrated when the baby is about 6-months-old.

When the baby turns his head to one side the arm and leg on this side are stretched while they are bent on the other side.

In the foetus the ATNR triggers kicking movements and gives the foetus proprio-ceptive and tactile stimulation. The reflex assists the child during delivery. It causes the

Asymmetrical Tonic Neck Reflex

newborn child to move his arms and legs depending on the position of the head. These movements are homolateral, i.e. the child moves one body half separately and stimulates the left and right hemisphere separately. The gradual modification of these movements assists the child in integrating the reflex: lying on his back and bending his arms or legs tracking the fingers or toes with his eyes and eventually putting them in his mouth is one way of integration; lying in a prone position lifting his head and chest, grasping things and putting them in his mouth is another. Further integration takes place by cross-movements causing nerve signals to pass through the corpus callosum and stimulating its nerve connections.

The movements that the infant makes to integrate this reflex train his binocular vision and the ability to track moving objects with his eyes.

If this reflex is not integrated well the child can have difficulties with the following activities:

- Making cross lateral-movements and being able to cross the midline
- Walking quickly, the child is more likely to walk in a slow amble
- Balance is affected when the head is turned to the side making it difficult for him to learn to ride a bicycle
- When the child turns his head to the right the right arm and fingers are extended and the child easily drops things or tips them over
- Gripping and pressing down hard on the pen when writing leads to poor handwriting
- In order not to have to cross the midline some of these children turn the paper 90 degrees and write vertically
- Many of them have challenges writing figure 8s
- Visual problems such as deficient binocular vision, astigmatism and sometimes strabismus and problems with tracking. Adults may have the same visual problems
- More often there is tension and pain in the back of the neck, shoulders, back and hips

The Importance of Working with the ATNR for Dyslexia

As the ATNR is responsible for laying down the foundation to work in the midline which is essential for reading and writing skills, it is important to work with this reflex so that the gross motor skills of the arms, shoulder and neck are well established, which means the fine motor skills have the best basis to work from.

The Hand-Mouth Babkin Reflex

Lightly pressing on the palms of a baby triggers the hand-mouth part of the Babkin reflex. The baby opens his mouth and bends his head forward or to the side and starts doing sucking movements. When the baby sucks you can also observe involuntary move-ments of the hands. The movements of

Hand-Mouth Babkin

the hand may stimulate the breasts when the baby is breast feeding. The reflex also helps the baby put his fingers and thumb or other things into his mouth.

The Babkin is developed during the third month after conception and is active during the first 3 or 4 months after delivery.

If the Babkin is not integrated the child will have challenges with the following:

- Motor control of his hands
- The fingers may be very floppy and over-flexible
- Fine motor skills will be impaired with challenges in tying shoe-laces, doing up buttons, etc
- Poor handwriting is common
- There may be challenges with speech and articulation
- There are often involuntary movements of the mouth and tongue when he writes, plays an instrument or uses scissors
- There may be hypersensitivity to touch on the palms and face
- The face may be hypersensitive to wind

Due to the difficulties of articulation the corresponding area of the sensory cortex of the left parietal lobe are not properly stimulated, which may cause impaired phonological ability and difficulties perceiving sounds. By working with motor integration of the Babkin articulation will improve as will phonological ability.

The Importance of Working with the Babkin for Dyslexia

Working at integrating the Babkin will help overcome phonological and speech challenges laying a better foundation for good auditory processing. It will also provide a firmer basis for establishing good writing skills.

The Grasp Reflex

Putting a finger in the hand of a baby triggers the Grasp reflex. The baby will grasp the finger and hold it. If you lift the baby his arms will stretch out.

The Grasp develops the third month after conception and should be integrated during the first year after delivery. This reflex is important for developing hand-eye coordination, binocular vision and cooper-ation between the hemispheres. The baby

Grasp Reflex

grasps and looks at the object then brings it to the mouth. Later the reflex is important for ear coordination and the ability of the auditory sense to judge distance and direction. When the baby has learned to support himself sitting up in a high chair he will start to throw objects around, practising throwing and releasing things at the same time. In this way the baby simultaneously integrates the Grasp and learns to judge direction and distance of the sound when the object hits the floor.

If the Grasp reflex is not integrated the child may have challenges with the following:
- Motor control of his hands
- Poor handwriting and poor fine motor skills
- Unusual or poor pen grip with a tendency to hold the pen too tightly

- Tension in the shoulders which makes writing difficult
- Shoulder tension and problems differentiating the movements of the hands and shoulders, in adults
- Difficulties in getting a firm grip on a golf club while making a swing resulting in unintentionally throwing away the club while hitting the ball

The Importance of Working with the Grasp for Dyslexia

An active Grasp reflex makes it difficult to relax the arms and shoulders enough to maintain focus and endurance when writing. So by working with this reflex we are able to improve muscle tone and decrease tension and when there is more stamina to write the child doesn't give up so easily.

The Hands Pulling Reflex

The Hands Pulling reflex is triggered by holding the baby around his wrists and pulling him towards you. Then the baby bends his arms and helps to get up into a sitting position. This reflex emerges 28 weeks after conception and is normally integrated 2 to 3 months after delivery.

Hands Pulling Reflex

At the age of two months the Grasp is integrated into the Hands Pulling reflex and they start to function as a unit. When you put your fingers into the palms of the baby he will clutch your fingers and bend his arms so you can help him get up into a sitting position. These two reflexes enable the baby to learn how to handle objects with his hands, pulling them toward him, putting them into his mouth, throwing them away, etc. They also assist with the integration of the Babkin.

An active Hands Pulling reflex causes:
- Tension in the forearms, making writing difficult
- The arms are constantly bent at the elbows in some people
- Others have problems bending the elbows and keeping them bent
- In adults tension in the forearms may cause elbow problems, e.g. tennis elbow
- Flapping of the forearms and hands when excited

The Importance of Working with the Hands Pulling Reflex in Dyslexia

Again, integrating this reflex is important for laying the foundation for good gross and fine motor skills, so it is important to work with this when there is too much tension in the arms. The child can then relax when writing and which allows an easier flow of ideas.

Chapter 19
A Selection of Rhythmic Movements

There are 17 basic movements used in RMT. The programme also includes isometric pressure techniques and other movements that do not contain rhythmic elements. The movements and other techniques and how they are used to integrate the primitive reflexes and help better establish the postural reflexes are taught in the RMT workshops.

The movements in this chapter are ones that seem to be useful for many people. As the child gets used to the stimulation you can add movements and time. Passive movements are especially useful to start with, and many children like them as they don't have to participate actively and find them very relaxing.

There are a number of things to keep in mind when working with the movements so as obtain optimal results. A few things to be aware of when working with the movements:

- Be comfortable
- Get feedback about the speed and pressure you are using
- Start with only one or two movements
- Limit the time spent on movements. Start with 2 or 3 minutes (or even less) and work up to 10 to 15 minutes
- We work towards exactness

Exact movements have the following qualities:
- Rhythm
- Smoothness
- Effortlessness
- Coordination
- Symmetry
- Connectedness and flow throughout the body
- No compensatory and accessory movements
    - e.g. not breathing, locking the neck

All the movements are suitable at some level or other for all people. Often the movements have to be modified for people with disabilities.

Please do not do movements that move the neck with people with Down's syndrome who have instability of the first two vertebrae of the neck.

When a movement can be done actively 20 to 30 times without losing the exactness and flow then the whole body movement system has been established and is ready to be built upon for development.

1. Sliding on the Back – Passive and Active

Passive sliding on back

Lie on the back with arms resting on the floor with knees bent.

Passive – Put hands on top of the knees and push back and forth gently. If it is difficult to do from this position put hands behind the knees on the calves and pull from there.

There should be a flow throughout the body. If the flow stops at the neck you need to encourage the person to nod his head. If the head does not easily move in time with the rest of the movement it is an indication that the TLR and STNR reflexes are still active.

Active – The movement originates from the feet and there needs to be a flow throughout the body, with the back remaining flat on the floor, the pelvis doesn't tilt up and down, the neck is relaxed and the head nods gently.

Active sliding on back

This movement can make some people feel dizzy and disoriented. If this is the case stop the movement immediately.

This is a good movement for emotional relaxation, diminishing hyperactivity, and improving attention.

2. Foetal Rocking – Passive

Many children find this movement very relaxing. They need to lie on their side, with the head resting on a pillow or arm, whatever is most comfortable. Place your hand on their ischial

Passive foetal rocking

tuberosity (sitz bone) and gently push towards the head. Repeat on other side.

The whole spine and head should be involved in the movement. If the flow is blocked put your other hand on the shoulder and push rhythmically back and forth using both hands.

If there is dizziness or disorientation stop immediately. Often in the beginning you can only do the movement for 20 or 30 seconds before the vestibular system becomes overstimulated. By building up slowly the vestibular gets accustomed to the movement and starts to find it easier to process stimulation.

3. Rolling the Bottom from Side to Side – Passive and Active

Passive rolling the bottom
from side to side

Lie in a prone position with forehead resting on hands. The shoulders need to be as relaxed as possible, with the armpits resting on the floor.

Passive – Grab the waistband and roll the bottom from side to side. Get feedback about the speed and range of movement. Some like small movements, some bigger and faster.

The movement originates in the mid-back. Ideally the head and shoulders need to be naturally still, without tension (not always possible at the beginning). If there is a lot of tension in the shoulder area it is okay to rest the chest on a cushion. The feet should also be still without being tense and locked. If the feet flop around a lot it is also appropriate to rest them on a cushion.

Active – When doing this movement by yourself make sure that you get a rhythm and symmetry. The shoulders and upper spine need to be relaxed yet not moving. The feet need to be relaxed.

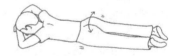

Active rolling the bottom
from side to side

This movement improves circulation of the cerebrospinal fluid, helps with emotional relaxation and stimulates the cerebellum.

The movement can produce phlegm and can cause difficulty with breathing, especially with asthmatics, so caution is highly recommended.

4. Windscreen Wipers - Active

Windscreen wipers

Lie on your back with your feet about 10 cm (4 inches) apart. Rotate your legs and make the big toes touch in the middle, and then rotate them out to the floor. Do this as much as possible without losing a spontaneous rhythm. The movement is a whole-leg movement originating in the hip. The feet should not be moving side to side by themselves.

It is often difficult to do this movement to begin with and it is frequently necessary to help someone do it in a rhythmical way. You do this by holding just above the ankles and helping to rotate the legs in and out rhythmically, making sure the whole leg is involved in the movement.

In order to teach the rhythm it is often best done by repeating the movement a few times (perhaps only three to five times) counting out the rhythm, then making a pause and then starting again. Gradually the child will learn to repeat the movement more and more times before losing the rhythm.

5. Longitudinal Rocking – Active

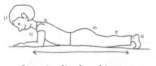

Longitudinal rocking

Lie face down with the hands at the level of the ears with elbows away from the body. The shoulders should be broad and the hands pressed onto the floor. Raise the head and chest from the floor. Tuck the chin *slightly*. Be up on the toes. Rock back and forward in a longitudinal direction.

The back of the body should be relaxed and the movement comes from the hands and the toes equally with a steady, even rhythm.

Some people find this very challenging and it is difficult to discover the rhythm and to move longitudinally. They will often bounce up and down rather than rock smoothly, finding it difficult to attain exactness.

Alternative ways of doing the movement are:

- Move from the hands and arms only, with chest and head lifted and feet relaxed
- Rest the forehead on the hands and move from the toes only
- Have arms resting by the sides, head and chest lifted, chin *slightly* tucked and move from the toes only

Feet resting and using hands and arms only	Head resting and using toes only	Head lifted using toes only

6. Rocking on Hands and knees – Active Sitting and Kneeling

Sit back on the heels, stretch the arms forward and press the hands onto the floor. Rock forward until the head is above the hands, then rock back on to the heels and bounce forward again. Repeat bouncing forward and back as rhythmically as possible,

The arms need to be slightly bent at all times. The back is relaxed and straight, with the lumbar spine slightly curved in and no

Rocking on hands and knees

tension between the shoulder-blades. The head should not be too bent back or hanging down.

If it is difficult to straighten the back move the hands back closer to the knees and make it a smaller movement.

If there is weakness in the upper arms because the STNR is still active then it will be difficult to acquire and maintain the rhythm of the movement.

7. Movements for the Fear Paralysis Reflex

Movements that replicate the movements a foetus makes are often good for working with the Fear Paralysis Reflex. Claire

Hocking in Australia teaches Pre-birth movements in her workshops. I also teach these movements.

The following are the leg movements that I find are a good place to start with many children.

Things to keep in mind when doing Pre-birth movements

- Do the movement one to three times only
- For many children you can only do them once every second or third day in the beginning
- Can be done individually or as a set
- Do as slowly as possible

1. Leg Swings

Feet are flat on the floor, slowly swing the knees down towards the floor, bring them back up to the middle, and then move them to the other side.

2. Side to Side Legs

Legs are straight. Slide one foot up the opposite leg to the knee, then straighten. Repeat with the other leg

3. Frog Legs

Start with legs straight. Join soles of feet and slide up then straighten legs.

4. Knees towards Chest

Start with legs straight, lift knees towards the chest then straighten legs.

5. Cross-over legs

Start with straight legs, cross one ankle over the other, uncross, and then cross the other ankle and uncross.

Appendix

Afterword
Sophia Lövgren, Ph.D.

Diagnoses and the Use of Social Phenomena to Explain the Existence of Certain Illnesses

I cannot stress strongly enough the importance of Harald Blomberg's book. The fact that he has already risked, and continues to risk, damage to his career because of both his book and his message doesn't detract from the importance of the book. It is in fact quite the contrary.

Dr Blomberg begins by drawing attention to the Swedish National Board of Health and Welfare's view of ADHD and their recommendation of treatment with drugs that stimulate the CNS. In a contrasting view, he discusses the fact that normal infants show attention difficulties and are also over-active due to deficiencies in the executive functions of the brain.

Developing the infant brain and its connections through all its different parts requires stimulation by the senses. If this stimulation is delayed or arrested then it can show itself in various ways such as having concentration difficulties. Development of the nerve nets can be stimulated by RMT. The author is clearly an expert in this area and there is really nothing more I can say.

However I can and I will, in my capacity as a Ph.D. in Sociology, say a few words about the SNBHW and other central players (read experts) actions against and motives behind diagnosing ADD/ADHD, and how diagnoses can be seen as an instrument of control from the perspective of the individual and also from the perspective of society.

In 2004 the SNBHW published a survey called "In brief - about ADHD in children and adults". In this booklet we discover, among other things, that between three and six percent of all children of school age are considered to suffer from ADHD, and show symptoms such as concentration difficulty, impulsivity and overactivity.

The reasons for ADHD are considered to be primarily hereditary with some possible involvement of environmental factors and also complications during pregnancy and childbirth. However the genes assumed to be significant for these problems explain only a smaller portion of the symptoms. To begin with ADHD should be treated with psychosocial support measures, but if these measures show themselves to be inadequate then drug treatment should be considered, by using central nervous system stimulants that affect the neurotransmitters.

Here we can establish that Sweden leans towards the strategy, the one that US among others prefers, where we anticipate having to medicate around 10% of children. The large drug companies have been the primary instigators in this strategy and strangely enough their campaign has been successful despite their critics pointing out how central nervous system drugs kill brain cells and cause permanent brain damage.

So how is it possible that the SNBHW and other players continue to recommend a treatment that critical researchers consider actually makes things worse?

Separation Strategies with Regard to Divergent Groups

In order to understand this conflicting behaviour we have to go to the root of the whole thing and see how illnesses are created in accordance with a specific objective. Illnesses are created by:
- Us individuals
    - we must consider that we have symptoms that disturb us and seek help for these
- Medical experts
    - the doctor must consider you to be ill and be able to give you a diagnosis
- Surrounding society
    - the state must accept the diagnosis as an illness and, for example, give you sick pay

The word diagnosis comes from Greek and means "separation knowledge" or "judgement". The National Encyclopaedia defines diagnosis as "demarcation and description of a particular state of ill health". We can see here that a rather fluid spectrum of symptoms and signs is transformed into something distinct and demarcated. If you have pains in the stomach, teeth and head you receive a certain diagnosis. If you have pain in the stomach and arms you get another diagnosis and, if you have pain in the teeth and arms you will get a third diagnosis. The diagnosis, in other words, makes the illness real. The illness wasn't there from the beginning - the pain was there, and the problem, but not the illness. The illness became visible with the help of the diagnosis.

Illnesses and diagnoses are, in other words, social constructs. The problems are of course real, at least to those of us who have them, but the illness - i.e. the diagnosis - is constructed by others. There must also be a number of people having a certain illness for it to be known as such. If you are the only person with a sickness, with specific symptoms, no diagnosis is going to be made.

Illnesses and diagnoses are also cultural phenomena. What existed during the time of Jesus wasn't in existence during the Middle Ages, and what existed during the Middle Ages isn't present today. Culture, time period, religion, politics, etc. all govern what is considered to be an illness. During the 19th century the place was crawling with hypochondriacs, hysterics, neurasthenics and nostalgics. These diagnoses don't exist today. Other diagnoses, such as fibromyalgia and whiplash existed not so long ago but have considerably decreased in number today. We now have anorexia, DAMP, ADHD, Asperger's syndrome and Tourette's syndrome.

Illnesses are also *socially contagious and socially controlled.* When a certain diagnosis is in fashion, the place is suddenly crawling with people showing typical symptoms of the diagnosis. Naming creates its own power. When a certain diagnosis becomes unfashionable, there are radically fewer people with these symptoms. Diagnoses also have a different level of status depending on whether or not they are controversial, which group carries them, what sex, class, lifestyle, sexuality, etc.

The myths of diagnoses also play a role with which area of the body the diagnosis refers to: the head is superior to the lower abdomen. Tuberculosis and AIDS are examples of diagnoses with myths. And finally, illnesses and diagnoses are *dependent on the economy.* New client groups are created when there is a cutback in the economy. For example, in regard to children with school problems, an individualized social categorizing results in the problem being treated on the individual level. Societies at large, or the school, are not required to fix the problem even if it becomes apparent that it is so common that it should be termed an epidemic. Large resources are involved in helping society. This can be seen not least in the US where in respects to health the economic interests of private insurance companies exercise much control.

An Explanation of ADHD that Cannot be Substantiated

The current model attempting to explain the cause of disturbances in children and adolescents represented by DAMP and ADHD/ADD is the neuro-psychiatric/biological model of illnesses; this is the one that the prevailing medical establishment represents. It is this explanation model that has created the need to medicate children with central stimulants such as amphetamines, Ritalin or Strattera.

In Sweden it is estimated that approximately 15,000 children and adolescents under the age of 19 are on medication. Some doctors within the prevailing medical establishment are of the opinion that around 10% of all children in Sweden have some kind of neuropsychiatric problem. For example, the psychiatrist Christoffer Gillberg considers that there is "a child in every class". The doctor Björn Kadensjö has come to the conclusion "that 5% of all children in Sweden have Asperger's, Tourette's or ADHD/DAMP of a serious nature...which can perhaps imply that 5% have a 'mild form'." (I have to say that this has never appeared in the texts I have read.) Whichever it is, a large proportion of children are considered to have these problems.

Eva Kärfve Ph.D. found to her, and my, surprise that when she looked more closely at the studies of the doctors mentioned above that had created these opinions that 8% of the 10% of the children referred to belonged to the lower socioeconomic groups. It is natural for a sociologist, and maybe even for many others, to wonder what it is that gives rise to such a high representation from this group. There are no obvious explanations why just biological malfunctions of the brain should primarily affect children from lower socioeconomic groups.

What then is neuropsychiatry? It deals with a biological malfunction of the brain that creates difficulties with motor planning, perception, activity and concentration. It is important to understand here that there is no possibility at all to prove malfunctioning of the brain using this model. No blood test, no genetic test, in fact no test at all that can prove the existence of the alleged malfunction. The fact is that there are a large number of experts who don't consider there to be any proven connection between organic brain malfunction and specific behaviour patterns. In addition to not being able to demonstrate any biological causes of the problems, it has not been demonstrated that other explanations are wrong.

These are the two most fundamental factors within science: you must be able to prove that your thesis is correct and you must be able to disprove the theses of others. If you can't do this then there is really nothing to discuss. You haven't put forward anything of scientific interest. Despite this, the SNBHW have swallowed the whole thesis, which isn't even a scientific thesis, and which furthermore involves rather large interventions in the lives of children and families using medication.

Environmental factors in the family or school, or the child's social or cultural class, for example, are thus not taken into consideration, not at least consciously. We could say, for example, that a lack of book reading or alternatively a lack of being read to, something observed in lower socioeconomic groups, can create a difficulty with learning how to read at day nursery and school. We could also say, for example, that the beginning or progress of a divorce in the family could create anxiety, restlessness, out-bursts and concentration problems for a child.

What critics of the neuropsychiatric explanation actually mean is that because such a high proportion of the children who they consider to have DAMP, ADHD, ADD, etc are to be found in the lower socioeconomic groups, it could be more a question of a problem within the community. That is to say that the fact that the family is clearly segregated in different ways (housing, economy, power) has created a child with "DAMP characteristics" (i.e. the child is showing stress reactions that are normal for the circumstances). We can also describe it by saying that we have taken children who are living through a period of stress with, for example, impaired concentration, and categorized them as ill. It is also true that economic cutbacks create new client groups when, through the social categorization of children with school difficulties, the causes are transferred to the individual level and not that of society. Then there is no need for the pro- vision of large resources to "help" the whole community. This explains, at least in part, the American strategy which is steered by the economic interests of private insurance companies. We can in addition keep control over deviating groups by means of a social categorization at the same time as seeming to provide help.

Why then would the individual accept such a classification, given to them as a neuropsychiatric explanation? A diagnosis can provide some kind of answer for the families where instead of having no identity at all they are given an identity which in some way can moderate their uneasiness and anxiety, although at the same time, of course, the child gets locked into a role of "ill- health".

Thus a diagnosis has its own power. For the patient, doctor and society many benefits (or not) can arise:

- For patients:
  - It represents an acknowledgement of their problem in the eyes of the world around them - family, work, the social insurance office
  - It can relieve their anxiety and guilt - why did this happen to me?
  - It can function as comfort - now I can get better
  - But it can of course also be stigmatizing and result in the feeling of being an outsider - I am different
- For doctors:
  - Their professional competence is confirmed - I found the solution - and an explanation for the causes is created
  - A diagnosis can also signify a concrete solution -

this is what we will do

- o Reward, and extra resources
- o They can bring together strange symptoms into one diagnosis
- For society:
  - o Patient associations can be created around the diagnoses
  - o A political agenda and involvement can perhaps be constructed – think of AIDS, smoking, obesity

However, above all of these, a diagnosis creates a border between normal and deviant. During the 19th century a demanding woman was termed hysterical; during the 20th century a homosexual as perverse and during the 21st century a troublesome child is medicated. In a complex society going through large and revolutionary changes at a fast pace (which is one way we can describe the experiences of our society since industrialization) categorization between deviant and normal provides a possibility for discipline, structure and normalization. In other words, citizens become obedient, conscientious and predictable in their behaviour.

The Power to Categorize Problems and Win Authorization

The fact is that it is possible to throw a historical light on this explanation of social phenomena as illnesses, and the cruel treatment of society's weaker groups. We can, for example, look at the forced sterilizations from the beginning of the 1930's, or "inspections" of prostituted women during the late 19th century as a tendency to explain social phenomena as illnesses. For example, many women, who were either mentally deficient or underage, never agreed to being sterilized, which in these cases often contained a racial hygiene indication as its foundation because, according to Swedish politics, it was important to prevent the "inferior race" from multiplying faster than the "more thoroughbred one". With regard to the prostituted women, they were judged to demoralize men and were seen as some kind of bestial half-humans who spread venereal diseases through their degeneracy, and by doing so gave gynaecologists a perfect opportunity, through the help of new legislation - and aggressive techniques - to test new methods or carry out new operations.

We can also observe doctor's authorization battles, where they show themselves to be people with egoistic motives just like the rest of us, visible in the study of caries done on mental defectives at Vipeholm in the middle of the 20th century or the mass removal of women's wombs at the beginning of the 20th century: At Vipeholm the doctors gave mentally defective patients, over a period of 4 years, and sometimes against their will, approximately 20,000 kilos of sweets, to elucidate the causes of caries. The connection to diet was already understood at an early stage, but the sweets industry bought itself time, and publication of the results was delayed by several years.

During the beginning of the last century a woman was considered to be a weak but dangerous creature, whose female sexuality could cause physical illnesses. The womb was something that wandered around the body, giving rise to such problems as kleptomania, hysteria, sexual frenzy, etc. The gynaecologists moved forward like steam-rollers, and operated on all the women they could get their hands on, without the use of anaesthetics and with an appallingly high death rate.

We can also pick out a more current example. The drug company Novartis, the maker of Ritalin, having increased their sales of this drug by about 800% over the last 10 years, have, together with other drug companies, hit on a very good strategy where the safety of the medicine can be introduced in scientific articles. Firstly, the drug company itself revises the results, for example, about how good (according to them) Ritalin is. Novartis are undoubtedly very objective and honest about any eventual harmful effects. Then they send the text to a writing agency, e.g. Current Medical Directions (CMD), who take a substantial fee, and then write the scientific article. But it isn't possible for CMD to publish the article because it wouldn't be accepted by the more eminent scientific journals. So, it is sent to an eminent researcher who is asked if he will put his name on the article. Thus everyone wins! Novartis have their results on Ritalin published and sell more amphetamines to children. CMD gets money. The clever researcher gets merit for publication of yet another article and perhaps now has a chance to obtain, for example, the title of professor or a new research grant. I have tried, with the help of different examples to show how ultimately, "truths" surrounding illness, standards and power strategies strike at subordinated groups who are categorized, problematized and corrected. So what can we now do in the future?

Which Method of Treatment Shall We Choose?

Perhaps Electro-Convulsive Therapy, also known as electric shock treatment (ECT), instead of amphetamines, Ritalin and Strattera, could be effective in "the modification of deviant brain function" in the eyes of a neuro-psychiatrist. ECT is an old and well-tried method of treatment. ECT creates powerful responses on an EEG, followed by a straight line, before the pattern returns to normal. It was invented in the 1930's by an Italian psychiatrist who noticed how electric shocks were given to pigs prior to slaughter, and realized that this could also be used on humans, where one would permit a specific number of volts to affect a small area of the brain so that a convulsive fit is triggered. These days the treatment is given under anaesthesia, and muscle-relaxant drugs and oxygen are also given, because the body jerks and cramps and at times is quite simply out of oxygen.

ECT is used in the case of serious psychotic depression accompanied by delusions and hallucinations. ECT can also be used on hyperactive patients. In Sweden about 2,000 people a year receive ECT, and it is said that 11% of these treatments are given by force. And some of these people die from the treatment through cerebral haemorrhage, because the ECT alters the blood flow. ECT's side-effects almost always involve muscle pain and pain-relieving drugs are given for this. Other side-effects are headache and memory deterioration. Critics also consider that ECT causes minor brain damage, but its representatives are of the opinion that this is prevented by oxygen. In former times an ECT treatment could produce violent cramps resulting in very serious complications. Patients could, for example, break their backs (something illustrated in the film *One Flew over the Cuckoo's Nest*). It is, however, unlikely that ECT treatments will be introduced as a solution, not least because the drug companies would never accept it.

So what can we do instead? Above I pointed out that when new professions, for example, neuro-psychiatrists, want to give themselves an air of authority, they create a new area of expertise which provides them with a reason for their existence. Historically we can see this with, for example, gynaecologists. The new area has to be "acute and alarming", in order that members can get hold of research grants and so that they can grow in number and influence.

It must also be of interest to the public, and here ADHD fitted in just perfectly, by explaining the problem of "rowdy children in nursery school and school", without having to give in to the increasing demands for more staff and smaller groups of children. A "rowdy and different" group becomes categorized and corrected through the individualization of a community problem and one escapes having to act at a community level.

The price we pay for this is children with incurable brain damage, as drugs are used to "control" children instead of using, for example, RMT, which is a far safer method. What we need to do as soon as possible is to place the problem where it truly belongs, i.e. as a community problem.

We also need to broaden our view of, and develop more tolerance to, what is considered "normal" and the same with our view of those experts who judge what is normal. We need to save our children from a diagnosis that negatively affects their view of themselves and points out possible shortcomings. We also need to create a space for alternative and sound methods, such as the method so dedicatedly represented by Harald Blomberg which leads me to finish with hearty applause for such an essential book!

References and Further Recommended Reading

Börjesson, Mats, Palmblad, Eva, & Wahl, Thamas (2005): *I skötsamhetens utmarker: berättelser om välfärdsstatens sociala optik*, (In well-behaved suburbs: the stories of the welfare state social optics), B. Östlings bokförlag Symposion

Börjesson, Mats & Palmblad, Eva (2003): *I problembarnens tid: förnuftets moraliska ordning,* (The problems of children in this time: Reason - moral order), Lund, Studentlitteratur, Stockholm, Carlsson

Börjesson, Mats & Palmblad, Eva (2003): *Problembarnets århundrade: normalitet, expertis och visionen om framsteg,* (Problem Child's Century: normality, expertise and vision of progress), Lund, Studentlitteratur, Stockholm, Carlsson

Hallerstedt, Gunilla, Ed., (2006): *Diagnosens makt: om kunskap, pengar och lidande,* (Diagnostic power: the knowledge, money and suffering), Göteborg, Daidalos

Johannisson, Karin (2004): *Tecknen: läkaren och konsten att läsa kroppar,* (Willingness to characterize: the doctor and the art of reading the body) Stockholm, Norstedt

Johannisson, Karin (2002): *Medicinens öga: sjukdom, medicin och samhälle - historiska erfarenheter,* (Eye medicine: disease, medicine and society - historical experience) Stockholm, Norstedt

Kärfve, Eva (2001): *Hjärnspöken: DAMP och hotet mot folkhälsa,* (Delusions, DAMP and the threat to public health), B. Östlings, Symposion

Lövgren, S. & Johansson, K., Eds. (2007): *Viljan att styra: individ, samhälle och välfärdens styrningspraktiker,* (The desire to control: individual, society and welfare management practises), Lund, Studentlitteratur, Stockholm, Carlsson

Sophia Lövgren

Sophia Lövgren has a Ph.D. in Sociology. Her thesis, "To create the future people, Governmentality and environmental discourse in modern Swedish housing policy: the suburban area of Navestad", was published in 2002. She has a background as a treatment assistant (social pedagogic) and has worked with families with severe social problems and children who have been physically, emotionally and sexually abused. She now works as a "free" researcher, author and lecturer. She calls herself a *Societal Doctor,* because she sees herself in a role as a "Genuine and Serious Visionary" in her goal to improve society.

Rhythmic Movement Training Stories

My Story – Harald Blomberg

It was 1971 when having completed my training to be a doctor that I found myself in a quandary because I thought my medical training had been based on extremely oversimplified and limited scientific explanations. The loss of faith that I experienced in scientific, western medicine had me seriously contemplating changing professions. However after some thought I decided not to leave and instead started to work in child psychiatry as it seemed to be the least "scientific" branch of medicine and therefore the least prestigious, being concerned mainly with the mind at a time when the mind was considered by other branches of the medical profession to be nothing more than the effect of molecules and nerve impulses.

In 1975 I became part of a group studying Soviet psychology and psychiatry. I visited the Soviet Union many times investigating the abuse of psychiatry for political purposes. I wrote many articles about what was happening culminating in my book *Opposition – a mental disease?* This was also at a time when I was completing my specialist training in general psychiatry which I had begun in 1976.

In 1978 I put forward a proposal to the Swedish Psychiatric Association (SPA) that it condemn the abuse of psychiatry in the Soviet Union. This was defeated with only four votes in favour. During the next four years I published my book and numerous articles written in conjunction with Amnesty International and Swedish solidarity groups exposing the Soviet abuse and the viewpoint of Swedish psychiatrists. 1982 the SPA changed its position and voted to condemn the Soviet abuse.

In 1984 I commenced training in clinical hypnosis. One of the principal teachers was Peter Blythe, the founder of the Institute of Neuro-Physiological Psychology (INPP) and so I also took the opportunity to attend his class on primitive reflexes and learning disabilities.

In 1985 I was introduced to Kerstin Linde, a self-taught body therapist. She was using movements inspired from those that infants make before they learn to walk, to work with people with severe neurological and physical handicaps. As a child I had contracted polio and I wanted to do something about the motor difficulties that I experienced because of this, so I attended sessions with her.

The treatment method had a very strong impact on me and I asked if I could sit in on her sessions, which she generously allowed me to do. I was especially interested in her work with children who suffered from neurological handicaps such as cerebral palsy. As I followed Kerstin I saw the most incredible improvements that contradicted all my medical education and experience. I also followed her work with Alzheimer patients and people with psychosis and other psychological and emotional disturbances. Even in these cases I was stunned by the positive effects of her treatment.

I'd finished my specialist psychiatric training in 1982 and had been working as a consultant in a psychiatric out patients' clinic since then. In 1986 I introduced the rhythmic movements at my clinic for both neurotic and psychotic patients. I had excellent results with this treatment. We even saw amazing recoveries in some cases of protracted schizophrenia. The patients were very grateful and happy about the treatment, however when my superior heard about it he forbad me to continue using the movements. I refused and he felt he had no alternative but to report me to the SNBHW and an investigation was started in 1988.

In his report to the Board my superior argued that he had forbidden me to use this treatment method because "it was not based on reliable experience and scientific evidence and moreover was not accepted or especially well known." I wrote a 50 page report with 10 case studies documenting the effects of the treatment and some 20 of my patients wrote to the Board to express their appreciation. Representatives for the SNBHW also inspected the out-patient clinic where I worked. In its formal report the Board established that the treatment was "experienced very positively by many patients" and that the "movement treatment was a worthwhile contribution in a situation that had appeared to be deadlocked or stagnant." They wrote that "if every element of treatment should be called upon for a full scientific documentation psychiatric treatment would probably be sterile which would totally contradict the humanistic values and expressions that psychiatry also had to defend." In the report I was strongly urged to assist in the initiation of a scientific examination of the treatment method. The Board concluded its report by criticizing my superiors for the lack of cooperation between treatment of in-patients and out-patients and urged the medical superintendent to take actions to improve this co-operation.

In 1989 I resigned and started private practice. A colleague invited me to introduce the movement therapy to some severely ill chronic schizophrenic patients, most of whom had been hospitalized for 10 years or more at the psychiatric hospital where he worked. In 1991 this work developed into a research programme supervised by a professor of psychology at the University of Umeå in Sweden. The research programme was designed to continue for 5 years but was unfortunately interrupted in 1994 when I had to quit my work at the psychiatric hospital for private reasons. However, in 1993 a report was compiled dealing with "short term changes in chronic schizophrenic patients treated with Rhythmic Movement Training." The report was an examination paper by two students of psychology. In it they concluded that "the study indicates that the patients treated with movement therapy had displayed the greatest positive changes... Among other things the changes manifested themselves in the fact that these patients were to a greater extent able to take part in social activities, participate occupational therapy and their daily tasks in the ward. They had also become more interested in their surroundings".

In 1990 I started to work once every 2 weeks as a psychiatric consultant at a Rudolf Steiner anthroposophical special school for mentally handicapped youths aged between 15 and 23 years. I still work at that school. Some of the pupils are mentally retarded; others suffer from autism or ADD. I introduced RMT to this school in combination with movements for inhibition of primitive reflexes taught by Peter Blythe at his INPP institute. Some of the therapists at the school have learned these methods, which are now being offered to the pupils who are thought will benefit from them. Our experience of this work has been that pupils with movement disabilities, learning disabilities due to psychosis, ADD, and to some extent autism are the ones that gain the most benefit.

In my private practice I use RMT in combination with movements for inhibition of primitive reflexes. This approach has been especially beneficial for patients who as children had suffered from dyslexia and/or ADD. But all patients who have agreed to do the movements have benefited since they stimulate the therapeutic process and especially the dreams of the patients.

After quitting my part time work at the psychiatric hospital in 1994 I started to work full time in my private practice. It was then that I finally found time to start writing books about Rhythmic Movement Training. In 1998 I published *Helande Liv* (Healing Life), and in 2008 I completed this book in Swedish.

Since 1990 I have given many lectures and courses in Rhythmic Movement Training for therapists, teachers and nursing staff. During the last 5 years I have given courses frequently and regularly. The emphasis of these courses has been on working with children with dyslexia, ADHD and severe motor problems.

I now work in the "Centrum för Rytmisk Rörelseträning" (Rhythmic Movement Training Centre) that I opened in 2009 in Stockholm. I train RMT instructors in Sweden and I now teach regularly in many parts of the world. An international organization has been set up to teach instructors of RMT and there are now many people training in this method.

Harald Blomberg, Stockholm Sweden, October 2010

Rhythmic Movement Training and Personal Development - Lauren

I attended my first RMT course in January of 2009, after an RMT flyer came up while I was searching online for information on neurodevelopment and modalities that incorporated movement into their programmes. I went to the class hoping to find additional modalities to use with the special needs children I work with. I can honestly say that I left that course with many new resources - only the resources weren't just for my clients, they were for me.

After 2 days of class, I realized that the painful foot cramps that had plagued my feet for over a year had stopped. In fact, I hadn't had a single cramp since the Babinski balance we learned on day one of class, when our instructor asked us, "How do you want to walk through life?" For me, that question touched on so many different levels and I found myself excited about an opportunity to change how I had been walking through life. After the experience with my feet, I started to take a closer look at my own development and found that there were several other reflex areas that were impacting my life and my ability to manage stress, particularly the Fear Paralysis & Moro reflexes, the STNR and the ATNR.

I began to do the movements for about 10 minutes a day, focusing on the rhythm, symmetry and exactness of each movement. At first, they were very difficult to perform. I often found myself frustrated with my inability to perfect them. However I continued to practise daily. After about 2 months, I decided to incorporate the balance formats into my daily practise. I found that when I incorporated an intention, the movements were easier! I now realize the healing power that can come from combining kinaesthetic and intentional energies in the balance format and the profound effect these rhythmic movements have on the nervous system and on development.

The most significant change that I have noticed in myself after doing RMT for over a year is in my ability to respond to stress instead of reacting to it. Before I found RMT I had an enormous need to control almost everything in my life. Through the RMT process I have learned more about myself and how operating reflexively from a survival standpoint was impacting my efficiency, stress level, emotional health, productivity and overall well-being. I now do things very differently. I will continue to be a student of this work and to use it as a resource for myself, as well as those around me. I am known to stop in the middle of an activity and slide on my back for a few minutes when I need to.

To this day, I am foot cramp free and overall a much happier person.

Lauren Harrington, Houston USA, April 2010

Jack's Story

The pregnancy with Jack was very stressful and the birth fast. He had a stressed mother in his infancy and was confined quite a bit in either a car capsule or a baby lounge. He was sometimes left to cry and was only breast-fed for a few months. During a seaside holiday when he was about 8-months-old his father repeatedly threw him into the air and let him plunge underwater (misguidedly thinking he was helping him) before catching and lifting him. Jack was terrified and hysterical.

Jack's language was delayed – four words by his second birthday, and his articulation was poor. He was terrified of loud sounds, e.g. trucks, vacuum cleaner, thunder and he was absolutely petrified of water.

When he was 3-years-old he injured his foot and had to have surgery. The surgical staff said he was the best-behaved child they had ever had because he didn't make a sound and he didn't move; only his eyes, his terrified little eyes.

Kindergarten at age four did not bring the hoped for social development and it was noted that his fine motor ability was poor. He didn't talk much and his behaviour was difficult. We started looking very carefully at his diet. Pre-primary was better. He participated in a structured motor programme as well as some Primary Movement and was passed up into Grade One.

Grade One was disastrous. By mid-year he knew 20 sounds (which were two more than he knew at the start of the school year) and could spell three words. A very stressed little boy. He spent his lunch-times sitting behind the rubbish skip bins in an isolated area. We were incredibly careful with what we fed him as he had reactions to many additives and some foods; even the air would set him off if the mines were pumping out high levels of sulphur dioxide. We were used to him getting frustrated easily and emotionally melting down but it had reached a new high. He seemed unable to connect or identify with how he was feeling. When he was upset he would lash out or I would find him hiding, curled up in a foetal position under a blanket, bewildered and distressed. He was not an aggressive child but often hurt other children when playing and was generally non-compliant. He was still wetting the bed nightly. He ground his teeth, he chewed his shirt, bottle caps and bits of plastic, and his handwriting was terrible. He did not seem to possess an imagination and I had never seen him engage in imaginary play. We took him out of school.

We commenced home schooling. Jack could learn only if lessons were presented as relaxed games. We began to work with Rhythmic Movement. Firstly we needed passive movements for 5 weeks for the Spinal Galant Reflex. This was followed a few days later by Moro and 9 weeks of isometric movements. His bed wetting decreased. We worked with the Amphibian and Babinski reflexes and started active movements. By this stage Jack was quite volatile. We did a kinesiology balance for "I feel happy" and the emotional stuff cleared straight away.

The next day I broke down in tears when I saw Jack playing a "pretend" game with his sister. He also started reading. We worked with Tendon Guard (35 minutes of rolling his head brought up disturbing images for him) and did more active movements for homework. A 42-muscle balance (from Touch for Health) picked up multiple switched-off bladder muscles along the deep muscle line leading from a prior foot injury site. Since doing all these things Jack has not wet the bed.

Next came the need to work with the cerebellum and neural chassis and *lots* of rolling the bottom. Then we started on work for the hands and the face. Jack's first Facial reflexes massage put him to sleep for six hours. At weekly intervals the Facial reflexes massage continued to put him into a deep sleep. By now we had hit end-of-year school holidays and he had about 40 small sight words. Still no spelling. It seemed for every three steps forward, we took two back. We had a complete break over the December-January Christmas holiday.

New Year – Grade Two and still home schooling. More Moro work. Landau and Amphibian reflexes had us working actively again. Even though Jack had earlier tested as being right-ear dominant, when we switched to speaking into his left ear while doing school-work, his work with sounds improved significantly. More work with grasp, TLR, and Limbic system – more active movements. Facial massages again. Jack could now tell us how he felt, could play with other children without hurting them, had stopped grinding his teeth, sucking his shirt and chewing bottle caps. His fine motor skills (i.e. handwriting) had improved amazingly and we had finished two thirds of the Grade One literacy curriculum in only 10 weeks. He was still having difficulty discriminating some sounds and short-term memory sequencing with some sounds was problematic.

We had Jack tested for heavy metals and he was positive for lead, cadmium, barium and aluminium. We started a biomedical protocol to support his gut function and progressed to chelation of heavy metals. Jack had low cellular mineral status due to heavy metal blockade of key nutrients.

Perhaps one of the most valuable skills Moira Dempsey taught me was the Facial reflexes massage. With it we could unlock the stress from his TMJ, change/soften the shape of his face and restore sensory processing somewhat. For the first time the Facial massage didn't put him into a deep sleep.

We started Grade Two literacy and had Jack assessed for central Auditory Processing Disorder (CAPD) along with hearing tests. His hearing was normal but he was border line for CAPD with very low scores. From May through to September we focused on school-work with the occasional Facial massage. We had STNR work to do but again we were hit-and-miss and didn't finish. We also commenced the Listening Programme with Bone Conduction for Jack's auditory processing difficulties. We completed all the Grade Two school-work by the end of the year. It had been quite a roller-coaster ride, especially when Jack was so unsettled at times by all the CNS stimulation. He was now able to hear all the phonetic sounds and was reading and spelling beautifully. Apart from the STNR which we didn't seem to be able to get our act together about, we didn't get any RMT work to do. We had hardly any challenging behaviour anymore and he was socially confident.

For Grade Three we enrolled Jack back into school. He had a fabulous teacher and settled in well. Socially he was happy and he was coping with the class work. Challenging behaviour was almost non-existent. In September we had an incident at school which resulted in us having to balance events from the past as well as needing to work with the STNR; however we again avoided doing this. By November we realized he wasn't keeping up with the spelling being taught at school so we worked with the foot reflexes and this time we did the movements quite diligently.

Grade Four and he had trouble from day one. I did a multi-sensory assessment and reflex testing to find out what was still affecting him. Surprise, surprise! The STNR! Also traces of hands, feet and mouth reflexes and some auditory Moro. We did a month's worth of very intensive motor work which included some RMT exercises and lots of Facial massages again. His story writing improved. I think his spelling has gone backward and his handwriting is scary. I am due to work with him again and see now what is left to do. I wish we had done the STNR work any of the first three times we got given it to do! However, he's come a long, long way from where he started from and if a bit of spelling and messy handwriting is all we have left to overcome, then that is what we shall do. He has friends and where once we would have had at least 10 meltdowns a day, now we might have one in 3 months.

Davina Fraser, Kalgoorlie Western Australia, May 2010

Calming Meltdowns

Autistic children are very much the-here-and-now live in the moment kind of kids. When they start moving towards a meltdown you usually only have a few minutes, at most, before it hits. The meltdowns are uncontrollable and the child is inconsolable. It's an ordeal for the parent every time and it can happen once or multiple times a day. These episodes almost always last a minimum of 2 hours and the child either eventually falls asleep from exhaustion or slowly winds down. Once the meltdown is in full swing, depending on the child, you may not be able to touch him, make any sound or talk to him, change the lighting, have any motion in the room - you get the idea, because if any of these things occurs the meltdown intensifies.

The first time I discovered that rhythmic movements would stop the meltdowns was with my own child. It was the first time I had attended an RMT class. Our routine had been different for several days, we had guests in our home, and my son had spent his days with his dad or friends instead of with me. I came home late on the third night and instead of finding my son in bed asleep he was still dressed sitting in the corner of his room. At this point we had recovered him from autism probably about halfway so meltdowns were no longer daily but they still occurred a few times a week. I asked him if he was okay and he shook his head. I calmly told him I understood he was feeling stressed because of all the changes that had happened in the last few days. He nodded. I asked him to come over and lie down on the floor and to let me try something. He did. I began to rock him in one of the RMT positions. I was surprised he let me. By this point we would normally have been into meltdown. As I rocked him I asked him how it felt, if he wanted it faster or slower, etc. After about 4 minutes he told me he felt better. He said I could stop and then he stood up with a smile on his face. He said he needed to get ready for bed and off he went on his own to brush his teeth and put his pyjamas on. Usually he wouldn't do this even on a good night. Then he crawled into bed and with a smile said goodnight. To say I almost fainted would be an understatement. This was nothing short of a miracle in our home!

With the autistic children I've worked with I show the parents how just to use the rhythmic movement when the child is beginning to get agitated, begins to talk or move too fast, becomes stressed, flaps his arms, etc. As soon as they see signs of trouble just get the child to lie down and start rocking immediately (assuming the child will lie down). Some of my parents have shared that they'd ask their child to lie down and they'd start doing a rhythmic movement in the doctor's waiting-room, at home, in school. Receptionists would get up and watch in amazement as the impending meltdown stopped, or others would watch as an autistic child who was being disorganized or anxious would get up from doing the rhythmic movement after a few minutes and go sit quietly and smile and giggle. The behaviour completely changes within minutes.

For some children with autism using the passive movements at night have allowed them to finally sleep through the night, something that many of them find difficult to do.

Laura Parker, Washington USA, August 2010

Painful Hamstrings

For two years I dedicated my physical work-outs to lengthening my seemingly short hamstrings. I tried yoga, Classical Stretch, Power 90 work-outs, and exercises from my chiropractor - all to no avail. When I bent forward, my hamstrings would begin to hurt by the time my hands reached my knees, and then the pain behind my knees became intense. It was the kind of pain that made me nearly sick to my stomach. I listened to everyone's advice, I tried many different techniques, I consistently worked at lengthening my hamstrings 5 days a week for 2 years - but still no improvement.

Then I took my first RMT class. During the training, we practise the techniques on ourselves and other classmates, getting many opportunities to heal different issues. One of the procedures is for releasing the Tendon Guard Reflex. At the time, I was solely focused on what I was learning in class and didn't take a moment to think about how this reflex was apparent in my life. I did the procedure then continued on with the next one, having to cover a great deal of information in a short period of time, and never giving it a second thought.

After arriving home the next day, as I unpacked from the trip, I suddenly noticed that I was picking things up off the floor with my legs straight and *no pain*! The Tendon Guard Reflex had been integrated during the training and now I could reach an additional 16 inches beyond my previous limit -pain free! I had spent two years working on lengthening my ham-strings when what I really needed was to do rhythmic movements.

Susan Phariss, Oklahoma USA, May 2010

A Mother's Story - Using RMT with other Modalities

For many years I have been searching high and low for answers for my now 23-year-old son's many challenges. He had tactile defensiveness; his personality was fairly rigid, took things very literally and in great detail. While he loved "The Three Stooges", he was acutely uncomfortable with interpersonal humour or whimsy. He was unable to stay focused on tasks in this world, preferring to live in a dream-world of his own, and despite a stratospheric IQ, was unable to do homework or pass tests in college. He mentally processed and moved quite slowly. His goals were to know himself and his preferences, to be able to drive, to be successful in school, and able to stay productive without drifting off into a dream-world or playing a complex binary game of his own making, and to have enough initiative to be independent.

We had done a few things, including Brain Gym and Bal-A-Vis-X, which had helped him cope better, however the basic symptoms were still there.

I took my first RMT classes in March last year, and repeated them in May. At first there was not a lot of difference, though this could be partially because while there was a lot of initial enthusiasm we didn't practise faithfully every day. In the beginning of July I did some more advanced training and then we began to see some loosening of his rigidity and an increasing joviality. So while there did not seem to be a big change I was still certain that somehow RMT was his way out.

So I re-took RMT 3 and Facial Reflexes later that July, and finally things started to come together more. The key was the admonition that we should do this with great attention to the client, to be aware of any small changes in them that would indicate a shift in energy, need to integrate, or for a different exercise. Mind you, these things had been said to me before, I can now think back and remember - but this time, they sank in.

This time, I came back to Nebraska with a gleam in my eye, steel in my spirit, and joy in my heart. And this time, I decided a few things.

1. I noticed that every time I attended an integration class (BG, RMT or BAVX) I came back feeling so different because of the intense barrage of integrating stimulation I had received. Also aware of how much submersion goes with learning a new language and having read somewhere that all an autistic person needs is 1½ hours a day of someone being totally present with them, and they'd be all right - I decided to be *totally present* with my son. I felt that as long as I was being present, that changes would happen for him in much the same way being submerged and present had changed me. So submergence was what he was going to get.

2. Because he couldn't find sorrow at a co-worker's death or particular joy in something, I opted to go back and *start at the very beginning*, as I felt it was *a very good place to start*. This meant we weren't starting with reading, but with the brain stem/neural chassis and working towards linking up the limbic system, and we would do this 1-3 times a day, for 10 days.

So for 10 days in August we did Brain Gym's PACE, all the RMT movements, and whatever BG exercises my son felt like doing at the time. After this initial 10 days we then went on to work specifically with the neural chassis and then on to the linking up the limbic system. On the days he had a lot of classes and/or homework, we would do it once; on other days, three times.

This is when I noticed that being *present* made all the difference in the world. Within 1½ seconds of my forgetting to concentrate on him, his body would resist. When I focused loving, joyful, grateful thoughts, his body loosened up!

In a month, we saw some lessening of his escaping to the dark basement to daydream. He began to initiate doing house-work, and took a bit of responsibility for his homework schedule. However in the meantime I was doing a lot of travel, getting BG classes in and trying to get a Master's in social work. It wasn't until October that things *really* started changing around.

We again did a 10-day immersion, again with the limbic system, as the majority of his symptoms were still there. Again, the more *present and coherent* I was able to be the more progress he made. In 3 weeks, when I asked him to stand with his feet evenly underneath him, he *balanced on one foot with the other behind him a la karate kid* (this previously ponderous and stolid young man), *put his hands together in a praying posture* and in his best "Yoda" voice, *said "Yes mother. You wanted me mother?"*

And her cup ranneth over with grateful joy

In December, we did another 10 days of limbic system balances (with occasional facial and grasping balances) with further progress.

And then two things happened: I read Carla Hannaford's *Playing in the Unified Field*, and my son confided that he felt he might be this way because he didn't get enough attention as a child.

So taking on the information in Carla's book I started having mental conversations with my son, both when we were working with integrating the system and when he was at school, 7 miles away. I also practised being coherent even when he was not only in the same room, but when he was at school or when I was out of town, and *things really started happening*. On days and times when I was stressed or distracted, things didn't go so well for him. But when I could be coherent and present, he was more productive, and could think more clearly.

Today, my son is still very much himself, only more spontaneous. He laughs out loud at things he finds funny, and spontaneously cracks jokes which he both enjoys and loves that we enjoy. He revels in deep-pressure hugs. We believe he is thinking faster; he gets homework done more quickly, while understanding material more easily. He is much more aware of other people around him, and of the social mores that he used to ignore. His reflexes are much better; his driving practise goes much more smoothly now as he multi-tasks better (snow coming at you, traffic lights, other cars and potholes - all at one time!) He is able to see more than just details; he includes at least awareness of the whole picture. His ability to start homework and stay with it has absolutely soared. He is able to state preferences for one balance over another. He initiates physical contact at least once a day with his mom. He now prefers to go to a hockey game rather than read or hang about in his dream-world. He keeps track of things in his area of study that come up in the real world. He can appreciate views other than his own. Friends and neighbours are astounded at his transformation.

We know that there is more to do, and we will continue - not only with my son's transformation, but with my own.

Ruth M, Nebraska USA, February 2010

Stewart's Story – Learning to Live with Asperger's

I first became aware of having Asperger's in the middle of 2008. Once I became aware I started researching and one of the first things I realized was that I walked homo-laterally instead of cross-laterally. At the time I used to go for a walk of about 2 to 3 kilometres every day and I decided that I needed to practise walking cross-laterally and it felt like I was waddling... I was sure people would think I was strange... I wasn't waddling of course... it was just the way it felt. After a week or two it started to feel normal walking cross-laterally and now I wouldn't walk any other way.

That was the start of what has turned out to be an amazing journey. The next major step was on Wednesday 8 October 2008 when I met and had my first session with Moira Dempsey.

With Moira's help I learned about autism and ASD. Slowly but surely all the pieces started to drop into place and I began to realize the impact Asperger's had had on me. I put everything I could into following her advice about doing the movements and exercises.

Social anxiety has always been a major problem for me all my life. It has caused numerous hardships and very nearly destroyed me. I have been to numerous psychologists, psychiatrists and complimentary therapists in an attempt to deal with it and none of them had the answer.

In the middle of 2009 I attended a workshop with Dr Harald Blomberg. In it he taught a movement of chest beating to integrate the Primitive Withdrawal or Fear Paralysis Reflex. I have found that the Rhythmic Movements are very powerful, so powerful I had to be careful not to overdo them at first.

For about the last 6 months I have been progressively increasing the amount I do the chest beating movement, and have now reached a point where I can do it as much as I like. Often when anxiety comes up the chest beating stops it immediately. It is one of the very valuable tools I am using that is progressively setting me free.

After 59 years of being trapped in fear, I can't thank Moira and Harald enough for setting me free. My life can now really begin.

Stewart Coad, Melbourne Australia, January 2010

A Rhythmic Movement Story from Indonesia - The Sangadi Family Story

It all began when our youngest son was diagnosed at the age of four as having PDD-Nos. The symptoms were autism and ADHD behaviour; lack of communication, very minimal social interaction, lack of eye contact, impulsivity and hyper-activity. We were then introduced to RMT and began using it to support his development. After doing it for two years on a daily basis, he is now coming all together. His development is tremendous, and he is catching up on all the things that he was behind in. He is now 6½-years-old, and is drawing many things using his imagination, whereas before he would draw the same thing over and over again obsessively. He is able to tell stories. There are no problems any more with making eye contact. His communication is excellent and his social interaction is very different as he has started to connect with people around him, not just his direct family members. The way he behaves is also more all together.

As I have seen so many improvements in my son I decided to also apply RMT on a daily basis with my two girls. My second daughter is very sweet and nice; however she has difficulty in showing her feelings and communicating clearly. This was starting to be a real problem for her, and at the age of seven she began to have nightmares almost every night. I then worked with her for 6 months using RMT for these difficulties. The result was surprisingly amazing. She no longer had bad dreams, she began to be able to express her opinion and react accordingly. Now at eight she is a role model among her classmates.

In contrast my oldest daughter tired easily, had headaches when reading, lost focus when doing tasks, and was always falling and bumping into things. These all challenged her to live up to her actual ability. I have used RMT since last year to help her with these things. It turns out that not only has her ability studying and reading improved, but also her maturity, her self-confidence and ability to manage her behaviour. Now at 11 years of age, she is continuously acknowledged as a smart leader and very trustworthy person.

There is no better statement to show my gratitude to God except "What was impossible is possible".

Mia Sangadi, Jakarta Indonesia, July 2010

Harry's Story

Harry is one of my students, and was 10 when we started to do rhythmic movements together.

Harry has autism, and his family had tried many popular treatments to help him, with some success. However Harry still had many challenges including "freezing" when in new and unfamiliar environments, and when seeing someone in distress. He had poor posture, accommodation was a real challenge, his handwriting was poor and he pressed down really hard when writing.

While he loves music and pattern games Harry would need to be prompted to give results when asked to initiate or repeat the rhythm or patterns. He had a moderate vocabulary, yet could only string three to five words together, and often used "scripted phrases" that he'd learned from video games or TV. He spoke robotically with little intonation or inflection. He often seemed to live in his own little world, and it would be hard to get his attention.

After assessing Harry's primitive and postural reflexes it became clear that he had many infant reflexes still active that were having an impact on his sensory processing, movement, and efficient brain integration.

When we first started doing passive sliding on the back we could only do it for between 30-60 seconds, however this would relax him for several minutes and allowed him to become still and quiet. Harry quickly began to ask for more and more movements as his tolerance to them increased, and he was soon able to do the movements actively. He was so proud the first time he slid independently and announced, "Ms. Lauren, I like sliding on my back!"

Harry now initiates the movements he wants to do in his twice daily 10-15 minute sessions, and can now do most of them easily and with so much more symmetry and rhythm. He has even incorporated some of the FPR pre-birth movements into his active sliding; his favourite is the "frog" slide!

A year after we started there are many changes. Harry is not so scared of the new, and he has made friends with quite a few people. He continues to feel sad when someone else is distressed however not nearly to the same degree as before. He is learning empathy and how to respond in a loving way. His posture has improved, as has his reading and his accommodation; he keeps place on the page; his pencil pressure has eased; and he is now able to erase and make corrections.

Music and patterns are even more enjoyable now that he doesn't have to be prompted to respond. He now participants in group activities; has started playing the piano and making up his own songs; is talking and communicating in ways he could never do before; and, has a greatly improved ability to move in more mature ways.

Harry still struggles with sustaining attention and focus; however he is now able to refocus after having been interrupted.

Harry is truly a changed child!

Lauren Harrington, Texas USA, April 2010

RMT Workshops
As at January 2011 – Subject to change and additions

General Classes
Introduction to RMT
RMT One (RMT and ADD/ADHD)
RMT Two (RMT, Emotions and Inner Leadership)
RMT Three (RMT and Dyslexia)

Other Classes
RMT, Dreams and Inner Healing
Face the Fear (RMT, Fear Paralysis and Facial Reflexes – for Language and Bonding)
RMT for Cerebral Palsy
RMT for Autism
RMT for the Pre-school and Kindergarten

Learning Rhythmic Movement Training

To find worldwide RMT classes, instructors and providers go to: www.rhythmicmovement.com

In Spain go to:
   www.reflejosprimitivos.es

In Sweden go to:
   www.rytmiskrorelsetraning.se

Dr. Blomberg's website is:
   www.haraldblomberg.com

Moira Dempsey's website is:
   www.integratedbeing.com

Other Resources

Some other movement based programmes that look at the role of retained primitive reflexes on learning and behaviour are:

Claire Hocking
    www.wholebrain.com.au

Peter Blythe and Sally Goddard Blythe
    www.inpp.co.uk

Brendan O'Hara
    www.movementandlearning.com.au

Martin McPhillips
    www.primarymovement.com

Brain Gym® – Paul and Gail Dennison
    www.braingym.org

Cecelia Koester
    www.movementbasedlearning.com

Body-Mind Centering – Bonnie Bainbridge Cohen
    www.bodymindcentering.com

Feldenkrais
    www.feldenkrais.com

Handle - Judith Bluestone
    www.handle.org

Glossary

Accommodation–The ability of the eye to change its focus from far to near distance and vice versa, this is achieved by the lens of the eye changing shape.

Accommodative Convergence–The inward rotation of the eyes (convergence) that happens in response to accommodation.

Adrenalin–Hormone produced by the adrenal glands and secreted as part of the fight-or-flight reaction. It causes a quickening of the heart beat and opens up the bronchioles in the lungs, and helps get us ready to stay and fight and to run away at times of stress. Also called epinephrine.

Amino Acids–The building blocks of protein. The body has 20 different amino acids that act as these building blocks. Nonessential amino acids are those that the body can synthesize for itself, provided there is enough nitrogen, carbon, hydrogen, and **oxygen** available. Essential amino acids are those supplied by diet since the human body either cannot make them at all or cannot make them in enough quantities to meet its needs. Under normal conditions, 11 of the amino acids are nonessential and 9 are essential.

Amyotrophic Lateral Sclerosis (ALS)–A rapidly progressive neurological disease that attacks the neurons responsible for controlling voluntary muscles. Sometimes called Lou Gehrig's disease.

Angular Gyrus–A region of the parietal lobe that is involved in a number of processes related to language, mathematics and cognition.

Anthroposophical Schools–Schools that follow the educational philosophy of Rudolph Steiner. Also called Waldorf Schools.

Asperger's Syndrome–A disorder on the autistic spectrum that is characterized by an inability to understand how to interact socially, clumsiness and uncoordinated motor movements, social impairment with limited interests and unusual preoccupations, repetitive routines or rituals and speech and language disorders.

Autism Spectrum Disorder (ASD)–Autism is a developmental disorder that is characterized by impaired development in communication, social interaction, and behaviour.

Axon–A long fibre of a neuron that carries messages as electrical impulses from one neuron to another.

Basal Ganglia–A region located at the base of the brain composed of four clusters of neurons, or nerve cells. This area of the brain is responsible for body movement and coordination.

Binocular Vision–The ability of both eyes to work together, maintain steady focus on an object, then to be able to create one clear image of that object.

Brain stem–The stemlike part of the brain that is connected to the spinal cord, it consists of the medulla oblongata and pons. It manages messages going between the brain and the rest of the body, and also controls basic body functions like breathing, swallowing, heart rate, and blood pressure. The brain stem also controls consciousness and determines whether you are awake or sleepy.

Broca's area–An area of the cerebral motor cortex in the left frontal lobe of the brain responsible for speech development. Damage to Broca's area can cause speech disorders.

Central Auditory Processing Disorder (CAPD)–A condition in which there is an inability to differentiate, recognize or understand sounds even though both hearing and intelligence are normal.

Central Nervous System (CNS)–The part of the nervous system that consists of the brain and spinal cord, it is important for coordinating the activity of the entire nervous system, and is the part from which sensory impulses are received and motor impulses pass out.

Cerebellum–The part of the brain at the back of the head between the cerebrum and the brain stem and sometimes called the little brain. The cerebellum controls balance for walking, standing and other complex motor functions.

Cerebral Cortex–A thin layer of gray matter covering the surface of each cerebral hemisphere, the cerebral cortex is crumpled and folded, forming numerous convolutions called gyri and crevices called sulci. The cerebral cortex is responsible for the processes of thought, perception and memory and serves as the seat of advanced motor function, social abilities, language, and problem solving.

Cerebral Palsy (CP)–An abnormality of motor function and postural tone that is acquired at an early age, even before birth. These abnormalities are caused by non–progressive brain lesions.

Cingulate Gyrus–A part of the brain that transverses longitudinally deep within the frontal lobes. The front part coordinates smells and sights with pleasant memories. The cingulate also participates in the emotional reaction to pain and helps regulate aggressive behaviour.

Convergence–The ability of the two eyes to move inward, coordinate and fixate at a near point.

Corpus callosum–The thick bridge of nerve fibres that connect the two hemispheric cortices and that allows the hemispheres of the brain to work together.

Cortisol–A hormone produced by the adrenal glands which is present during the day, usually in higher levels in the morning, and helps with regulating blood sugar, suppressing the immune system and aiding in metabolism. However at times of stress cortisol is released in higher doses to give the quick burst of energy needed to fight or flee.

DECT Phones –Digital Enhanced Cordless Technology

Dentate Nucleus–The largest of the nuclei deep within each cerebellar hemisphere and is responsible for the planning, initiation and control of volitional (conscious choice) movements.

Dopamine–An important neurotransmitter in the brain that affects the processes that control movement, emotional responses and the ability to feel pleasure and pain. Neurons that contain dopamine are clustered in the Substantia Nigra, one of the basal ganglia.

Epinephrine–See Adrenalin

Esophoria–An eye muscle condition that happens when the eyes are at rest they turn inward, however when both eyes are open they are able to point accurately and focus. This means that while binocular vision is possible it is a strain to maintain it. Also called over-convergence.

Exophoria–An eye muscle condition that when the eyes are at rest they turn outwards, however when both eyes are open they are able to point accurately and focus. This means that while binocular vision is possible it is a strain to maintain it. Also called under-convergence.

Functional Magnetic Resonance Imaging (fMRI)–Uses magnetic resonance imaging (MRI) to learn which areas of the brain are active while performing specific functions, e.g. speech

Fovea–A tiny hollow located in the macula of the retina of the eyes that provides the clearest most accurate vision. In the fovea there are only cones – the cells that provide the sharpest image. Also called the Central Visual Field

Frontal Lobes–The part of each hemisphere of the cortex located behind the forehead they serve to regulate and mediate the higher intellectual functions. The frontal lobes have intricate connections to other areas of the brain.

Gamma-Aminobutyric Acid (GABA)–The chief inhibitory neurotransmitter in the Central Nervous System of mammals and plays a role in regulating neuronal excitability. Also responsible for the regulation of muscle tone.

Hyperphoria–An eye muscle condition that happens when the eyes are at rest they turn upwards, however when both eyes are open they are able to point accurately and focus.

Hypophoria–An eye muscle condition that happens when the eyes are at rest they turn downwards, however when both eyes are open they are able to point accurately and focus.

The Institute for Neuro-Physiological Psychology (INPP)–Founded by Peter Blythe and based in Chester, UK. INPP has pioneered research into early development and retained reflexes.

Kinesiology–The art and science of testing the strength of certain muscles to determine areas of physical imbalances, neurological deficits, certain types of nutritional deficiencies, emotional imbalances or behavioural challenges.

Lability–Being susceptible to change, error or instability.

Multiple Sclerosis (MS)–An autoimmune disease where the body's immune system attacks myelin and affects the CNS and produces numbness, weakness, loss of muscle coordination and problems with vision and speech.

Muscle Checking–Used by kinesiologists as a bio feedback mechanism that uses muscles as a tool to assess the nervous system.

Myelin–The fatty substance that covers and protects the axons like a sheath and acts like a conduit in an electrical system that ensures that nervous system messages are not lost in transmission.

Myelination–The process whereby the protective myelin sheath is formed around the axon. Also known as myelinization.

Neocortex–The newer part of the cerebral cortex that in humans serves as the centre of higher mental functioning that permit vision, hearing, touch, balance, movement, emotional responses, etc to be understood. The neocortex contains some 100 billion cells, each with 1,000 to 10,000 synapses (connections), and has roughly 100 million meters of wiring, all packed into a structure the size and thickness of a large dinner napkin.

Neural Pathway–The white matter of the brain is bundles of elongated myelinated neurons connecting relatively distant areas of the brain together.

Neuron–A nerve cell that sends and receives electrical signals over long distances. Motor neurons send messages from the CNS to the body; sensory neurons send information from the sensory receptors to the brain; and interneurons between sensory and motor neurons.

Neurotransmitters–Chemicals within the nervous system that transmit information from or between neurons.

Occipital Lobes–The posterior part of each cerebral hemisphere, concerned with the interpretation of visual sensory impulses.

Parietal Lobes–The part of each cerebral hemisphere concerned with the perception and interpretation of sensations of touch, temperature, taste and with muscular movements.

Parkinson's disease–A disease characterized by progressive loss of muscle control, which leads to trembling of the limbs and head while at rest, stiffness, slowness, and impaired balance. As symptoms worsen, it may become difficult to walk, talk, and complete simple tasks.

Paul MacLean–An American physician and neuroscientist who through his work at Yale University and the National Institute of Mental Health (NIMH) in the USA proposed the evolutionary triune brain theory that the human is in reality three brains in one, the reptilian, limbic system and neocortex.

Peptidase–A naturally occurring enzyme that helps to metabolize proteins. These enzymes break down proteins by destroying the chains between their amino acids, and they can usually be found in the digestive tract.

Peptide–Peptides occur naturally in the body and are composed of amino acids. When a chain of amino acids is over 50 acids long, it is usually called a protein, when it contains less than 50 amino acids in the chain it is a peptide. So, a peptide is a portion, or a building block, of a protein.

Pervasive Development Disorder–Not otherwise specified (PDD–Nos)– Refers to a group of conditions that involve delays in the development of many basic skills, most notably the ability to socialize with others, to communicate, and to use imagination. Children with these conditions often are confused in their thinking and generally have problems understanding the world around them.

Positron Emission Tomography (PET) Scan–A highly specialized imaging technique that uses short-lived radioactive substances to produce 3-dimensional coloured images of the brain.

Postural reflexes–Life-long reflexes that allow us to move and be stable while being upright in gravity.

Prefrontal Lobes–The anterior (front) part of the frontal lobe.

Primary Motor Cortex–Areas in the parietal lobes that work in conjunction with the pre-motor areas, basal ganglia and cerebellum in the conscious planning and refining of movement.

Primary Sensory Cortex–Part of the parietal lobes that receive somatic sensory information from the thalamus.

Primitive Reflexes–Reflexes that develop during uterine life and are fully present by the time of birth or very shortly after.

Proprioception–The unconscious perception of movement and spatial orientation from within the body.

Psychosis–A mental illness which interferes with a person's capacity to meet life's everyday demands and where the sense of reality is impaired. Symptoms can include seeing, hearing, smelling, or tasting things that are not there; paranoia; and delusional thoughts.

Purkinje cells–A specific type of nerve cell that carries all information from the cerebellum, these cells are responsible for a great deal of control over the refinement of motor activities.

Reticular Activating System (RAS)–The system of cells of the reticular formation of the medulla oblongata that receive information from the ascending sensory pathways and sends it to higher centres; they control the overall degree of CNS activity, including wakefulness, attentiveness, and sleep.

Schizophrenia–A chronic, severe, debilitating mental illness. It is one of the psychotic mental disorders and is characterized by symptoms of thought, behaviour, and social problems. The thought problems associated with schizophrenia are described as psychosis, in that the person's thinking is completely out of touch with reality at times.

Strabismus–Commonly known as cross-eyed or wall-eyed, is a vision condition in which a person can't align both eyes at the same time. One or both of the eyes may turn in, out, up or down.

Suppression–When there is strabismus or other eye challenges the brain can ignore the images of one of the eyes so it can eliminate double vision.

Synapses–These are specialized junctions between neurons where one neuron can communicate with the other.

Temporal Lobes–Part of the cortex that lies at the sides of the brain, and are involved in auditory processing, speech and memory.

Vergence–The simultaneous movement of both eyes in opposite directions to maintain binocular vision, and are closely connected to accommodation.

Vermis –The middle lobe connecting the two halves of the cerebellum.

Vestibular–The system in the body that is responsible for maintaining balance, posture and the body's orientation in space. The vestibular system keeps visual focus on objects as the body moves.

Visual Acuity–The acuteness or clarity of vision which is dependent on how well the retina can focus and how well the brain can interpret the information sent from the eye.

Wernicke's area–Wernicke's area is a region of the brain that is important in language development. It is located in the temporal lobe on the left side of the brain and is responsible for the comprehension of speech.

Notes and References

Introduction

1. According to an article in the Swedish newspaper *Svenska Dagbladet* 29 April 2007

2. Jan Wållinder, *Transmittorn*, No 7

3. "Kort om ADHD hos barn och vuxna (2004) En sammanfattning av Socialstyrelsens kunskapsöversikt", Page 31 (Swedish National Board of Health and Welfare (2004), briefly about ADHD in children and adults)

Chapter 1

1. Andrew Bridges, Associated Press, 6 January 2004

2. Peter Breggin (2001): *Talking back to Ritalin*, Da Capo Press, page 259

3. Breggin, page 68

4. Breggin, page 24

5. BBC "Panorama", *What next for Craig*, 12 November 2007

6. BBC "Panorama", *What next for Craig*, 12 November 2007

7. Breggin, page 52

8. Breggin page 49 referring to Rie, H.E., Rie E.D., Stewart, S., and Ambuel, J.P. (1976): "Effects of Methylphenidate on underachieving children", *Journal of Consulting and Clinical Psychology*, 44, pages 250-260

9. Breggin, page 130

10. Breggin, page 97: referring to Drug Enforcement Administration (DEA) October 1995. *Methylphenidate* (a background paper)

11. Breggin, page 97

12. Breggin, pages 71–72

13. Breggin, page 24

14. *Dagens Nyheter* 7 June 2008

15. *Dagens Nyheter* 7 June 2008

16. *Dagens Nyheter* 7 June 2008

17. *Dagens Nyheter* 7 June 2008

Chapter 2

1. Robert Winston (2004), *The Human Mind*, Bantam Press, page 78

2. Paul D. MacLean (1990): *The Triune Brain in Evolution*, Plenum Press

3. Jean Ayres (2000): *Sensory Integration and the Child*, WPS, page 72

Chapter 3

1. Breggin, page 217

2. Kärfve, Eva (2001): *Hjärnspöken: DAMP och hotet mot folkhälsa*, (Delusions, DAMP and the threat to public health), B. Östlings, Symposion

3. Breggin, page 74

4. Breggin, page 74

5. Jaffe, Jerome from Kaplan H.I & Sadock B.J. (1995): *The Comprehensive Textbook of Psychiatry*, Williams & Wilkins, page 796

6. AP 4 January, 2006

7. Eli Lilly, "Poster" presented at a conference in Florence, 28 August 2007

8. MHRA (2005): *Preliminary Assessment Report*, December

9. FDA Report, 3 March 2006

Chapter 4

1. Mats Lindqvist & Gerd Pettersson, "Rytmiska rörelseterapi med kroniskt schizofrena patienter", (Rhythmic movement therapy with chronic schizophrenic patients), *Examensarbete 20 poäng*, Umeå University, 1993

Chapter 6

1. MacLean, page 23

2. Sally Goddard (2002): *Reflexes, Learning and Behavior*, Fern Ridge Press, page 89

3. En Bok om Hjärnan (A Book on the Brain) (1995): *Tiden*, Rabén Prisma, page 149

4. Svetlana Masgutova with Nelly Akhmatova (2004): *Integration of Dynamic and Postural Reflexes into the Whole Body Movement System*, Warsaw

5. Frank A. Middleton and Peter L. Strick: "Cerebellar Projections to the Prefrontal Cortex of the Primate", *Journal of Neuroscience*, 21(2): 700-712

6. Torleiv Höien, Ingvar Lundberg, "Dyslexi", *Natur och Kultur* 1999, page 182

Chapter 7

1. James Purdon Martin (1967): *The Basal Ganglia and Posture*, Pitman Medical Publishing Co. Ltd, chapter 15

2. Purdon Martin, chapter 8

3. Salford L. G. et al.: "Nerve Cell Damage in Mammalian Brain after Exposure to Microwaves from GSM Mobile Phones", *Environmental Health Perspectives,* 2003:11

4. Divan et al.: "Prenatal and Postnatal Exposure to Cell Phone Use and Behavioral Problems in Children", *Epidemiology,* Vol. 19, No 4, July 2008

5. According to an article by Bertil Wosk, Pelle Randberg: "Konstgjort sötningsmedel ett hot mot vår hälsa" (Artificial Sweeteners a Threat to our Health), *Näringsråd och Näringsrön,* 2001, 6.

6. Wosk, Randberg, page 6

7. Bryan Jepson (2007): *Changing the Course of Autism,* Sentient Publications, page 115

8. Paul Dennison Ph.D.: *Total Core Repatterning* and *Movement Re-Education,* Edu-K Workshops Ventura CA

9. Masgutova with Akhmatova, page 50

Chapter 8

1. By this time the embryo has already developed the beginning of the eyes, ears, mouth, feet, hands and neural tube.

2. What I mean by integrated is that the reflex no longer plays an immediate role in our movement patterns and the role these patterns play in development. They are still available to us at times of stress or trauma as a way of providing us with ways of dealing with the event when the higher cortical responses become unavailable to us.

3. Goddard, page 18

4. Thie, John D.C. & Thie, Matthew M.Ed. (2005): *Touch for Health* DeVorss and Co, CA USA, page 229

Chapter 9

1. Ayres, page 39

2. Ayres, page 55

3. MacLean, page 327

4. Berit Heir Bunkan (1980): *Muskelspänningar,* Universitetsforlaget Oslo, page 43

5. Ayres, page 137

6. Zimmerman, Frederick J. et al. "Associations between Media Viewing and Language Development in Children under Age 2 Years". *Journal of Pediatrics,* April 2007

7.   MacLean, page 396

Chapter 10

1.   Goddard page 142

Chapter 11

1.   Elkhonin Goldberg (2001): *The Executive Brain*, Oxford University Press, page 34

2.   Goldberg, page 36

3.   Frank A. Middleton and Peter L. Strick: "Basal-ganglia 'projections' to the Prefrontal Cortex of the Primate", *Cerebral Cortex*, September 2002. Vol. 12, No 9

4.   Goldberg, page 139

Chapter 12

1.   Jepson, page 34

2.   Jepson, page 25

3.   Nature: *Functional impact of global rare copy number variation in autism spectrum disorders*. Published online 9 June 2010

4.   Windham, G., Zhang, L., Gunier, R., Croen, L., Grether, J., "Autism Spectrum Disorders in Relation to Distribution of Hazardous Air Pollutants in the San Francisco Bay Area". *Environ Health Perspect.* September 2006, 114(9):1438-44

5.   Robert Kennedy, Jr., "Autism, Mercury and Politics", *Boston Globe* 1 July 2005

6.   William Shaw (2002): *Biological Treatments for Autism and PDD*, pages 5 & 102

7.   Beezy Marsh, Sally Beck: "US scientists back autism link to MMR", **www.telegraph co.uk.** Updated: 29 May 2006

8.   Kawashima H., Mori T., Kashiwagi Y., Takekuma K., Hoshika A., Wakefield A.: "Detection and sequencing of measles virus from peripheral mononuclear cells from patients with inflammatory bowel disease and autism", *Digestive Disease and Science,* 2000 April;45(4): 723-29

9.   Walker S.J., Hepner K., Segal J., Kriegsman A.: "Persistent ileal measles virus in a large cohort of regressive autistic children with ileocolitis and lymphonodular hyperplasia: revisitation of an earlier study.", *IMFAR* June 1, 2006, Montreal, Canada

10.   Jepson, page 86

11. Reichelt. K.L. et al.: "Childhood Autism: A Complex Disorder", *Biol. Psychiatry* 21, 1986

12. "Risk Evaluation of Potential Environmental Hazards from Low Frequency Electromagnetic Fields using Sensitive in vitro Methods", 2004

13. www.bioinitiative.org

14. Jepson, pages 172 & 252

15. Yasko, Amy (2009): *Autism: Pathways to Recovery*, Neurological Research Institute, page 68

16. Yasko, page 59

Chapter 13

1   David H. Ingvar & Goren Franzén: "Abnormal Distribution of Cerebral Activity in Chronic Schizophrenia", *The Lancet*, Vol. 304 Issue 7895, 21 December 1974, pages 1484-1486

2. Reichelt, K.L. et al.: "Urinary Peptides in Schizophrenia and Depression", *Stress Medicine* 1, 1985

3. Dohan F.C. & Grasberger J.C.: "Relapsed Schizophrenics: Earlier Discharge from Hospital after Cereal-Free, Milk-Free Diet", *American Journal of Psychiatry*, No 130

4. Mårten Kalling, *Gap junctions, Kanalerna mellan celler*, (Gap Junction, channels between cells), Unpublished manuscript, June 2007

5. Robert G. Heath: "Modulations of Emotions with a Brain Pacemaker", *The Journal of Nervous and Mental Disease*, No 5, 1977

6. Robert G. Heath: "Gross Pathology of the Cerebellum in Patients Diagnosed and Treated as Functional Psychiatric Disorders", *The Journal of Nervous and Mental Disease* No 10, 1979

7. MacLean, pages 527-534

8. According to an article by Anna-Lena Haverdahl: "Var sjätte dog efter lobotomi", (Every Six Dies After Lobotomy), *Svenska Dagbladet* 30 April 2007

9. MacLean, page 529

10. Mats Lindqvist & Gerd Pettersson

Chapter 14

1. Myrberg, Mats Ed. (2003): *Att skapa consensus om skolans insatser för att motverka läs- och skrivsvårigheter* (Building consensus on the school's efforts to combat dyslexia)

2. Myrberg, page 51

3. Boder, E. (1973):" Developmental dyslexia: A diagnostic approach based on three atypical reading-spelling patterns", *Developmental Medicine and Child Psychology*, 15, 663-687

4. Gjessing, H. (1977): *Dysleksi*, Oslo, Universitetsförlaget

5. Aaron, P.G. (1978): "Dyslexia, an imbalance in cerebral information processing strategies", *Perceptual and Motor Skills*, 47, 699-706

6. Hellige, Joseph B.: *Hemispheric Asymmetry*, Harvard University Press, 1993, page 36

7. According to Kandel, E.R., Schwartz, J.H., & Jessell, T.M. (1991): *Principles of Neural Science*, 3rd edition, Connecticut US, Appleton & Lange

8. Goldberg, page 49

Chapter 15

1. Dr David Cook (2004): *When your child struggles. The Myths of 20/20 Vision*, Invision Press, Atlanta Georgia, pages 72-73

2. Lasse Müller (2006): *Optometri vid läs- och skrivsvårigheter*, (Optometry and Reading and Writing)

3. Cook, pages 107-108

4. "Klinisk optometri: Visuella faktorer i läsprocessen", (Clinical Optometry: Visual factors in the reading process), by Swedish optometrist Jan Wikander

5. Masgutova with Akhamatova, page 66

6. McPhillips M., Hepper P.G., Mulhem M.: "Effects of replicating primary-reflex movements on specific reading difficulties in children: a randomised, double-blind, controlled trial", *The Lancet*, Vol. 355, No 9203, pages 537-541

7. McPhillips M. & Jordan-Black J-A.: "Primary reflex persistence in children with reading difficulties (dyslexia): A cross-sectional study", *Neuropsychologia, 2007*, 45, pages 748-754

8. Gesell A., Ilg F.L., Bullis G.E. (1948): *Vision: Its Development in Infant and Child*, New York, Harper & Row

Chapter 16

1. Johansen, Kjeld V. (1993): *Lyd, hoerelse og sprogudvikling*, (Sound, Hearing and Language Development), Denmark

2. Moats, L. (1996): "Phonological spelling errors in the writing of dyslectic children", Reading and Writing: An Interdisciplinary Journal, 8, pages 105-119

3. Hamilton, Gregory et al.: "Psychiatric Symptoms and Cerebellar Pathology", *American Journal of Psychiatry*, 14:10, October 1983

4. Nicolson, R. & Fawcett, A.: "Comparison of deficits in cognitive and motor skills among children with dyslexia", *Annals of Dyslexia*, 44, pages 147-164

Chapter 17

1. Steen Larsen (1996): *Laesningens mysterium*, (Readings mystery), Hellerup, page 112

2. Goldberg, page 24

3. Goldberg, page 114

4. Berg, Lars-Eric & Cramér, Anna, (2007): *Hjärnvägen till inlärning* (Brain road to learning), Brain Books, Sweden

5. Stern, J.F., and Walsh, V.: To see but not to read: The magnocellular theory of dyslexia *TINS* 20: 147-152 1997

6. Witton, C., Talcott, T.B., Hansen, P.C., Richardson, A.J., Griffiths, T.D., Rees, A., Steen, J.F., Green, G.G.R.: Sensitivity to dynamic auditory and visual stimuli predicts nonword reading ability in both dyslexic and normal readers, *Curr. Biol.* 8: 791-797, 1998

7. Fawcett, A.J., Nicolson, R.I. and Dean, P.: Impaired performance of children with dyslexia on a range of cerebellar tasks, *Annals of Dyslexia*, 46, 259-263, 196

8. Rae, C., Harasty, JA., Dzenrowskyj, T.E., Talcott, J.B., Simpson, J.M., Blamire, A.M., et al.: Cerebellar Morphology in developmental dyslexia, *Neuropsychologia*, 40 (8): 1285-1292, 2002

9. Visser, J.: Developmental coordination disorder: a review of research on subtypes and comorbidities, *Human Movement Science*, Vol 22, Issues 4-5, Nov 2003, Pages 479-498

10. Iverson, S., Berg, K., Ellertson, B., Tonnessen, F.E.: Motor cordination difficulties in a municipal group and in a clinical sample of poor readers, *Dyslexia*, Vol. 11, Issue 3, pages 217-231, Aug 2005

Bibliography

Ayres, Jean (2000): *Sensory Integration and the Child*, WPS

Berg, Lars-Eric & Cramér, Anna (2007): *Hjärnvägen till inlärning*, (Brain road to learning), Brain Books, Sweden

Blomberg, Harald (1998): *Helande Liv*, (Healing Life), Cupiditas Discendi, Sweden

Breggin, Peter (2001): *Talking back to Ritalin*, Da Capo Press

Brewer, Chris and Campbell Don G (1991): *Rhythms of Learning*, Tucson, AZ, USA, Zephyr Press Inc

Bunkan, Berit Heir (1980): *Muskelspänningar*, (Muscle Tension), Universitetsforlaget Oslo

Campbell, Don (1997): *The Mozart Effect*, New York, USA, Avon Books

Campbell, Don (2002): *The Mozart Effect for Children*, London, UK, Hodder & Staughton

Dehaene, Stanislas (2009): *Reading in the Brain-The New Science of How we Read*, NY, USA, Penguin

Doidge, Norman (2007): *The Brain that Changes Itself*, New York, USA, Viking Penguin

Edwards. Betty (1989): *Drawing on the Right Side of the Brain*, New York, USA, Jeremy P. Archer/Perigee Books

Erickson, Carol Ann (1999): *Movement Exploration*, Ventura, CA, USA, Educational Kinesiology Foundation

Elliot, Lise (1999): *Early Intelligence*, Penguin

Gesell A., Ilg F.L., Bullis G.E. (1948): *Vision: Its Development in Infant and Child*, New York, Harper & Row

Goddard Blythe, Sally (2004): *The Well Balanced Child*, Stroud, UK, Hawthorne Press

Goddard Blythe, Sally (2009): *Attention, Balance and Coordination – The ABC of Learning*, Chichester UK, Wiley-Blackman

Goddard, Sally (2002): *Reflexes, Learning and Behavior*, Oregon, USA, Fern Ridge Press,

Gold, Svea J. (1997): *If Kids Just Came with Instruction Sheets!* Oregon, USA, Fern Ridge Press

Goldberg, Elkhonin (2001): *The Executive Brain*, Oxford University Press

Greenfield, Susan (2008): *i.d.–The Quest for Identity in the 21st Century*, London, UK, Spectre

Hackney, Peggy (2002): *Making Connections*, New York, USA, Routledge

Hartley, Linda (1995): *Wisdom of the Body Moving*, Berkeley, CA, USA, North Atlantic Books

Hannaford, Carla (1995): *Smart Moves–Why Learning is not all in Your Head*, Arlington, VA, USA, Great Ocean Publishers

Hellige, Joseph B (1993): *Hemispheric Asymmetry*, Harvard University Press

Harald Blomberg M.D.

Höien, Torleiv & Lundberg, Ingvar (1999): *Dyslexi,* (Dyslexia) Sweden, Natur och Kultur, (Nature and Culture)

Jepson, Bryan (2007): *Changing the Course of Autism,* Sentient Publications

Johansen, Kjeld V (1993): *Lyd, hoerelse og sprogudvikling,* (Sound, Hearing and Language Development) Ålöcke, Denmark

Kanner, Leo: "Autistic Disturbances of Affective Contact", *Nervous Child 2,* 1943 pages 217-250

Kaplan H.I. & Sadock B.J. (1995): *The Comprehensive Textbook of Psychiatry,* 6th Ed. Baltimore, US, Williams and Wilkins

Koester, Cecilia (2006): *Movement Based Learning For Children of All Abilities,* Reno, NV, USA Movement Based Learning, Inc.

Kort om ADHD hos barn och vuxna - En sammanfattning av Socialstyrelsens kunskapsöversikt,(2004): (A Map of ADHD in Children and Adults. A sampling of the Board's Knowledge Review, 2004)

LeDoux, Joseph (1998): *The Emotional Brain,* New York, USA, Touchstone

McManus, Chris, (2002): *Right Hand Left Hand,* Massachusetts, USA, Harvard University Press

Melillo, Robert and Leifman Gerry (2009): *Neurobehavioral disorders of childhood: An Evolutionary Perspective,* NY, Springer

Müller, Lasse, (2006): *Optometri vid läs - och skrivsvårigheter,* (Optemetry and reading and writing) Svenska

Nilsson, Mona, (2010): *Mobiltelefonins hälsorisker,* (Health risks of mobile telephones) Miljöbyrå, Sweden

Nilsson, Mona & Lindblad, Maria, (2005): *Spelet om 3G,* (The game on 3G) Medikament Faktapocket

Ornstein, Robert (1997): *The Right Mind,* Orlando, FL, USA, Harcourt Bruce

Oschman, James (2000): *Energy Medicine – the scientific basis,* Churchill Livingstone

Redfield Jamison, Kay (1996): *An Unquiet Mind,* New York, USA, Vintage Books

Schiffer, Fredric (1998): *Of Two Minds,* New York, USA, Free Press
Teitelbaum, Osnat, and Teitelbaum, Philip (2008): *Does Your Baby Have Autism?* New York, Square One Publishers

Upledger, John (2010): *A Brain is Born: Exploring the Birth and Development of the Central Nervous System,* North Atlantic Books

Wolf, Maryanne (2007): *Proust and the Squid,* New York, USA, Harper Perennial

CPSIA information can be obtained
at www.ICGtesting.com
Printed in the USA
BVHW030205110619
550688BV00001B/73/P

9 781791 985127